ZOMBIES AND CONSCIO

By definition zombies would be physically and behaviourally just like us, but not conscious. This currently very influential idea is a threat to all forms of physicalism, and has led some philosophers to give up physicalism and become dualists. It has also beguiled many physicalists, who feel forced to defend increasingly convoluted explanations of why the conceivability of zombies is compatible with their impossibility. Robert Kirk argues that the zombie idea depends on an incoherent view of the nature of phenomenal consciousness. His book has two main aims. One is to demolish the zombie idea once and for all. There are plenty of objections to it in the literature, but they lack intuitive appeal. He offers a striking new argument which reveals fundamental confusions in the implied conception of consciousness. His other main contribution is to develop a fresh and original approach to the true nature of phenomenal consciousness. Kirk argues that a necessary condition is a 'basic package' of capacities. An important component of his argument is that the necessary cognitive capacities are not as sophisticated as is often assumed. By focusing on humbler creatures than ourselves he avoids some of the distracting complications of our sophisticated forms of cognition.

The basic package does not seem to be sufficient for phenomenal consciousness. What is also needed is 'direct activity' - a special feature of the way the events which constitute incoming perceptual information affect the system. This is an integrated process, to be conceived of holistically, and contrasts sharply with what is often called the 'availability' or 'poisedness' of perceptual information.

This original, penetrating, and highly readable book will be of interest to all who have a serious concern with the nature of consciousness: not only professional philosophers and students, but also many psychologists, neuroscientists, and zoologists.

Robert Kirk is Emeritus Professor in the Department of Philosophy at the University of Nottingham. His other books are *Translation Determined* (OUP 1986), *Raw Feeling* (OUP 1994), *Relativism and Reality* (Routledge 1999), and *Mind and Body* (Acumen 2003).

Zombies and Consciousness

ROBERT KIRK

CLARENDON PRESS · OXFORD

OXFORD
UNIVERSITY PRESS

Great Clarendon Street, Oxford OX2 6DP

Oxford University Press is a department of the University of Oxford.
It furthers the University's objective of excellence in research, scholarship,
and education by publishing worldwide in

Oxford New York

Auckland Cape Town Dar es Salaam Hong Kong Karachi
Kuala Lumpur Madrid Melbourne Mexico City Nairobi
New Delhi Shanghai Taipei Toronto

With offices in

Argentina Austria Brazil Chile Czech Republic France Greece
Guatemala Hungary Italy Japan Poland Portugal Singapore
South Korea Switzerland Thailand Turkey Ukraine Vietnam

Oxford is a registered trade mark of Oxford University Press
in the UK and in certain other countries

Published in the United States
by Oxford University Press Inc., New York

British Library Cataloguing in Publication Data

Data available

Library of Congress Cataloging in Publication Data

Kirk, Robert, 1933–
  Zombies and consciousness / Robert Kirk.
    p. cm.
  1. Consciousness. 2. Zombies—Miscellanea. 3. Other minds (Theory of
knowledge) 4. Mind and body. 5. Materialism. I. Title.
B808.9.K58 2005   126—dc22   2005020194

Typeset by Laserwords Private Limited, Chennai, India
Printed in Great Britain
on acid-free paper by
Biddles Ltd., King's Lynn, Norfolk

ISBN 978–0–19–928548–8 (Hbk.)   978–0–19–922980–2 (Pbk.)

1 3 5 7 9 10 8 6 4 2

To Fay

Preface

Zombies (the philosophical sort: this is not about voodoo) would be exactly like us in all physical and behavioural respects, but completely without consciousness. This seductive idea threatens the physicalist view of the world dominant in philosophy and science today. It has led a number of philosophers to reject physicalism and take up dualism. More surprisingly, it has beguiled many physicalists, who now feel forced to defend increasingly convoluted explanations of why the conceivability of zombies is compatible with their impossibility. But the zombie idea is a major source of confusion and distorted thinking.

I have two aims in this book. One is to dispose of the zombie idea once and for all. There are plenty of objections to it in the literature, but they lack intuitive appeal. I have an argument which I think demolishes it in a way that is intuitively appealing as well as cogent. The other aim is to set out an explanation of what it is to be phenomenally conscious. Both aims need to be pursued in the same work, since the anti-zombie argument on its own would have left us still wondering how on earth there could be such a thing as phenomenal consciousness; while my account of consciousness is in the end dependent on the anti-zombie argument.

Three things about my approach are distinctive, I think. One is the argument showing that zombies are inconceivable. Another is the attention given to humbler creatures than ourselves, which helps to avoid some of the distracting complications of our exceptionally sophisticated forms of cognition. The third is my development of the notion of a 'basic package' of capacities to pick out a special class of creatures: 'deciders'. When this idea is properly de-sophisticated, it makes a solid conceptual framework for an account of the crucial feature: 'direct activity'.

I hope the book will appeal to anyone seriously interested in problems of consciousness: not only to professional philosophers, research students, and philosophy undergraduates, but to zoologists, psychologists, and neuroscientists tackling the empirical questions which consciousness raises.

I am grateful to colleagues and students at Nottingham for stimulating discussions of these topics over many years; to Ned Block, Peter Carruthers, and David Chalmers, who kindly read the whole or parts of a draft and generously offered very helpful comments and suggestions; and to OUP's two anonymous readers for their constructive suggestions. I would specially like to thank Bill Fish for acute detailed comments on the entire draft, and Janet, my wife, for unfailing encouragement and support.

R. K.

April 2005

Contents

1

Introduction

A cook was charged with cruelty to animals. He had put live prawns on a hot plate, where they wriggled and writhed, apparently in pain. The case was dropped because it proved impossible to get expert advice on whether or not prawns could feel pain. Although the prawns' behaviour made it easy to suppose they were really suffering, perhaps there was no more to it than behaviour—perhaps they really had no sensations at all, any more than a twisted rubber band, writhing as it unwinds, has sensations. Perhaps there was *nothing it was like* for the prawns.

Can we make progress in this area? I think so, provided we resist some seductive but radically mistaken ways of thinking. The philosophical idea of zombies is the most dramatic manifestation of these, highly significant in spite of its strangeness. There is much to be said for the view that the seeming possibility of zombies entails the falsity of physicalism; and it matters whether physicalism is true. Even more importantly, I think, the zombie idea reflects a fundamentally wrong conception of consciousness and provokes much misguided theorizing. In this book I have two main aims. One is to expose the incoherence of the zombie idea in what I think is a cogent and intuitively appealing way. The other is to build on that result to develop a fresh approach to phenomenal consciousness: to explaining how there can be such a thing as *what it is like*.

1.1 TWO KINDS OF IGNORANCE ABOUT PRAWNS

It is easy to imagine that prawns feel pain. And since they have eyes and other sense organs, it is easy to imagine they are capable of other kinds of 'phenomenal' consciousness too. (Expressions like 'phenomenal consciousness' will be examined later.) It is also easy to imagine that they don't feel pain but only behave as if they did, and that they have no conscious perceptual experiences at all. Regardless of what we might be able to imagine, though, there is surely a matter of fact to be right or wrong about. Either there is something it is like for a creature or there isn't, or so we tend to assume. In our own case, surely there is. I might pretend to have toothache when I don't; but sometimes I really do have toothache—and lots of other phenomenally conscious experiences: visual experiences of the lines of blue writing on my computer screen, auditory experiences of the chugging of a diesel van in the road, olfactory experiences of the faint smell of coffee drifting past my door. Knowing that we ourselves are subjects of such phenomenal consciousness, we are ready to believe that many languageless animals are too, perhaps even quite humble ones. But the prawn case exposes our ignorance.

We need to distinguish two different kinds of ignorance in this area. One concerns the physiological details of creatures' perceptual systems. We know prawns have sense organs whose stimulation affects their behaviour in various ways, but it seems there is still quite a lot we don't know about these animals. That is one kind of ignorance.

The other kind is less tractable. Suppose we knew all the discoverable facts about the workings of prawns' visual and other perceptual systems—all about their neural mechanisms and their roles in the creatures' lives. Would that enable us to tell whether they were phenomenally conscious? What if all their behaviour were explicable in terms of mere built-in reflexes? That would at least make it problematic whether there was 'something it is like' for them. Or, to return to the example of pain, suppose prawns have a certain kind of sensory receptor which, when stimulated, causes writhing and wriggling. Does it follow that those are *pain* receptors, in which case the animals can suffer? Surely not straightforwardly, if at all. One thing we need to get clear about is the relevance of such facts. Which facts about a creature *matter* from the point of view of an interest in whether it is phenomenally conscious? Why do they matter? Those questions are not empirical, at least not obviously; they are largely philosophical. That is the second kind of ignorance exposed by the prawns case; perhaps not so much ignorance as a lack of understanding.

In thinking about these problems we tend to be dazzled by features of specifically human consciousness, for example language, self-consciousness, 'mind-reading'. To make it easier to concentrate on what matters for perceptual consciousness in general I shall often focus on relatively humble creatures. Since our problem is general we should have to do that in any case; my point is that it will make the task easier. An incidental advantage of this approach is that it may help to make some of my suggestions practically useful, perhaps for those interested in the problem raised by the prawns.

How can philosophy contribute to a scientific question? Isn't it up to zoologists to determine whether prawns can feel pain, and up to neuroscientists to determine which processes actually constitute pain? Well, yes, up to a point. But there are two worries. One is that, to the extent that zoologists and other scientists apply everyday psychological concepts to non-human animals, they don't tend to say much about what really matters when it comes to determining whether those concepts apply. They reasonably assume that if the animal's behaviour is sufficiently like that of human beings to whom a given psychological description applies, then that description applies to the animal. In any case biology, neurobiology, neurochemistry, and related sciences are concerned with the actual workings of living creatures: ourselves, chimps, rats, fruit flies, nematodes, bacteria, and the rest. In contrast, those philosophical questions about which facts matter, and why, are general. They apply not only to human beings and languageless creatures like prawns; not only to terrestrial creatures but to whatever creatures there might be anywhere; not only to evolved organisms but to artificial systems like robots. For that reason they cannot be adequately answered exclusively in terms of human or terrestrial nervous systems. Nor could they be answered by specifying any particular type of mechanism. You might wonder whether we have an appropriate framework for answering such general questions. Is the project feasible? Read on.

The idea that the prawns might be just behaving without feeling comes to mind naturally; it doesn't have to be prompted by philosophical argumentation. Plenty of things just behave without feeling: the twisted rubber band is one example; most if not all existing robots are another. On the other hand, we unhesitatingly treat other people as no less subject to conscious feelings than ourselves. So the questions of what matters from the point of view of an interest in phenomenal consciousness, and why it matters, are not necessarily driven by exclusively philosophical preconceptions. However, the other worry I mentioned is unmistakably—even extravagantly— philosophical. Even if we knew all the scientific facts about the workings of the human nervous system, some people would say: 'Yes, but we can imagine that all those physical facts might have been true while there was no consciousness at all'. The idea of zombies throws an eerie light on our innocent-seeming questions.

1.2 THE ZOMBIE IDEA

I said 'the' idea of zombies, but there is more than one even if we ignore Caribbean folklore. To make sure we agree on the relevant zombie idea, imagine that somewhere in this or another world there is an exact physical double of yourself. It not only looks and behaves like you, it matches you in every detail of body and brain: it is a particle-for-particle duplicate. So (we can assume) it says and writes exactly the same things as you do. In my own case this creature talks a lot about consciousness, which it apparently regards as a deep philosophical problem. It even writes articles and books on the subject. Naturally everyone treats it as if it were conscious. Not only is that attitude natural; it seems to be supported by overwhelming evidence. How could this creature talk and write about consciousness unless it were conscious? But the example is strictly philosophical, and this particular physical duplicate is a philosophical zombie. By definition philosophical zombies are supposed to have no conscious experiences at all: 'all is silent and dark within'.[1]

All the philosophers I know—indeed all the sane people I know—agree that in fact there are no philosophical zombies. Not only that: they agree they are ruled out by the laws of nature. But the question is whether zombies are possible at all. Is

---

[1] The words are Iris Murdoch's in a discussion of behaviourism: *The Sovereignty of Good*, 13. The idea of zombies will be explained more fully in the following chapters.

there a possible world where there are zombies in the sense explained: a world physically like what we tend to assume the actual world is, including organisms physically just like ourselves, but where there are no 'qualia' (to introduce a word I try to avoid if possible, and will say more about later)? If zombies are so much as a bare possibility, the world is a very paradoxical place. That possibility doesn't just imply that there is more to us than the behavioural or other physical facts can provide for. It implies that our part of the world involves something non-physical, on top of the molecules, atoms, and subatomic particles that compose our bodies and those of other sentient creatures. If on the other hand zombies are not possible, then if we can make clear why that is so, we shall have solved the hardest part of the mind-body problem.

I shall discuss those claims in the next three chapters. For the present, it is enough that the question of whether zombies are a genuine possibility takes us to the heart of the problem of the nature of phenomenal consciousness.

Many people find the accounts of consciousness currently on offer hard to swallow. How could experiences be just a matter of behavioural dispositions, for example, or the mere performance of functions, or information being processed, or representations, or higher-order thoughts? Such accounts, to be considered in Chapter 11, don't seem up to the job. As Thomas Nagel (1974) argued, they seem to leave out something essential; there seems to be what Joseph Levine calls an 'explanatory gap'—something he rightly links with the zombie idea (1983; 2001). Any adequate account of phenomenal consciousness must deal illuminatingly with that apparent gap.

1.3 OUTLINE

The project of this book has two phases. The first consists of an examination of the zombie idea and its eventual unmasking as radically misconceived. In order to establish its potential significance for physicalism, the next chapter considers physicalism's basic commitments. I argue that even the most minimal physicalism involves commitment to the 'strict implication thesis'. If that is right, to establish the bare possibility of zombies would be to disprove physicalism. Chapter 3 examines the main arguments for the zombie possibility, all of which appear to fall short. There are of course also plenty of arguments *against* the zombie possibility in the literature; but they lack intuitive appeal. I think the argument to be presented in Chapter 4 has a good deal of intuitive appeal, and exposes the fundamental incoherence of the conception of phenomenal consciousness implied by the zombie idea—together, it is worth emphasizing, with quite a few other views, including epiphenomenalism, parallelism, and the notion of an 'inverted spectrum' without physical differences.

If that first phase of the project is successful it will help to correct a lot of desperate and confused thinking about these matters. Much effort and ingenuity have been devoted to reconciling physicalism with the seeming conceivability of zombies. Indeed, the zombie idea and its relatives seem to have been responsible for much that is hard to accept in the theories of consciousness now on offer. The zombie idea also seems to have made the main objections to functionalism, and indeed to physicalism, look more appealing than they ought to be. If my argument against the conceivability of zombies is sound, the 'explanatory gap' can be seen to be either not genuine, or not a problem.

That brings us to the harder task: to explain *how it is* that zombies are not possible: equivalently, to explain what matters for phenomenal consciousness. Although my anti-zombie argument shows that the idea of zombies reflects a fundamentally mistaken way of conceiving of phenomenal consciousness, it doesn't make clear how we ought to conceive of it. The second phase of my project is an attempt to provide a suitable understanding. No doubt there is more than one acceptable way to do that; but we need at least one. There is a vital preliminary question. What sort of illumination can we reasonably hope to achieve? Do we for example have to define consciousness-involving concepts in physical or neutral terms? Chapter 5 will discuss what a solution must do, and what it does not need to attempt.

Chapters 6 to 9 will set up a framework in terms of which suitable explanations can be given, using reasonably unproblematic everyday or folk-psychological concepts. This framework treats perceptual consciousnesss as central, presupposing that it is also phenomenal. The task of extending our understanding to phenomenal consciousness in general will then, I claim, be relatively straightforward, and will be only briefly considered. To introduce the framework I shall outline a scheme for classifying organisms and other behaving systems from the point of view of an interest in perceptual consciousness. I shall argue that a necessary condition for perceptual consciousness is the 'basic package' of capacities, possession of which makes a behaving system a *decider*.

Philosophical discussion of these matters is distorted not only by our tendency to think in terms of inappropriate or even grossly misleading models, but by unwarranted theoretical assumptions. Among the former are the 'Cartesian Theatre' fallacy, made familiar by Ryle (1949), and what I call the 'jacket' fallacy. The latter include, I think, the assumption that concept-possession is a unitary, all-or-nothing matter, and that it requires a high level of cognitive sophistication. In Chapter 8 I shall examine such assumptions and explain how we can de-sophisticate the framework in terms of which the relevant cognitive capacities are to be conceived.

Being a decider is at least necessary for perceptual consciousness, but apparently not also sufficient. In Chapters 9 and 10 I shall explain what further is required. It is 'direct activity': a special feature of the way incoming perceptual information is processed. Again this feature is characterized in terms of a relatively unproblematic subset of everyday or folk-psychological concepts: cognitive-functionally in a broad sense. Direct activity as I shall explain it is an integrated process, to be conceived of holistically, and to be contrasted with what is often called the 'availability' or 'poisedness' of perceptual information.

Once the crucial notion of direct activity has been explained it will be possible to state necessary and sufficient conditions for perceptual consciousness. I hope the reasoning that runs through Chapters 6 to 10 will gradually make clear how it is that, necessarily, anything satisfying those conditions is thereby perceptually and phenomenally conscious.

'Ha!' you may be thinking, 'Functionalism. Read no further. Functionalists are a bunch of circle-squarers.' But even if you choose to describe my position as a variety of functionalism, it is not open to the usual objections. One of these is that functionalism leaves open the logical possibility of zombies (as I argued, regrettably, in Kirk 1974*b*) while here I am trying to make clear that, and how, zombies are not even conceivable in any useful sense. Further, unlike some varieties of functionalism, my position does not require mental concepts to be *definable* in terms of functions. Also unlike some varieties, it requires us to take account of the nature and causal character of the behaver's internal processing. These features enable my approach to deal with what many regard as a fatal objection to all forms of functionalism: that they treat 'intrinsic' properties as if they were relational. Chapter 10 confronts that and the other objections that have been and may be expected to be raised to the account offered here.

You may reasonably challenge my reliance on everyday or 'folk' psychological concepts. Some will surely fall into disuse with the progress of scientific psychology, to be superseded by concepts better attuned to our accumulating scientific knowledge. However, the concepts I actually depend on for the central notions of 'deciders' and 'direct activity' are ones for which I don't know of any promising potential substitutes. Much of the work of refining our folk concepts has been focused on specifically human cognition, while I am aiming at something more general. You will have to decide whether there is a serious deficiency here.

The concluding chapter is devoted to briefly considering rival accounts of phenomenal consciousness and explaining why I think mine has the edge over them.

2

Zombies and Minimal Physicalism

The zombie idea is strangely alluring, but is it worth bothering with? Some philosophers regard it as a ridiculous waste of time (Dennett 1991; 1995). I think there are two good reasons to give it close scrutiny. One is that the zombie idea reflects misconceptions which must be exposed if we are to understand the nature of phenomenal consciousness. The other is that if zombies are even possible, physicalism is false. In this chapter I will try to make clear why that is so. (Note that my eventual account of consciousness will be neutral between physicalism and dualism: I am not aiming to defend physicalism here, at least not directly.)

2.1 CAUSAL CLOSURE AND EPIPHENOMENALISM

Descartes contrasted us strongly with other animals. They are automata whose behaviour is explicable wholly in terms of physical mechanisms. It might be possible to construct a machine which looked like one of us but, he argued, it could not behave like one of us because it could not use language creatively rather than producing stereotyped responses; and it could not behave appropriately in arbitrarily various situations. Distinctively human behaviour, he thought, depends on the immaterial mind, interacting with processes in the body (*Discourse* v). If he is right, there could not be a world that was physically like the actual world while its human-like inhabitants lacked consciousness: their bodies would not work properly. If we suddenly lost our minds our bodies might continue to run on for a while; our hearts might carry on beating, we might breathe, sleep, and digest food. We might even walk or sing in a mindless sort of way (*Reply to Objections* IV). But without the contribution made by immaterial minds our behaviour would not show characteristically human features. So although Descartes seems to have thought up the idea of something like zombies, it could not be slotted into his explanatory scheme.

The situation changed when nineteenth-century scientists began to think there were grounds for supposing that the physical world is 'closed under causation': that every physical effect has a physical cause. If the developing science of neurophysiology fulfilled its promise, and physical explanations could be extended so as to apply to human behaviour, then the human body could plausibly be regarded as a machine, capable on its own of producing the whole range of human behaviour. In that case substantial minds would be redundant, leaving us with the serious problem of how consciousness fitted into the story. One response was that consciousness too is just a matter of physical processes. But then, as now, that struck many people as absurd. T. H. Huxley and others continued to insist on the causal closure of the physical world; but they didn't see how consciousness could be purely physical either. Hence the notion of epiphenomenalism: consciousness is a mere by-product of the brain's churnings, with no effects on the physical world. Human beings are 'conscious automata'.

Clearly epiphenomenalism entails that zombies are possible. For what would bind the 'epiphenomena' of consciousness, including 'qualia', to the churnings of the neurones? At most it could only be a matter of natural necessity. On this view, therefore, the relevant laws of nature could have been absent—and if they had been absent, the actual world would have been a zombie world. As G. F. Stout pointed out, if epiphenomenalism were true, then it ought to be 'credible' that the entire physical history of the universe should have been 'just the same as it is if there were not and never had been any experiencing individuals. Human bodies would still have gone through the motions of making and using bridges, telephones and telegraphs, of writing and reading books, of speaking in Parliament, of arguing about materialism, and so on'. The idea of such a world struck him as 'incredible to Common Sense' (1931: 138 f.).

I take it there are no good reasons to think that human behaviour requires contributions from a Cartesian mind. All the evidence we have suggests that the physical events in human brains and bodies are physically caused. Indeed, the evidence suggests that the whole physical world is closed under causation. (Papineau 2002 assesses the evidence.) However, we need not commit ourselves to this view. All that matters here is that even if the physical world is not causally closed, the zombie idea depends on its being *possible* that it should have been; which no one disputes. So if it is also possible that the alleged epiphenomena of consciousness should be connected to physical events in a causally closed physical world by merely natural necessity, then possibly a zombie (a particle-for-particle duplicate of a normal human being which totally lacked consciousness) could still behave like a human being. (Other conceptions of zombies will be noted later: 3.1.) If such creatures are indeed possible it follows, I think, that any kind of physicalism is false. To see why, we first need to get reasonably clear about physicalism, at least as far as it concerns mental states.

2.2 REDESCRIPTION AND STRICT IMPLICATION

The rough idea of physicalism, of course, is that nothing exists but the physical. Since the zombie possibility is supposed to demolish all varieties of physicalism, it will be useful to try to isolate what I shall argue is a basic commitment of them all. We can start by imagining we have an idealized version of today's physics. The point of idealization is to think away the multiplicity of competing theories; and the point of confining ourselves to today's physics rather than invoking an imagined ideal future physics, or a completed true physics, is to avoid the familiar objection that we cannot tell what kinds of things and properties some remotely future physics might appeal to: conceivably it might even be dualistic. For that reason we had better stipulate that our idealized contemporary physics includes none of the current dualistic interpretations of quantum mechanics. By appealing to an idealized physics we can sidestep some difficulties that are irrelevant in the present context. The decisive consideration is that the main philosophical objections to physicalism are neutral with respect to the details of physical theory. All the emphasis is on the supposed impossibility of facts about consciousness being accommodated in a purely physical world of *any* recognizable sort.

Given the austere vocabulary of idealized contemporary physics, then, let P be the conjunction of all actually true statements in that vocabulary. Since P includes all truths about the spatiotemporal locations of things, events, and processes throughout spacetime, it represents the entire physical universe past, present, and future.[1] And since all true physical laws are also expressible in that vocabulary, P includes them too.

If you maintain that nothing exists but the physical you will probably accept that the following statement conveys an important truth:

If there are any true statements about the world not expressible in the austere physical vocabulary of P, then those statements are different ways of talking about—different ways of describing, explaining, and so on—the same world as is specified by P, and their truth does not depend on anything other than what is provided for by P.

An example will explain the last clause. We could describe a certain historical event truly, though not very informatively, by saying that 'a man fired a pistol at another man'. Redescriptions of that event include this: 'Gavrilo Princip assassinated the Archduke Franz Ferdinand at Sarajevo in 1914.' The first description does not by itself imply the second because the second depends on further facts. By itself, the first description implies only such statements as 'Two men existed', 'A pistol existed', 'A shot was fired'. We can call the statements so implied 'pure redescriptions', since their truth depends purely on whatever items or situations have been specified by some base description. That gives us a convenient way to state the following *redescription thesis*:

(R) Any true statements about the world not expressible in the austere physical vocabulary of P are pure redescriptions of the world specified by P.

(R) does not imply that truths not statable in austerely physical terms must pick out exactly the same aspects of the world as the truths in P do. Still less does it

---

[1] Perhaps the details of the underlying physical structures are impossible to convey by finite descriptions. (Thanks to Robert Black for indicating this possibility.) However, details could still be expressed down to any arbitrary degree of resolution; and the broad points I want to make still stand.

imply that we must be able to construct counterparts in P to all non-physically statable truths. Typically the non-physically statable truths classify and select things and properties in different ways from those provided by physics. These points will be illustrated shortly.

To reject the redescription thesis would imply that there were truths which were about the actual world, yet not made true by the world specified by P. In that case something other than the world specified by P must provide for the truth of those statements, contradicting the physicalist thesis that there is nothing in the world but the physical.[2] That is a prima facie case for the view that physicalists ought to endorse the redescription thesis. Although that thesis needs further clarification, I don't think many physicalists would object to it.

However, some who call themselves physicalists would certainly object to a related thesis, which I think follows from the redescription thesis and helps to clarify it. I will argue that all physicalists, whether they like it or not, are committed to a thesis according to which the purely physical truths about the world *strictly imply* many other truths, including psychological truths. Strict implication here is to be understood as follows:

A statement A strictly implies a statement B just in case 'not-(If A then B)' is inconsistent or incoherent for broadly logical or conceptual reasons.

Let Q be the conjunction of the totality of actually true statements in psychological language about the individuals whose existence physicalists suppose to be provided for by P.[3] Then the *strict implication thesis* is:

P strictly implies Q.

In other words, 'P and not-Q' involves inconsistency or other incoherence of a broadly logical or conceptual kind, so that it is absolutely impossible that P should be true and Q false. In still other words, in every possible world where P is true, so is Q. Unfortunately the vocabulary of possibility and necessity has become very slippery. Kripke in similar contexts uses 'logical possibility' and 'metaphysical possibility' interchangeably; some apply 'logical' to a kind of possibility that others prefer to call 'conceptual' (Chalmers 1999: 477); others use 'logical' for 'metaphysical or conceptual' (as noted by Yablo 1999: 457 n.; Latham 2000: 72 f.). I will try to avoid these adjectives except in quotations. By 'possible' without qualification I will mean just that the worlds, descriptions, situations or states of affairs in question involve no inconsistency or other incoherence of a broadly logical or conceptual

---

[2] The redescription thesis allows for worlds where P is true but there are intelligent non-physical beings. Suppose there are exactly twenty billion intelligent beings in the actual world. Then 'There are exactly twenty billion intelligent beings' will be false in such other worlds, but P will make it true in the actual world *if* this is purely physical.

[3] Like the redescription thesis, the strict implication thesis does not rule out possible worlds where P is true but there are intelligent non-physical beings. But I need only consider those psychological statements which are true of individuals whose existence, according to physicalism, is already provided for by P.

kind. If the context forces explicitness, I will use 'c-possible' and its cognates in this sense. Thus P strictly implies Q just in case it is c-impossible that P should be true and Q false.[4]

The inconsistency need not be obvious, any more than it is in mathematical cases. There is no obvious inconsistency in maintaining that there is a greatest prime number; but inconsistency is entailed all the same. However, mathematical examples are significantly unlike the cases that chiefly concern us; here is one that is a bit more to the point:

(M) There are mountains.

M is true; and we may assume that landscape features such as mountains involve nothing beyond the physical. But the vocabulary of landscape features is by definition not part of the austere vocabulary of our idealized version of contemporary physics. Does P (the conjunction of all true statements in that austere vocabulary) leave scope for M to have failed to be true? Of course not. Why? Because the world specified by P has features which just are describable in those terms. There is nothing mysterious about this. Truths such as M are, in the sense explained, *pure redescriptions* of the reality that P specifies: different ways of talking about it—and nothing but it. P describes a certain world in its own special vocabulary, and M describes an aspect or component of that same world in its own vocabulary, without having to take account of anything beyond what is specified by P. P specifies a whole universe, where among other things there are galaxies, stars, and planets. In particular it specifies the physical details of our own planet's surface, including those large masses of dense materials which project relatively far from their surroundings, and which we call 'mountains'. If we knew and accepted that much of what P specifies (always in its own terms, of course, not in the terms I have just used) then for us to deny that there were mountains on our planet would be inconsistent with our understanding of those words and our grasp of the concepts involved. It is in that sense that it would be incoherent to assert 'P and not-M', and it is in that way that P's strict implication of M is to be understood.

The argument can be extended to cover the strict implication thesis proper. If the redescription thesis is true, and all the true psychological statements conjoined in Q are pure redescriptions of the reality specified by P, then that reality contains all that is needed to ensure that those descriptions apply to it. Note especially that no natural laws are required other than those either included in P or strictly implied by P.

Although it is not an empirical question whether P strictly implies Q, the strict implication thesis itself is empirical. This is because P includes empirical statements that just happen to be true in our world. In different possible worlds

---

[4] Versions of this approach are defended in Kirk 1974*b*; 1979; 1982; 1994; 1996*a*; 2001. Lewis defends a similar view, implicitly in his (1966), explicitly in his (1994). See also Chalmers 1996; 1999; Jackson 1994; 1998; Chalmers and Jackson 2001. Kirk 1996*a* advocates strict implication and descriptions in preference to supervenience and properties.

different statements are true; but the strict implication thesis says nothing about those worlds. 'P' is not a variable, standing for whatever the physical facts may happen to be in any old possible world; P is the conjunction of those austerely physical statements that are actually true in our world. The following statement should remove hesitation over this point: 'The first statement of the last paragraph strictly implies the second.' That statement is empirical even though, when the two other statements have been identified, it is not an empirical question, but logical or conceptual, whether the one strictly implies the other.

If P does indeed strictly imply Q, then it is not c-possible that P should be true and Q false: it is not c-possible that the physical universe should have been as physicalists suppose it to be, while the psychological facts were in any respect different.[5] So if all physicalists are committed to the strict implication thesis, they are committed to the impossibility of zombies. More to the point, they are committed to the *c-impossibility* of zombies: to their impossibility for broadly logical or conceptual reasons. It follows that to establish even the bare possibility of zombies would be to refute physicalism.

Many philosophers accept that physicalism involves commitment to something like the strict implication thesis and the consequent c-impossibility of zombies (for example Byrne 1999; Chalmers 1996; Jackson 1994; Lewis 1966; 1994). But since there is also resistance to this view (Block and Stalnaker 1999; Hill and McLaughlin 1999; Hill 1997; Loar 1997; 1999; Papineau 2002), it will be worth elaborating the points made above and dealing with some rather more detailed worries about physicalism and the strict implication thesis. The next two sections may be skipped by readers willing to accept what has been said so far.

2.3 MORE ABOUT PHYSICALISM AND STRICT IMPLICATION

It seems obvious that 'mountain' is just a pure redescription of certain features of the physical world specified by P. But you may object that although the argument in the last section shows there are no c-possible worlds where P holds in the absence of mountains, it does not also show that 'P and not-M' is actually inconsistent or incoherent, which is what strict implication requires. This thought may appear to be reinforced by a suggestion from Block and Stalnaker. They say that 'for at least some names for substances or properties that are in fact physical, the reference-fixing definition might be a functional one that did not exclude on conceptual grounds the possibility that the substance or property be non-physical' (1999: 18). If being a mountain is such a property, so that in some possible worlds

---

[5] By my definitions the statement 'If P then M' is c-necessary. Does that make it a case of what people mean by 'metaphysical' necessity? I don't know; which is why I won't use that expression. The relation between P and M seems too straightforward and unmysterious to be labelled in such a problematic way.

mountains include non-physical items, you might suspect that 'P and not-M' is not incoherent. But that would be a mistake. For two main reasons, Block and Stalnaker's point does not undermine the argument of the last section.

One reason is that even if the strict implication thesis holds in our world, it does not rule out the possibility of dualistic worlds. As noted earlier, P simply specifies the actual physical facts in the actual world: 'P' is not a variable. In a dualistic world, to be sure, whatever conjunction of physical statements is true of *that* world (the conjunction which may be said to correspond to P) may fail strictly to imply the psychological truths about that world because those truths may depend on non-physical items. But that is irrelevant: the strict implication thesis has P itself as one of its components, not some different conjunction of statements.

The second reason why Block and Stalnaker's suggestion does not affect the present argument is that (to recall) P includes a complete specification not only of the entire actual physical universe throughout space and time, but all true physical laws—on the assumption that physicalists are right about the actual world, including the causal closure of the physical. It follows that in any possible world where P is true, whatever non-physical items may also exist in it have no physical effects. They make no difference to the physical structures provided for by P, some of which we call 'mountains'. In particular, they cannot *prevent* those structures from being mountains. Conceivably there are possible worlds where mountains are somehow significantly involved with non-physical items (mountain-sprites?) and perhaps P holds in some of those worlds. But that would not prevent P from strictly implying that there are mountains. It is not as if our concept *mountain* risked being discovered to require mountains to have non-physical properties. We know (I am assuming) that our concept is not like that—even if we might conceivably have possessed different concepts, which did require what then counted as 'mountains' to have non-physical properties.

I have argued that physicalists about mountains are committed to the view that 'P and not-M' is inconsistent or incoherent in the sense explained. By similar reasoning, physicalists about the mental are committed to the view that 'P and not-Q' is inconsistent or incoherent in the same sense, hence to the strict implication thesis. (Thomas Nagel has remarked that 'There is no hidden verbal contradiction in the description of a zombie—even if in reality a zombie is logically impossible' (1998: 345). Perhaps the last few paragraphs help to make it intelligible that he should have put his point in those terms.[6])

The same goes for psycho-physical identity theorists as well as other physicalists. Bald assertions of psycho-physical identities do not dispense physicalists from commitment to the strict implication thesis; they do not provide a basis on which physicalists can allow zombies to be so much as c-possible.

---

[6] In other respects his position on the zombie threat to physicalism is not much like the one advocated here. See also 5.4, 5.5 below.

2.4 A POSTERIORI NECESSITY AND PHYSICALISM

That last claim is controversial, however. Plenty of physicalists still hold that zombie worlds are only 'a posteriori' impossible, in a sense identified by Kripke (for example Block and Stalnaker 1999; Hill and McLaughlin 1999; Hill 1997; Loar 1997; 1999; Papineau 2002). I will briefly explain why I think they are wrong. (For fuller discussions see Chalmers 1996; Chalmers and Jackson 2001; Jackson 1998; Kirk 2001.)

A lot of philosophers follow Chalmers in distinguishing two kinds of physicalism: 'type A' and 'type B'. Type-A physicalists hold that 'phenomenal truths (in so far as there are such truths) are necessitated *a priori* by physical truths'. Type-B physicalists 'accept that phenomenal truths are not necessitated *a priori* by physical truths, but hold that they are necessitated *a posteriori* by physical truths' (Chalmers 1999: 474 f.). Chalmers's definitions include further clauses; but I find them problematic, so will avoid talking of type-A and type-B physicalism.[7] Instead I will use the clauses quoted to define the following two theses:

The strong thesis: Phenomenal truths are necessitated a priori by physical truths.
The weak thesis: Phenomenal truths are not necessitated a priori by physical truths, but they are necessitated a posteriori by physical truths.

If we postpone a (quite significant) worry over just what a priori necessitation is supposed to be, it seems clear that the strict implication thesis, which I maintain is part of physicalism's minimal commitment, is at least close to the strong thesis. If that is right, then since the weak thesis is defined as ruling out the strong thesis, my position seems to entail that *the weak thesis is not physicalism at all*—a claim which contradicts what many philosophers seem to assume. I will reinforce that claim.

For the moment, let us assume that what is 'a priori possible' coincides with what I am calling 'c-possible': in other words, that a truth B is 'a priori necessitated' by a truth A if 'not-(if A then B)' would involve inconsistency or other incoherence in the sense explained above. (The assumption is not trivial. I will qualify it at 5.4 below.) Evidently, if the weak thesis is not to collapse into the strong thesis, what is a posteriori possible must not coincide with what is a priori possible or, on our assumption,

---

[7] Chalmers (2002*b*) links other claims with the strong thesis. According to what he calls 'type-A materialism', [1] 'there is no epistemic gap between physical and phenomenal truths; or at least, any apparent epistemic gap is easily closed' [while I think there is such a gap]; [2] 'there are no phenomenal truths of which [Jackson's] Mary is ignorant in principle from inside her black-and-white room' [while I think there are such truths: 5.4]; [3] when Mary leaves the room, 'she gains at most an ability' [while I think she gains more: 5.4]; [4] 'on reflection there is no "hard problem" of explaining consciousness that remains once one has solved the easy problems of explaining various cognitive, behavioral, and environmental functions' [while I think it really is a hard problem to explain consciousness philosophically]. As well as avoiding the type-A/type-B vocabulary, I avoid the expressions 'a priori physicalism' (because it doesn't differentiate between the strong thesis and Hobbes-type materialism, which rules out dualism a priori) and 'a posteriori physicalism/materialism' (because it is not physicalism at all).

c-possible. Since what is a posteriori possible cannot involve inconsistency or other incoherence, it must be at least c-possible. So weak-thesis physicalists who wish to distinguish themselves from strong-thesis physicalists must hold that some c-possible worlds are not a posteriori possible. And typically, so-called 'a posteriori' physicalists do indeed say that such things as zombie worlds, and pairs of worlds differing only in that they are spectrum-inverted relative to each other, are impossible yet not 'a priori impossible' (Block and Stalnaker 1999; Papineau 2002). Let us consider the position they seem committed to, focusing on the case of zombie worlds: that the c-possibility of zombie worlds is consistent with the view that consciousness in our world involves nothing other than the physical.

I have already argued that physicalism involves commitment to the redescription thesis, and that the redescription thesis entails the strict implication thesis—which directly rules out the c-possibility of zombie worlds and spectrum-inverted worlds. Not having come across any persuasive counter-arguments to the reasoning in the last two sections, I think that conclusion stands. However, some readers may find one or both of the following slightly different arguments more intuitively appealing. Neither appeals to the redescription thesis.

First argument. Assume for argument's sake that:

(a) consciousness in our world involves nothing other than the physical (as physicalists without exception maintain); and
(b) z is a c-possible zombie world where P holds.

By (a) it is only the purely physical facts about our world (or, if you find talk of facts problematic, the purely physical realities in our world) which make true the consciousness-involving statements in Q. Those physical realities 'make true' those statements in the same sense as that in which they also make true the statement that there are mountains: nothing other than those realities is involved in those statements being true. At the same time, by (b) z is in all physical respects exactly the same as our world, and, being a zombie world, contains nothing other than the physical. So if, as all physicalists must maintain, those physical realities make it true that there is consciousness in our world, the same physical realities cannot fail to make the same thing true in z. In that case there is consciousness in z, which contradicts (b). Thus (a) and (b) are mutually inconsistent, and physicalists cannot consistently accept the c-possibility of zombies.

Second argument. This argument, like that of the last two sections, has the more general conclusion that all physicalists are committed to the strict implication thesis, according to which P strictly implies Q.

Let a 'purely physical twin' of our world be a c-possible world where:

(c) P is true;
(d) nothing exists whose existence is not strictly implied by P.

And suppose that someone claiming to be a physicalist asserts that, c-possibly, in one such purely physical twin w of our world:

(e) Q is not true.

Since Q does not hold in w, there must be a difference between w and our world. But all purely physical differences between w and our world have been ruled out by definition. Therefore our purported physicalist implies that there is a *non-physical* difference between our world and w. Since w is purely physical, and both worlds answer to exactly the same physical description P, the difference must be that there is something non-physical in our world. Since that is inconsistent with the view that our world is purely physical, our purported physicalist cannot consistently deny the strict implication thesis.

If either of those two arguments is sound, or if the reasoning of the last two sections is sound, then those who maintain the weak thesis, and thereby (on our temporary assumption that a priori necessitation is the same as c-necessitation) reject the strict implication thesis, are committed to the view that there is more to our world than the physical. Although they may call themselves physicalists, they are not. The arguments do not prevent them from endorsing a posteriori psycho-physical identity statements, but they prevent such statements from serving as substitutes for the strict implication thesis itself: physicalists can consistently endorse such identity statements only if they are strictly implied by P. (The a posteriority of such statements would be provided for by P.)

There is no need for P to include the statement that it itself is about the actual world, by the way. The strict implication thesis is a physicalistic claim about the actual world, and specifically about the relations between the actual physical truths or facts, and certain others. So when we consider the statements in P, we already know they are supposed to be about the actual world.

Do physicalists have to follow Chalmers and Jackson (2001) in maintaining that we could in principle get from P to Q a priori? They do *if* the strong thesis is indeed logically equivalent to the strict implication thesis, and *if* we are supposed to take seriously the occurrence of 'a priori' in the strong thesis. However, the true position is more complicated, as we shall see.

Of course there is much more to be said on the topic of strong-thesis and weak-thesis physicalism. I have touched on it here partly because I think it is important that physicalism is committed to the strict implication thesis; also because the strict implication thesis helps to define what I take to be the task of explaining the nature of phenomenal consciousness. (For fuller discussions see Byrne 1999; Chalmers 1996; 1999; Chalmers and Jackson 2001; Jackson 1994; 1998; Kirk 1994; 1996*a*; 1996*b*; 2001.[8])

---

[8] Chalmers and Jackson's position is broadly in line with mine. However, there are significant points of difference, including the following. (1) They start from *micro*physical facts alone: their 'P' stands for 'the conjunction of microphysical truths about the world' (2001: 316). My minimal physicalism maintains only that the psychological truths in Q are strictly implied by what I call 'P': the totality of truths expressible in the austere vocabulary of an idealized version of today's physics. And it is the conjunction of truths about our world, the *actual* world: a point which obviates any need to worry about indexicals. (2) They are neutral as to whether P 'implies' phenomenal truths. Their discussion is confined to the question whether, when P is conjoined with all phenomenal truths, it 'implies' all macro-truths. The strict implication thesis, in contrast, has it that P strictly implies all

For our purposes it is enough that the strict implication thesis is *necessary* for minimal physicalism. I had better add that it is not also sufficient. It has to be supplemented by at least one further thesis, for example:

(N) nothing exists other than what is strictly implied to exist by P.

(N) is clearly implied by the redescription thesis: it does essentially the same work as is done in the statement of that thesis by the word 'pure'. But unless dualism is c-impossible (as Hobbes may have held) P by itself does not strictly imply (N). Together, the strict implication thesis and (N) seem jointly sufficient for a minimal kind of physicalism.[9]

2.5 PSYCHOLOGICAL AND PHYSICAL EXPLICABILITY

If the idea of zombies is to do useful work against physicalism, zombie worlds must be assumed to be subject to the causal closure of the physical. That is, in zombie worlds all physical effects must be physically caused. I have been arguing that if such worlds are possible, physicalism is false because in that case conscious-ness in the actual world involves something non-physical. However, if physicalism is *true* of the actual world, and this world is subject to causal closure, it does not follow that psychological events must be somehow physically explicable *as* psychological events. This is not always recognized.

Barry Stroud, for example, starts a critical discussion of physicalism with the assumption that a 'full semantic reduction' of the psychological vocabulary to equivalent physical terms is not available (2000: 78). Many physicalists will agree with that assumption, but they will not regard it as a difficulty. To see why, sup-pose we need to explain some phenomenon in terms of mountains. 'Relief rain' is a good illustration. Relief rain occurs when the prevailing winds are forced upwards by mountain sides, as a result of which condensation leads to precipita-tion. And that is a perfectly good explanation of relief rain. If we think it is a purely physical phenomenon, do we have to produce a 'full semantic reduction' of the relief rain vocabulary to the vocabulary of physics, by means of which we could translate that explanation into the vocabulary of fundamental particles,

---

macro-truths about the mental states of the individuals whose existence is supposedly provided for by P, including phenomenal truths. (3) They offer a particular view about what they call 'reductive explanation'; I do not. I find what they say on this topic plausible, but do not see why it must be a component of minimal physicalism. (4) Strict implication is different from a priori entailment as explained by Chalmers and Jackson, as we shall see at 5.4. The difference is hardly relevant in the context of their (2001); but in the context of a discussion of the minimal commitments of physicalism it matters a lot. (5) Finally, Chalmers and Jackson find it useful to explain their position with the help of 'two-dimensional semantics'. I have not found that useful, mainly because I find it tends to distract attention from the decisive arguments.

 [9] There is no need to pursue this matter here: my point is that the strict implication thesis is a basic commitment of any physicalism.

strings, or whatever? No. We know that mountains involve nothing beyond the physical; but our explanation of relief rain is fine as it stands: only confusion and obfuscation would result from trying to express it in terms of quarks and so on. Nor is there any need to attempt a 'semantic reduction' of the macro-vocabulary and concepts of mountains, winds, and so on, to microphysics. Certainly, for any given case of relief rain there will be an explanation in those terms. But if you want to understand what relief rain is you had better steer clear of microphysics. The best explanation will be on the lines sketched above. Details of the fine structure of mountains and moving air are irrelevant.[10]

Analogously, I suggest, physicalists can look for explanations of how psychological descriptions apply without having to find austerely physical equivalents for them. Stroud wonders how physicalists can do without such 'semantic reductions'. The idea cannot be that 'only the sentences expressed in physical terms are true. The psychological sentences about perceptions and beliefs are true as well; ...' (2000: 79)—a remark with which only eliminativists would disagree. He finds it obscure if physicalists want to say (as they surely do) that 'the physical facts in question are all that it takes to "make it true" that' the psychological descriptions apply. He objects that the physicalists' position 'involves the obscure idea of one sentence "making true" a different non-equivalent sentence *which it does not imply*' (80, my emphasis). His example is: 'The sentence in purely physical terms, "Processes P1, P2, P3 ... are occurring", does not imply the sentence "Smith is buying a house from Jones"' (83). There seem to be misconceptions here.

Certainly house-buying involves a lot of things besides the physical processes inside buyer and seller. It involves everything which makes it the case that there are legally instituted practices of contracting and purchasing. But why shouldn't a sufficiently broad range of purely physical truths describe enough of the world to provide for the existence of those institutions? Why shouldn't they also describe enough to ensure that Smith is buying a house from Jones? If I am right, that is what physicalists have to claim, like it or not, because they have to claim that the totality of purely physical truths strictly implies such other truths as that Smith is buying a house from Jones. It is not obvious that P strictly implies such things; but we have been given no reason to suppose that if the strict implication thesis is true it must be obvious. On the contrary, there is every reason to expect it will be far from obvious. But Stroud makes physicalism look more puzzling than it is. Physicalists don't have to say that a sentence might make true 'a different non-equivalent sentence which it does not imply'. They need only say that a sentence might describe or specify a world, a reality, which makes true a different non-equivalent sentence—and actually does imply the latter in the sense I have been explaining.

[10] This is the moral of Putnam's well-known example of the square peg and the round hole (1975c).

2.6 SEEING WHETHER DESCRIPTIONS FIT REALITY, VERSUS LOOKING FOR ANALYTIC CONNECTIONS

Many people share Stroud's assumptions about what physicalism requires. The reasoning behind these and related assumptions seems to go like this:

(1) Physicalism needs necessary links from the physical to the mental.

(2) If the necessity in question were merely natural, the resulting view would be compatible with dualism; so the necessity has to be logical, conceptual, or otherwise a priori.

(3) For any pair of truths A and B, if A implies B by logical, conceptual, or other a priori necessity, then it must be possible to construct a deductive argument in which A is shown to follow from B by strict logical steps.

(4) If the vocabularies used in A and B are significantly different (as with the physical vocabulary of P and the mental vocabulary of Q), such a deductive argument will require equivalences, or at least conditionals, to supply the necessary connections from A-expressions to B-expressions.

(5) Such equivalences or conditionals must be meaning-explicative. That is, they must be 'analytically' or 'conceptually' necessary (as these expressions are used by those who make the assumptions I am arguing are mistaken). In yet other words, B-expressions must be capable of 'full semantic reduction' in terms of A-expressions.

(6) One consequence is that the concepts involved in B must be capable of being acquired purely on the basis of knowing A.

I have no objections to (1) and (2) apart from reservations over the wording. But I hope the example of 'There are mountains' has loosened the grip of (3), (4), (5), and (6). To reinforce the points made in this chapter, a different example will make it particularly easy to bring out the assumptions those moves embody, and to show that they are in fact mistaken.

My digital camera produces images consisting of two-dimensional arrays of a large number of pixels, each pixel being either white or black in any given image. Every image it can produce is therefore completely specifiable by Cartesian co-ordinates and the letters 'W' and 'B'. ('W(3,4)' means that the pixel three places in from the left and four up from the bottom is white, 'B(0, 22)' means that the 22nd pixel up on the left-hand edge is black, and so on.) Suppose, then, that we have a specification S of an image in those terms, and that a certain ordinary-language description D is true of that image. How might we show that S strictly implies D, if it does?

If D were 'The image is of a rectangle', or involved only some other simple geometrical shape, we could easily construct a deductive argument of the kind envisaged in (3). S itself would be one premiss; a definition of 'image of a rectangle' (or whichever other shape D involved) in terms of arrays of pixels would be another premiss. The definition would be meaning-explicative as required by (5), because anyone who knew what a rectangle was could work out that whatever satisfied the definition would be an image of a rectangle; and the conclusion would follow straightforwardly. Such a demonstration would be conclusive proof that S strictly implied D.

Could that method be applied to less straightforward cases, for example when the image was describable as being 'of a duck'? The trouble is that in general there will be neither definitions nor even useful meaning-explicative conditionals involving expressions such as 'image of a duck'. Definitions, in the sense of meaning-explicative conditions that are both necessary and sufficient, can be ruled out very quickly: it cannot be necessary for an image of a duck to be expressible in terms of pixels. However, strict implication does not require conditionals from right to left as well as from left to right; D is not required to imply S. At most, even a deductive argument on the lines suggested earlier would only have required *sufficient* meaning-explicative conditions expressed in pixel-language. Are such conditionals available?

Suppose my camera produces something identifiable as an image of a duck. Then a specification of that image in terms of pixels will strictly imply that description; as will indefinitely many such pixel-language specifications $S_1, S_2, \ldots$, each of which specifies something recognizable as an image of a duck. The statements 'The image specified by S_1 is of a duck', 'The image specified by S_2 is of a duck', and so on will all be true. But will they be analytic or otherwise meaning-explicative? Clearly not—or not as 'analytic' and related expressions are usually understood. That would require us to be able to tell that they were true purely on the basis of knowing their meanings; and it seems clear that we could fully understand the pixel-language specifications without being able to infer from them that they were of duck-images. If that is right, it will not generally be possible to establish such cases of strict implication by constructing a deductive argument on the lines suggested earlier.

However, that would not be the only way to establish that the specification S strictly implies 'The image is of a duck': here is another. Take a sheet of squared paper, ink in each square marked 'B' in the specification, and look at the result. Is it an image of a duck? If so, S strictly implies 'The image is of a duck'. This shows how very straightforward the idea of strict implication is. In the sorts of case that concern us, it is just a matter of seeing whether or not the description on the right-hand side fits the item specified by the left-hand side. You might suspect I am misrepresenting things. Doesn't looking at an image on a sheet of paper introduce empirical considerations? How can the look-and-see method show that S implies D 'for broadly logical or conceptual reasons'? That objection overlooks the fact that although it is not an empirical matter whether S strictly implies D, each such strict implication thesis is itself empirical. Certainly it is a question of empirical fact—decidable by simple inspection—whether we are faced by an image 'of a duck'; but that is just part of the empiricalness or a posteriority of the statement that S strictly implies D; it is analogous to the question whether a certain feature provided for by P is a mountain range. The question at issue now, though, is not the empirical question whether that particular image is or is not of a duck. It is whether, *given* it is of a duck, it could c-possibly have fitted the specification S and have *failed* to be of a duck. The answer to that question is a firm non-empirically based 'No'. Given that the present image is of a duck, any particular image-token which fitted that same specification S would also have been describable as 'of a duck', and that is something we know for broadly logical or conceptual reasons.

What if the specified image is subject to gestalt-switching: can be seen as an image of a rabbit and can also be seen as an image of a duck? How can S strictly imply that it is the one rather than the other? Duck-rabbit images are just a special type of ambiguity. S does not have to settle, for each image, either that the given description applies to it, or that it does not apply to it. In countless cases the answer will be indeterminate, and only descriptions conveying that indeterminacy will themselves be determinately true or false. Since what centrally concerns us is the strict implication thesis, where the statements conjoined in Q are supposed to be true, those other cases are beside the point.

There is an apparently more serious worry. In order to know that 'image of a duck' applies to a specified image, one must already possess the necessary concepts. Now, understanding a pixel-language specification of an image which is in fact of a duck will not by itself endow one with the concept *duck*. To acquire that concept calls for quite a lot of complicated knowledge of, and interactions with, other things and people. Its acquisition seems to be inextricably entangled with factual knowledge (just as Quine argued). For that reason it may seem impossible to come to know that 'of a duck' applies to the image specified by S without having acquired duck-relevant information empirically; which may appear to be another objection to the claim that S strictly implies 'The image is of a duck'. But that is a mistake. Certainly we couldn't acquire concepts like *duck* and *duck-image* purely from knowing pixel-language specifications. But working out that the given specification S strictly implies 'image of a duck' does not involve *acquiring* the concept on that basis. It is presupposed that we come to the task already in possession of the necessary concepts. There is no objection here.

It is worth emphasizing that we might be able to establish some cases of strict implication without dealing one by one with individual instances: certain general considerations could enable us to establish whole swathes at a blow. For example we can establish on the basis of a priori reflection on our landscape concepts and on the nature of P, that P by itself is enough to provide for truths about the terrestrial landscape. If so, that P strictly implies 'There are mountains' would be one among vast numbers of special instances not requiring piecemeal analyses of individual statements. Similarly for the case of meteorological truths. Thus physicalists are not compelled to subscribe to any strong doctrine of conceptual analysis: a point that will be relevant when we come to consider, in Chapter 5, what a philosophical account of consciousness must do.

To conclude this section it may be helpful to list the main points:

(i) Establishing that a description A strictly implies a description B does not generally require a deductive argument.

(ii) Nor does it require there to be meaning-explicative equivalents for B in terms of A, nor even meaning-explicative conditionals which take expressions in the vocabulary of A to expressions in the vocabulary of B.

(iii) The fact that it is often impossible to establish a case of strict implication by means of a deductive argument does not prevent us from establishing that it is indeed a case of strict implication. In many cases, general considerations may enable us to establish that strict implication holds, without piecemeal analyses.

(iv) The project of showing that A strictly implies B does not require the concepts involved in B to be capable of being acquired on the basis of a knowledge of A; it presupposes that the necessary concepts are already in our possession.

Many of the above points are in agreement with Chalmers and Jackson (2001). I don't claim that the only acceptable statement of the basic commitments of physicalism is in terms of the strict implication thesis. For most purposes Chalmers's statement in terms of what he calls 'logical supervenience' may be regarded as equivalent (Chalmers 1996: 32–89). Jackson (1998), and Chalmers and Jackson (2001), take a similar line (some differences are indicated in footnote 8).

2.7 CONCLUSION

It is easy to see how 'image of a duck' can be a pure redescription of an item specified in terms of pixels, hence strictly implied by such a specification. It is easy to see how 'mountain' can be a pure redescription of a feature of the purely physical world specified by P. But it is not at all easy to see how the psychological descriptions in Q could be pure redescriptions of that same physical world. The difference is of course a consequence of our relative lack of understanding of certain aspects of psychology, particularly of phenomenal consciousness. We know roughly what it takes for there to be mountains, what it takes for there to be ducks, and what it takes for something to be an image of a duck or of a mountain. That lets us see very easily how descriptions of such things are made true by a purely physical reality. But we have only shaky ideas about what it takes for something to be a case of phenomenal consciousness, and therefore only shaky ideas about how descriptions of subjective experiences might be made true by a purely physical reality. The arguments to be examined in the next chapter are often supposed to show that no purely physical reality could possibly make such descriptions true.

3

The Case for Zombies

I have been arguing that any kind of physicalism is committed to the strict implication thesis. It follows that if zombies are possible, physicalism is false. In this chapter I will examine the main arguments for the zombie possibility, in particular those urged by David Chalmers. We can start by clearing away any remaining uncertainties over what to count as zombies.

3.1 KINDS OF ZOMBIES

The philosophical zombies I am focusing on are of course very different from those seen in horror films, which seem to derive from voodoo beliefs. The idea there is that corpses are caused by magic to perform tasks for their controllers. Zombies of that kind don't seem to raise any special philosophical problems: they belong to the same broad class as marionettes. For the same reason no philosophical problems are raised if their behaviour is caused not by magic, but for example by control signals transmitted by radio.

Some philosophers, notably Dennett, have used 'zombie' for a 'behavioural' zombie: *any* internally controlled system that matches a human being behaviourally and dispositionally, regardless of the details of its internal workings. I don't think zombies in that sense raise any special philosophical problems. As I will argue later, something could have the right behavioural capacities but the wrong innards to be genuinely conscious (Chapter 7). Of course that is just what behaviourists deny; so the later argument will incidentally undermine behaviourism.

In common with most writers I am using 'zombie' in a more restricted sense. It is a crucial feature of these special philosophical zombies that their innards are just like ours, assuming the physical world is closed under causation. Zombies that are exact physical duplicates of human beings need not be the only sort. For if those are conceivable, so are ones which, though having nervous systems just like ours and being subject to the same physical laws, are not our twins and have different histories. At the same time zombies must be assumed to live in a world essentially like ours in other respects.

When the zombie idea first struck me many years ago,[1] it seemed enough to demolish not only behaviourism but functionalism. Once its implications had been properly explained—so it seemed in my excited state—not just Ryle's, but Smart's, Armstrong's, and Lewis's materialism melted away. Cooler colleagues pointed out that this was begging the question. Why should the apparent conceivability of zombies be enough to prove they are genuinely possible? I devised the following arguments for their possibility, but came to realize they were mistaken. Diagnosing the source of the trouble took longer.

3.2 TWO OLD ARGUMENTS

(a) Dan (Kirk 1974a)

One day Dan accidentally cut his hand and started to behave oddly. He winced, said 'Ouch!', nursed his hand, and so on, as you would have expected. But alongside such normal expressions of pain he showed astonishment and made remarks bizarrely at odds with his apparent situation. He said he felt no pain and seemed to have been anaesthetized, and that his complaints were happenings over which he had no control. A hypothesis that would apparently help to explain those phenomena is that Dan had really ceased to feel pain in situations where a normal person would have felt it; and that what appeared to be normal expressions of pain were the product of the normal operation of his central nervous system.

After six months, further behavioural oddities set in, this time concerning his sense of smell. On the one hand he appeared to appreciate the smell of roses; on the other he protested that, in spite of really having lost his sense of smell, his facial muscles formed, as appropriate, expressions of enjoyment or revulsion, and his vocal organs produced, puppet-like, appropriate comments. After each of the next few periods of six months an additional oddity, analogous to the first two, set in, affecting one sense after another. It seems—or rather it seemed to me as I was writing—at least coherent to hypothesize that what was happening was that Dan was successively being deprived of each category of sensory experiences. It was only with increasing effort that he managed to express (what on that hypothesis were) his own thoughts and feelings: most of the time, (as he effortfully complained) his seemingly normal utterances about experiences and otherwise normal behaviour occurred automatically: he was powerless to inhibit them. Eventually,

---

[1] But not so long ago as it had struck Stout. (Thanks to Bill Joynson for telling me about Stout's use of the idea.) In my case it started with one of my first tutorials with first-year students. After my brash exposition of a broadly Rylean line one of them said, 'But there are zombies, aren't there?' (She was thinking of the voodoo kind: the word had not become current for the philosophical kind.) Eventually I realized that although she was naive, so was I. The effect was to convert me from hard-nosed physicalist to zombie freak.

on the same hypothesis, Dan was reduced to just one genuine sense: let's say it was his sense of hearing. With prodigious effort he managed to shout, 'I can't see! My only link with the world is hearing, and I fear that too will go in another six months.' He was sent to a psychiatric ward, and after another six months or so was pronounced cured. However, friends who had been following his troubles feared he had been replaced by a zombie.

The point of this fantasy was not to describe compelling evidence that Dan had turned into or been superseded by a zombie, but to show that the hypothesis that there *was* a zombie in the final stage of the story was at any rate free from incoherence: that zombies were 'logically possible'. But apart from other difficulties, this argument, by silently presupposing a certain conception of the relation between experience and the physical, pushes out of sight what we shall later see is a fundamental defect of the zombie idea: that it lacks the resources to explain how it is possible for anyone to have conscious experiences at all.

(b) Zulliver (Kirk 1974*b*)

The second argument extends the story of Gulliver in Lilliput. It turns out that he had encountered a technologically very advanced race of people even tinier than the Lilliputians. A team of their scientists had invaded his head and disconnected the afferent and efferent nerves. They had then arranged to monitor the inputs from his afferent nerves and to send outputs down his efferent nerves that would produce behaviour indistinguishable from what it would have been had his brain still been connected. What the Lilliputians were dealing with was not Gulliver, but this special construction, Zulliver. Although Zulliver both behaves and is disposed to behave just as Gulliver would have done, he lacks sensations and other experiences: he is totally insentient—or so I argued.

Zulliver appeared to be a counter-example not only to behaviourism but to various versions of functionalism. In order to prove the possibility of zombies, the claim was that 'if Zulliver's internal constitution and functioning do not entail that he is sentient, there is no good reason to expect that modifying the contents of his head could fill the logical gap.' Although it would be reasonable to expect that if he were to be restored to his original state he would become a sentient human being once again, 'the question is whether his being sentient would be entailed by the fact that such modifications had been made' (147). I suggested that there was no rational principle on which a line could be drawn between those cases (such as that of Gulliver himself) where such an entailment held, and those where it didn't (such as Zulliver).

I think that was a mistake, and that there is such a rational principle. I will start explaining what it is in Chapter 6. But let us focus on the manner in which those two arguments exploit intuitions about what is possible. They presuppose that if there appears to be no inconsistency in the thought experiments, then genuine possibilities are being described. They rely implicitly on the 'argument from conceivability'.

3.3   THE ARGUMENT FROM CONCEIVABILITY

The simplest form of this argument goes:

(1) Zombies are conceivable.
(2) Whatever is conceivable is possible.
(3) Therefore zombies are possible.[2]

That is obviously valid. But both its premisses are obscure, and they are controversial even when clarified. The crucial question is how to understand 'conceivable'.

We could easily show that zombies were possible if we only had to feel we could imagine them reasonably clearly. I have no trouble thinking I can imagine a 'zombie twin': an exact physical duplicate of myself, behaving like me and living in a physically similar world, yet without phenomenal consciousness. If conceivability were taken in that sense the first premiss of the argument would be indisputably true; but then the second premiss would be indisputably false and the argument would not even appear to work. For no one thinks mere imaginability proves possibility: if it did, then since we can imagine there is a greatest prime number, possibly there *is* a greatest prime number—which has been proved to be false.

Many philosophers are willing to concede that zombies are conceivable in some stronger sense. Christopher Hill comments that 'Chalmers is clearly right to maintain that it is within our power to *conceive* of zombies' (Hill 1998: 26. See also Hill and McLaughlin 1999; Loar 1999; Yablo 1999). But this sense is still quite broad. Assertions such as the following are quite common: 'there are no substantive a priori ties between the concept of pain and the concept of C-fiber stimulation': a claim which Hill, for example, supports by saying that 'it is in principle possible to master either of these concepts fully without having mastered the other' (Hill 1997: 76; cf. Papineau 2002: 49). Conceivability in the sense implied by that remark would still be too loose for the purposes of the conceivability argument, which requires conceivability to entail possibility. We can master the concept *the ratio of the diagonal of a square to its side* without also mastering the concept *irrational number*. By the implied standard of conceivability, therefore, it ought to be conceivable that the ratio of a square's diagonal to its side is not an irrational number; and if conceivability entails possibility, then it is *possible* for that ratio not to be an irrational number. But it isn't possible. The lower the threshold for conceivability, the easier it is to accept premiss (1)—but the harder it is to accept premiss (2). Evidently, the kind of conceivability invoked in the argument needs to be strongly constrained.

Conceivability in the relevant sense needs to be an epistemic matter. Arguing from conceivability to possibility makes sense only so long as you don't already

---

[2] 'Descartes' argument for the separateness of mind and body has this form. Kripke used a similar argument in his 1972. Other versions are discussed in Chalmers 1996: 93–171; 1999; 2002; Levine 2001; Nagel 1974.

know that the situation in question is impossible: to prove c-impossibility (as I aim to do) must be a good way to prove inconceivability. For our purposes, therefore, it will be enough that a proposition or situation is conceivable only if no amount of a priori reflection on it would reveal contradiction or other incoherence.

I think that makes 'conceivable' clear enough for my purposes.[3] Shortly I will examine Chalmers's arguments for the conceivability of zombies; but now let us look at premiss (2) of the conceivability argument. Suppose zombies are conceivable in the relevant sense. Does it follow that they are possible?

3.4   DOES CONCEIVABILITY ENTAIL POSSIBILITY?

Arguably the burden of proof is on those who claim a given description involves an impossibility. Chalmers remarks, 'If no reasonable analysis of the terms in question points toward a contradiction, or even makes the existence of a contradiction plausible, then there is a natural assumption in favor of logical possibility' (1996: 96). That looks like a prima facie case for premiss (2) of the argument. But it faces a number of challenges. One source of objections is Kripke's ideas on necessary a posteriori truths.

Objections Appealing to A Posteriori Necessity

According to Kripke, statements such as 'Water is H_2O', in spite of being knowable only a posteriori, are necessary. This is because 'water' refers to H_2O in all possible worlds: it is a 'rigid designator'. He himself used these ideas to argue *against* the psycho-physical identity theory, suggesting that because it seems that our brains and the rest of the physical world could have existed without pain (for example), pain cannot be identical with anything physical (1972: 146). Kripke does not seem to endorse the conceivability-entails-possibility claim explicitly; but he does suggest that if it appears to break down for some particular identity thesis, that is because we are mistaking some different thesis for the one in question. If for example it seems to us that water might not have been H_2O, that is because we are not really thinking of water but of some other substance: something on the lines of 'the watery stuff'. Where no such alternative thought is available, as he supposed was the case with pain, he seems to think that conceivability does entail possibility.

A number of philosophers argue that these ideas actually facilitate the defence of physicalism. They urge that even if a zombie world is *conceivable,* that does not

---

[3] Levine (2001) discusses a version of the conceivability argument using a different conception of conceivability from this. For him, the conceivability of zombies is 'the principal manifestation of the explanatory gap' (79). What creates this gap is the epistemological problem of explaining how the phenomenal is related to the physical. He sees no way to solve this problem and thinks it remains even if zombies are impossible.

establish that it is *possible* in the way that matters. Conceivability is an epistemic notion, they say, while possibility is a metaphysical one: 'It is false that if one can in principle conceive that P, then it is logically possible that P; . . . Given psycho-physical identities, it is an "a posteriori" fact that any physical duplicate of our world is exactly like ours in respect of positive facts about sensory states' (Hill and McLaughlin 1999: 446. See also Hill 1997; Loar 1997: 1999).

Chalmers responds to this attack on the conceivability-entails-possibility thesis by exploiting a framework for elaborating Kripke's ideas which, he thinks, leaves the thesis substantially intact. On this account there is certainly a difference between a posteriori and a priori necessary statements, but only one underlying kind of necessity and possibility: one space of possible worlds. He then claims that if entailments from the physical to the phenomenal are not a priori necessary, this framework shows they are not a posteriori necessary either, and that therefore phenomenal properties involve something over and above the physical. He rejects the further suggestion that there is a 'strong' metaphysical possibility, 'distinct from and more constrained than logical possibility, and that arises for reasons independent of the Kripkean considerations' (1996: 136–8; 1999: 483–9).[4] Our discussions in the last chapter tend to support that view.

Several other objections have been raised to premiss (2) of the conceivability argument; some are noted below.

'Special factors'

One objection is that there are special factors at work in the psycho-physical case which have a tendency to mislead us. For example it is claimed that what enables us to imagine or conceive of states of consciousness is a different cognitive faculty from what enables us to conceive of physical facts: 'there are significant differences between the cognitive factors responsible for Cartesian intuitions (such as the intuition that zombies are logically possible) and those responsible for modal intuitions of a wide variety of other kinds' (Hill and McLaughlin 1999: 449; cf. Hill 1997). It is suggested that these differences help to explain the ease with which we seem able to conceive of zombies, and the difficulty we have in under-standing the claim that they are nevertheless impossible.

Must distinct concepts express distinct properties?

Chalmers's defence of the conceivability-entails-possibility thesis appeals to the view that if a zombie world is conceivable, then 'there are properties of our world

---

[4] In presenting his case Chalmers makes extensive use of 'two-dimensional' semantics; it would take us too far off our course to discuss it here. See Chalmers 1996: 131–8; 1999: 477–92; 2002; Chalmers and Jackson 2001; Jackson 1998; and for discussions Byrne 1999; Loar 1999; Hill and McLaughlin 1999; Perry 2001: 169–208; Shoemaker 1999; Yablo 1999.

over and above the physical properties' (1996: 133). Against this it is argued that even if a zombie world is indeed conceivable, it does not follow that there are non-physical properties in our world. If that is right, physicalists can concede the conceivability of zombies while insisting that the properties in question are physical. 'Given that properties are constituted by the world and not by our concepts', Brian Loar comments, 'it is fair of the physicalist to request a justification of the assumption that conceptually distinct concepts must express metaphysically distinct properties' (Loar 1999: 467; cf. his 1997).

Loar also argues that phenomenal concepts are 'recognitional', in contrast to physical concepts, which are 'theoretical'. Phenomenal concepts, he says, 'express the very properties they pick out, as Kripke observed in the case of "pain" ' (1999: 468). He thinks these points explain the conceivability of a zombie world, while maintaining that there is no possible world in which the relevant physical properties are distinct from consciousness. Chalmers objects that 'there is nothing in Loar's account to justify coreference' (1999: 489).

Conditional analysis

Some objections rest on conditional analyses of the concept of 'qualia': the properties which zombies supposedly lack and we have. The rough idea is that if there actually are certain non-physical properties which fit our conception of qualia, then that is what qualia are, in which case zombies are conceivable; but if there are no such non-physical properties, then qualia are whichever physical properties perform the appropriate functions, and zombies are not conceivable. It is argued that this approach enables physicalists to accept that although the *possibility* of zombies is conceivable, zombies are not conceivable (Braddon-Mitchell 2003. Stalnaker 2002 makes a related point).

The utterances of zombies

Consider an exact zombie duplicate of our world, in which philosophers who appeal to the conceivability argument have zombie twins. Katalin Balog (1999) argues that the utterances of these zombie-twin philosophers would be meaningful, although their sentences would not always mean what they do in our mouths. She further argues (to oversimplify) that if the conceivability argument were sound in actual philosophers' mouths, then it would be sound in the mouths of zombie philosophers too. Since by hypothesis physicalism is true in their world, their argument is not sound. She concludes that the conceivability argument used by actual philosophers is not sound either. If this argument works, it has the piquant feature that 'the zombies that antiphysicalists think possible in the end undermine the arguments that allege to establish their possibility.'[5]

[5] For other discussions of whether conceivability entails possibility see Block and Stalnaker 1999; Chalmers 1999; 2003; Gendler and Hawthorne (eds.), 2002; Jackson 1998; Perry 2001.

Naturally all these objections to the conceivability argument are contested; but at least they show it cannot be regarded as solid. However, I need not reach a decision on whether conceivability really does entail possibility: in the next chapter I shall argue that zombies are not even conceivable.

3.5 CHALMERS'S ARGUMENTS FOR CONCEIVABILITY

Now for the most systematic defence of the possibility of zombies in the literature: by David Chalmers in his book *The Conscious Mind* (1996). His aim is not limited to establishing the possibility of zombies; it is to show quite generally that the facts about consciousness do not 'logically supervene' on (or are not 'a priori necessitated by') the physical facts. He backs up what strikes him and many others as obvious with a series of five arguments designed to establish the conceivability of a world where the facts of consciousness do not logically supervene on the physical facts. He appeals to the conceivability argument to conclude to the failure of such logical supervenience. Early on he remarks:

... the logical possibility of zombies seems ... obvious to me. A zombie is just something physically identical to me, but which has no conscious experience—all is dark inside. While this is probably empirically impossible, it certainly seems that a coherent situation is described. I can discern no contradiction in the description. (1996: 96)

He acknowledges that the intuitive appeal of the idea cannot be relied on. The nature of consciousness really is hard to understand: what strikes some people as obviously possible could still turn out to be contradictory or incoherent. A powerful case for conceivability may still be defeasible.

His *first argument* takes as starting point Ned Block's idea of the population of a large country, or equivalently a population of homunculi, substituting for someone's brain (Block 1978; 1980). Suppose a population of tiny people disable your brain and replicate its functions themselves, while keeping the rest of your body in working order. Each homunculus performs the functions of an individual neurone: some receive signals from the afferent nerve endings in your head and transmit them to colleagues (using for example mobile phones); others receive signals from colleagues and transmit them to your efferent nerves; most receive and send signals to colleagues exactly as your own neurones do. Would such a system be conscious? Intuitively one may be inclined to say obviously not. Some functionalists may bite the bullet and answer 'Yes'. But the argument does not depend on showing that the system would not be conscious. It aims only to show that its not being conscious is *conceivable,* which many people find reasonable. In Chalmers's words, all that matters here is that when we say the system might lack consciousness, 'a meaningful possibility is being expressed, and it is an open question whether consciousness arises or not' (1996: 97). Possibly, then (as we might suppose for argument's sake) the system is not conscious. But if it isn't, then it is already much like a zombie. The only difference is that it has little people where a zombie has neurones. Why should that make a difference to whether the situation is conceivable? Why should switching from homunculi to neurones necessarily switch on the light of consciousness?

That argument is intuitively appealing, and makes a prima facie case for the conceivability of zombies. However, the fact that it seems intelligible that a system functionally isomorphic to a human being should lack consciousness does not prove it is genuinely coherent. We shall come back to this homunculus-head of Block's (7.8).

Chalmers's *second argument* appeals to the alleged possibility of the 'inverted spectrum'. It seems possible that you and I should—undetectably—experience colours in two systematically different ways. As it happens, I think something like that is genuinely possible. I think two individuals with similar behavioural dispositions and capacities, and even with largely similar functional organizations, should have transposed experiences in *some* possible sense modality: 'transposed qualia' of some kind, if not inverted spectra. But there is a crucial difference between that claim and Chalmers's. It will follow from what I shall be arguing later that if there were such a difference, there would also have to be a difference between the two people's innards. His claim, in crucial contrast, is that their experiences could differ in the way envisaged even if their innards were exactly alike in all relevant respects. Simply making that claim, however, is no more decisive than denying it: argument is needed in either direction. In the end, appealing to the inverted spectrum adds nothing to the admittedly strong intuitive appeal of the basic idea that the character of people's experiences could be different even if there were no differences between the underlying physical facts. Chalmers asserts that 'it seems entirely coherent that experiences could be inverted while physical structure is duplicated exactly' (1996: 100). We know it seems coherent; but we also know that cannot be enough.

His *third argument* goes as follows:

Even if we knew every last detail about the physics of the universe—the configuration, causation, and evolution among all the fields and particles in the spatiotemporal manifold— *that* information would not lead us to postulate the existence of conscious experience. (1996: 101)

It is true that the information he alludes to would not necessarily lead any arbitrary creature to ascribe conscious experiences to the organisms whose existence was provided for by the physical facts. Martians, for example, might be so different from us that the physical facts failed to suggest to them that we might be conscious. In that case they wouldn't take the trouble to examine whether those facts nevertheless did entail that we were conscious. So what? It doesn't matter whether there are individuals who are not inclined, or not able, to get to the facts of consciousness on the basis of the totality of purely physical truths. What matters is whether that totality *does* strictly imply that we are conscious. In Chalmers's terminology the question is whether the facts of consciousness logically supervene on that physical totality; so the statement quoted above ought to be put in those terms. It ought to be to the effect that the totality of physical facts about the world doesn't ensure that the facts of consciousness logically supervene on it. But since the purpose of his arguments is to establish that they do *not* supervene, the quoted passage falls well short of its aim.

Chalmers concedes that the physical facts about the world 'might provide some indirect evidence for the existence of consciousness'. Some organisms themselves might even claim to be conscious. But he asserts that 'this evidence would be quite inconclusive, and it might be most natural to draw an eliminativist conclusion—that there was in fact no *experience* present in these creatures, just a lot of talk'. Again, however, although that may be intuitively appealing it falls well short of proof. He is not entitled to claim that 'the epistemic asymmetry in knowledge of consciousness makes it clear that consciousness cannot logically supervene' (1996: 102).

3.6 THE 'KNOWLEDGE ARGUMENT'

Chalmers's *fourth argument* appeals to Frank Jackson's famous 'knowledge argument', inspired by some points made by Thomas Nagel. (For the argument see Jackson 1982; Nagel 1974. For discussion see for example Dennett 1991: 398–406; Kirk 1994: 226–31.) Since it has received a great deal of discussion I will state it only briefly. Mary is a superb scientist who has been brought up in an environment drained of all colours except black, white, and shades of grey. She knows all the physical facts about colour vision, but because she has never actually seen any coloured things she doesn't know what it is like to see red. She only discovers it when she is let out. Following Jackson, Chalmers claims that 'No amount of reasoning from the physical facts alone will give her this knowledge', and that 'it follows that the facts about the subjective experience of colour vision are not entailed by the physical facts' (1996: 103).

But it does not follow. Certainly it is plausible to say that Mary doesn't know what it's like to see red before she has had any actual experiences of red things: indeed I think it is correct. But consider what makes that claim plausible. It is that we tend to assume that in order to know what it's like to see a colour you must have had some experience of it or a similar colour, or at any rate be able imaginatively to construct an experience of an appropriate kind. Since Mary has had no such experiences, most of us will probably accept that she doesn't know what it's like to see red things because she lacks a full grasp of the colour concepts. (Not everyone accepts that: see for example Churchland 1985: 26; Dennett 1991: 399–401). On those assumptions the story ensures that Mary *lacks the right concepts* to have a full understanding of truths about subjective colour experiences. But it is one thing to say that, quite another to say the truths in question 'are not entailed by the physical facts'. The argument trades on a confusion between two distinct things: what an individual can come to know on the basis of the physical facts; and what is actually *entailed* by those facts. There are all sorts of reasons why someone who knows the relevant physical facts should lack the concepts needed for acquiring a knowledge of facts which are nevertheless entailed by those same physical facts. So someone who maintains that the facts about subjective experience are entailed by the physical facts can happily concede, as I do, that Mary cannot acquire a full knowledge of the experiential facts purely on the basis of her knowledge of all the relevant physical facts.

Chalmers goes on to say something which actually reinforces that objection to his argument. Alluding to Nagel's famous example of bats, he points out that

the physical facts about these systems [bats and mice] do not tell us what their conscious experiences are like, if they have any at all . . . . Once all the physical facts about a mouse are in, the nature of its conscious experience remains an *open question*: it is consistent with the physical facts about the mouse that it has conscious experience, and it is consistent with the physical facts that it does not. (1996: 103)

Consider what is supposed to show that both those possibilities are consistent with the physical facts. It is that because bats and mice are so different from us, we can reasonably assume we lack the ability to have experiences like theirs, hence lack the ability to acquire concepts in terms of which we might be able to describe what their experiences are like. We may conclude that knowing all the physical facts about bats and mice won't enable *us* to tell what their experiences are like— *nothing* will. But suppose there were language-using bats and mice. They would be able to describe batty (or microchiropteric, if you prefer) and mousy (or murine) experiences. So we have been given no reason to suppose that an intelligent scientific bat or mouse, given all the relevant physical facts, would not be able to see how they entailed the facts about batty and mousy experiences. I am not arguing here that the physical facts actually do entail or strictly imply the facts about experience. The point is that the knowledge argument fails to justify the claim that they do *not* entail them.

Chalmers returns to the knowledge argument later in his book, this time presenting it as a direct argument against materialism. He urges that 'ultimately, the strategy that a materialist must take is to deny that Mary gains knowledge about the world' (145). That is incorrect. He has overlooked the points noticed just now, together with something closely related. This is that there are indefinitely many different ways of describing one and the same world: different systems of concepts in terms of which it could be done. To acquire new concepts is to acquire new ways of thinking about the world, hence new knowledge. Even something as trivial for normally sighted people as learning the name of a particular colour enables us to say and believe things about the world we were not able to say or believe before. If I learn that this particular shade is called 'Antwerp blue', for example, I know something I didn't know before: that this and no doubt other things are coloured Antwerp blue. And that is unproblematically 'knowledge about the world'. For the reasons we noticed just now, when Mary comes out of her monochromatic prison she acquires new concepts, or at any rate a fuller grasp of concepts she already had some understanding of. She thereby acquires new knowledge about the world. But that additional knowledge is no embarrassment for physicalism. It is not a tenet of physicalism that perfect knowledge of all the relevant physical facts concerning colour vision would automatically equip you with all the colour concepts there are in the different cultures of the world. Physicalism is not committed to the view that someone with all the relevant physical knowledge could use it to acquire *all* the knowledge about colour vision, or about the world of colour, that could possibly be acquired.

Here we need to notice an important distinction, blurred by Chalmers in the argument under discussion (although he does it full justice elsewhere). It is between the question whether or not bats and mice have conscious experiences at all, and the question what their experiences are like. If we knew all the relevant physical facts about these animals, that would not enable us to tell what their experiences were like for the reason given. But it doesn't follow (as Chalmers seems to assume here) that such knowledge would not enable us even to tell whether they had experiences at all. I will return to these points in Chapter 5.

3.7 THE ARGUMENT 'FROM THE ABSENCE OF ANALYSIS'

Chalmers's *fifth and last argument* is 'from the absence of analysis'. He justifiably proposes that his opponents 'will have to give us some idea of how the existence of consciousness *might* be entailed by physical facts.' But, he goes on, 'any attempt to demonstrate such an entailment is doomed to failure' (104). By now his readers are agog—at any rate this one is, since this book is part of just such an attempt. But his reasons for his claim don't live up to the billing. He starts from the plausible assertion that 'the only analysis of consciousness that seems even remotely tenable for these purposes is a functional analysis.' He then asserts that what makes states conscious 'is that they have a certain phenomenal feel, and this feel is not something that can be functionally defined away'. 'On the face of it, it is entirely conceivable that one could explain all these things (such as are offered in functional analyses) without explaining a thing about consciousness itself' (105). Relatedly, Kripke (1972) emphasized that in his view, the feeling of pain is essential to pain, and can be conceived to be absent in the presence of the same physical facts, and present in their absence.

Chalmers's phrase 'functionally defined away' is revealing. It hints that a functionalist account seeks to show there is no such thing as conscious experience. In fact such accounts typically agree that there is conscious experience, and set out to explain its nature. If they were to prove successful, contrary to what Chalmers and many others expect, then the 'feel' would not have been 'defined away': its reality would have been acknowledged by the very fact of explaining its nature.

There are those who, like Chalmers, think no functional analysis is capable of doing the job, and there are others who think the first lot are begging the question, confused by the idea of zombies. Rather than take up Chalmers's assertions in detail now, I invite you to keep reading: my full reply is the rest of this book.

Chalmers accepts that his arguments are 'based on intuition' but suggests the intuitions in question are 'natural and plain', and that it is 'forced' to deny them. The main intuition involved, he says, is 'that *there is something to be explained*— some phenomenon associated with first-person experience that presents a problem not presented by observation or cognition from the third-person point of view'. That, at least, is something I can emphatically endorse, though it is hardly a mere intuition. He goes on to say that since first-person experience 'forces' an explanandum on us which third-person observation does not, 'what needs to be explained cannot be analysed as the playing of some functional role, for the latter phenomenon is revealed to us by third-person observation and is much more straightforward' (110). That last remark is too quick. It overlooks the possibility that philosophical or psychological explanations may be capable of revealing that what at first appear to be two distinct phenomena are in fact the same thing. The point is neatly illustrated by Chalmers's later assertion that 'the problem of consciousness goes beyond any problem about the explanation of structure and function, so a new sort of explanation is needed' (121). He is right that explanations of structure and function can't do the necessary work by themselves. He is also right that in a sense a new sort of explanation is needed. But he is wrong to conclude that such explanation necessarily requires 'radical changes in the way we think about the structure of the world' (122). What it requires is philosophical understanding, which is what I am aiming at.

3.8 CONCLUSION

I have argued that the arguments for the alleged possibility of zombies are far from conclusive. It is now time to look more critically at the zombie idea.

4

Zapping the Zombie Idea

The zombie idea does seem to fit in with some 'natural and plain' intuitions. And the friends of zombies are right to insist that we still need an explanation of phenomenal consciousness. But even though the idea appeals to some natural intuitions, it conflicts with others. As I will try to make clear, it seductively conveys what turns out to be an illusion. It both feeds on and feeds an incoherent conception of phenomenal consciousness.

4.1 CONFLICT AMONG INTUITIONS

Recall that the version of the zombie idea which concerns us here presupposes the causal closure of the physical domain: all physical effects are physically caused. For that reason the friends of zombies must concede that those properties which we have and zombies supposedly lack—the so-called 'phenomenal qualities' or 'qualia', whose occurrence ensures that there is 'something it is like'—play no essential part in the causation or explanation of behaviour.

The vocabulary of qualia is slippery. The notion is sometimes defined so as not necessarily to require consciousness (Crane 2003: 40); sometimes qualia are even identified with properties of external objects (Dretske 1995). For the purposes of this discussion we can follow Chalmers, who defines phenomenal qualities, or qualia for short, as 'those properties of mental states that type those states by what it is like to have them' (1996: 359 n. 2). If for example I am experiencing the scent of eucalyptus, I could describe the situation (not elegantly) by saying my olfactory experience has a eucalyptus quale. Note that Chalmers's definition of qualia is neutral as to whether having qualia involves anything non-physical. Of course he thinks it does; but he doesn't think the matter is settled by definition.

On Chalmers's view, then, the existence of (phenomenal) consciousness contributes nothing to explaining the fact that he and others talk and write a great deal about consciousness. But that is in violent conflict with some of our most natural and plain intuitions. Here is a simple example. As I type these words I see them showing up on the monitor screen. I notice I have just typed 'sceren' instead of 'screen', so I go back and correct it. Noticing that misspelling involved a visual experience. There is something it is like for me to see the blue characters on the white screen, and something it is like to see 'sceren', which is rather different from what it is like to see 'screen'; and so on. It certainly seems that what prompted the correction was my experience of seeing 'sceren'. Indeed, it *seems* as if having perceptual experiences quite generally makes a vital contribution to my being able to monitor and control my behaviour. True, we are learning that many of our movements, especially those involving rapid reactions, are controlled independently of conscious experiences: two distinct visual systems seem to be involved (Milner and Goodale 1995: see 10.8, 10.9, 10.13 below). But those who think zombies are conceivable—*zombists*—are committed to a lot more than that. They are committed to the view that even in cases where we have plenty of time to reflect on how things look, as when a painter studies the effect of recent brush-strokes and then thoughtfully adds another, conscious experiences make no contribution to the monitoring or control of behaviour. So although zombists appeal to ordinary intuitions in support of the zombie possibility, their position also conflicts with ordinary intuitions. We just do assume that our experiences affect our thinking, hence what we believe, hence how we behave.

Nor is this an optional extra, on the fringe of our ordinary intuitions. It reflects something vital about our understanding of ourselves. How *could* feelings play no part in explaining our behaviour? Yet epiphenomenalists and other zombists have to say it all rests on an illusion. They have to say we are hopelessly mistaken in supposing that our feelings and the character of our experiences often influence what we do. In spite of that, they agree that conscious experiences are extremely important, and they spend a lot of time talking and writing about them.

The fact that their position is in conflict with strong, centrally important intuitions means that zombists need positive arguments for it. I know of none which introduce considerations other than those discussed in the last chapter, which appeared to be at best inconclusive. However, to show they have nothing on their side beyond the intuitive appeal of the zombie idea is not to show they are mistaken. I shall now argue that the zombie idea entails an incoherent conception of phenomenally conscious experience.

4.2   THE JACKET FALLACY

A particular kind of mistake comes into play in this context. If you take off your jacket you retain all your other properties: it is still you who are now jacketless. If you strip the paint off your door the same door is still there, with all its other properties apart from that of being painted. Many other properties may similarly be possessed or not possessed by an individual without affecting its remaining properties. But there are plenty which are not jacket-like. A car's performance cannot be altered without tinkering with its engine or other physical properties. An economic depression cannot be reversed without altering patterns of production and distribution. In those particular cases you would have to be pretty confused to think otherwise. Consciousness, in contrast, can only too easily strike us as jacket-like, especially when we are in the grip of zombie fever. If the arguments that follow are right, that is a mistake. Zombists commit what we can call the 'jacket fallacy'. They mistakenly assume that phenomenal consciousness is a property which can be stripped off while leaving the individual's other main properties intact.[1]

There are many objections in the literature to the conceivability of zombies (indirect ones in Ryle 1949; Wittgenstein 1953; direct ones in for example Dennett 1991; 1995; Kirk 1994; 1999; Shoemaker 1981; 1999). But when you are a victim of zombie fever—I write as an ex-victim: I know what it is like to have zombie fever—you tend to feel there *must* be something wrong with the objections. To counter the intuitive allure of the zombie idea we need an intuitively appealing way of exhibiting its fundamental wrongness: the wrongness of the underlying conception of phenomenal consciousness. It is no use just pitting one lot of intuitions against another; we need a cogent argument with intuitive impact, which is what I think I can provide.

I call the underlying conception of phenomenal consciousness the *e-qualia story*. Broadly, the argument goes:

(I) The e-qualia story is not conceivable.

(II) If zombies were conceivable, the e-qualia story would be conceivable.

Therefore:

(III) Zombies are not conceivable.

4.3 THE E-QUALIA STORY

Stout was right to hold that epiphenomenalism entails the possibility of a zombie world. For according to epiphenomenalism, consciousness depends essentially on a special class of non-physical properties. Being non-physical, these special properties cannot depend logically or a priori on the physical world; therefore the physical world could have existed without them. So epiphenomenalism entails that a zombie world is not just conceivable but possible.[2]

But is the converse also true: does the possibility of zombies entail epiphenomenalism? Some have argued that it does; but that seems to be a mistake. Why shouldn't zombies be possible even if the actual world is interactionistic? What

---

[1] Not to be confused with the fallacy of assuming that an individual may exist without its 'essential' properties. That fallacy (if it is one) depends on there being properties without which the individual would not exist. The jacket fallacy consists simply of assuming that some property can be removed while leaving the rest in place, when it cannot.

[2] Or could there be a physicalist version of epiphenomenalism? (Thanks to Bill Fish for this thought.) Given causal closure, the special properties in question must have physical effects; the point is that these would not be mental or behavioural. However, this idea would still leave room for a modified variety of zombies, and is vulnerable to an extension of the argument which follows.

I am going to argue later is something different: that the *conceivability* of zombies entails the *conceivability* of the e-qualia story. This story is constituted by theses (E1)–(E5) below. Although the e-qualia story is close if not identical to epiphenomenalism as usually understood, it does not aim to be a fair reflection of epiphenomenalists' views. Nor does it aim to reflect any prevailing views about 'qualia' that there may be. (For example it doesn't have to reflect the views about 'epiphenomenal qualia' once defended by Frank Jackson (1982), although perhaps it does.) The point is that the conceivability of zombies entails the conceivability of *this particular story* about phenomenal consciousness. It doesn't matter that other stories about qualia are conceivable, and that some versions of epiphenomenalism need not be committed to it. Here, then, is the e-qualia story:

(E1)   The world is partly physical, and its whole physical component is closed under causation: every physical effect has a physical cause.
       (Note that even those epiphenomenalists who maintain that God intervenes in the physical world can accept that *conceivably* such causal closure might have obtained.)

(E2)   Human beings stand in some relation to a special kind of non-physical properties, *e-qualia*. E-qualia make it the case that human beings are phenomenally conscious.

(E3)   E-qualia are caused by physical processes but have no physical effects: they could be stripped off without disturbing the physical world.

(E4)   Human beings consist of nothing but functioning bodies and their related e-qualia.

(E5)   Human beings are able to notice, attend to, think about, and compare their e-qualia.

(E1) and (E3) spell out some of the main points noted earlier; I assume they are clear enough for our purposes. (E4) also seems clear enough, given (E2): it emphasizes the assumption that in order for organisms in the universe as conceived by physical science to be conscious, all that is needed is for these special properties to be appropriately associated with them. (E5) will be explained in the next section; (E2) needs comment now.

   The notion of e-qualia is significantly different from the broad one offered by Chalmers. The existence of qualia in his sense can be accepted even by physicalists, since his definition does not entail that these properties must be non-physical; nor, unlike the e-qualia story, does it entail that they could be stripped off without affecting the physical world. (Still less does the same widely used notion of qualia entail the remarkable conception defended by Michael Lockwood, according to which qualia may 'outrun awareness' (1998: 415).) To say qualia in the broad sense exist is just to say we are phenomenally conscious. Clause (E2) of the e-qualia story is crucially different from the claim that we have qualia in that sense. The point of (E2) is that what *makes* us conscious is our relation to these special, strictly non-physical, properties.

(E1)–(E5) are of course just a sketch of a metaphysical position; but my argument does not need anything more detailed.

Although perhaps not many philosophers would endorse the view represented by (E1)–(E5), many would assume it is at least coherent. My main argument in this chapter aims to show a priori that the e-qualia story is *not* coherent because clauses (E1)–(E4) are incompatible with clause (E5). If there were such items as e-qualia satisfying clauses (E1)–(E4), the epistemic intimacy provided for by (E5) would thereby be ruled out. Now, it is a familiar point that epiphenomenalism gets into trouble over our epistemic relations with qualia; but I think I have a new way of making intuitively clear that this difficulty is lethal. A necessary preliminary is to consider the relevant causal relations.

4.4 E-QUALIA, CAUSATION, AND COGNITIVE PROCESSING

(E3) spells out that e-qualia have no physical effects. In any case that seems to be a consequence of (E1) and (E2). (E1) (the causal closure of the physical) entails that if any items have physical effects, they themselves are physical. Since e-qualia are defined by (E2) as non-physical, it follows that they have no physical effects, hence (E3). You might suspect that there could be overdetermination, whereby some physical events were caused both physically and by e-qualia. There are two reasons why that suggestion will not work here. One is that, given causal closure of the physical, it seems self-contradictory. If all physical effects are caused physically, there is no room for non-physical items such as e-qualia to be even minor causal factors in their production. They would be completely idle, not causal factors at all (cf. K. Campbell 1970: 52; Kim 1993: 250–3; 1998). However, the main reason why there is no need to labour the point is that what matters for my argument is whether the e-qualia story, including (E3), is *conceivable*. I therefore don't have to rule out overdetermination as a possibility in some worlds; all I need is that there is none in the world described by (E1)–(E5). We can move on.

Suppose I am tasting two wines. I might compare what it is like for me to experience their flavours, which might cause me to change my preferences, hence my behaviour: I might stop drinking one and drink more of the other. It certainly seems that, contrary to the e-qualia conception of consciousness, the qualities of our experiences have physical effects. Naturally epiphenomenalists have devoted a lot of attention to this objection. They concede it seems as if the qualities of our experiences have effects on our behaviour, but maintain that we are mistaken. What really affects behaviour, on their account, is physical processes; but because some of these are caused by preceding physical processes which simultaneously cause qualia, it seems as if it were the qualia, not their correlated physical processes, that did the causing (see for example Jackson 1982). That response at least appears to leave epiphenomenalism and the e-qualia story coherent, if not plausible. So if we are looking for a persuasive refutation of the e-qualia story, more is needed than to point out that experiences seem to affect behaviour.

A first step in that direction is to consider whether there can be causation *among* e-qualia: does the e-qualia story permit e-qualia to have effects on other e-qualia? No. For suppose a certain e-quale were to cause an event that was either an e-quale or involved e-qualia. Since by (E3) all e-qualia are already caused to occur by physical events, there would be no work for that one to do: it could make no difference to the course of events. Thus e-qualia have no effects either on the physical world or among themselves. They are completely inert. But mightn't there be causal overdetermination? No: there is no room for it at this point any more than there was earlier. The causation of e-qualia by other e-qualia is ruled out by (E1)–(E5) because e-qualia are said to be caused by physical processes, not by other e-qualia. Again, a different story from (E1)–(E5) might have permitted overdetermination of e-qualia-like items; but again that is beside the point. It is this particular story that I am going to argue is not conceivable, yet would have had to be conceivable if zombies had been conceivable.

Could zombists hold that certain counterfactuals entail that *to all intents and purposes* e-qualia cause other e-qualia? Suppose that on their account a physical event p1 causes both an e-quale q1 and another physical event p2, and p2 causes q2. Why shouldn't they add the following counterfactual: if p2 hadn't occurred, q2 would still have occurred because q1 alone is sufficient? (Note by the way that this pattern could not be applied to all sequences of e-qualia because many e-qualia must be conceded to occur independently of their predecessors. Just now a swallow is flying past, making unexpected twists and jinks. The associated visual e-qualia could not be explained in terms of earlier ones: they depend on the swallow, not on their predecessors.) That suggestion will not work. If in the circumstances p2 had not occurred, p1 would not have occurred either, in which case q1 would not have occurred. For that reason q2 would not have occurred. The proposed counterfactual would therefore not have been true (or had whatever property corresponds to truth for counterfactuals). Given the causal closure of the physical, zombists could not consistently maintain that q1 was sufficient for q2: that would be to ignore the necessity of the physical events.

The all-round inertness of e-qualia has an important consequence. Wine-tasting illustrates how I can *notice, attend to, think about,* and *compare* the qualities of my experiences. If the e-qualia conception is to provide for the facts about consciousness, it must be able to account for these and related activities. They involve what Chalmers describes as an 'intimate epistemic relation' to our experiences, a relation he also calls 'acquaintance' (1996: 196f). I have reservations about the relevant notion of acquaintance, but surely there is a kind of epistemic intimacy. For our purposes it will be enough that the epistemic intimacy in question is exemplified by noticing, attending to, thinking about, and comparing the qualities of our experiences, as in the wine-tasting example. Can the e-qualia story account for this intimacy?

Noticing, attending to, thinking about, and comparing experiences are not simple matters: they involve cognitive processes such as conceptualization and the storing and retrieving of information. It is crucial that *e-qualia cannot perform such activities themselves.* They are in any case rather obviously not the category of thing to perform cognitive activities; more to the point, those cognitive activities involve the causation of changes. There can be no storage or retrieval of information without 'traces' or effects; no thinking or conceptualization without changes which cause other changes. Since e-qualia are causally inert, both with respect to the physical world and among themselves, it follows that they cannot perform cognitive activities of the kinds in question.

It might be suggested that, just as epiphenomenalists claim we are mistaken in supposing that some of our behaviour is caused by the qualities of our experiences, so exponents of the conceivability of the e-qualia story—*e-qualists*—could claim that we do not genuinely notice, attend to, think about, or compare those qualities: perhaps it is all an illusion. But that position is not open to them. Not even e-qualist ultras could adopt it, since it would imply that they could not really notice, attend to, think about, or compare the items they spend so much time discussing. The principal exponent of the zombie idea does not suffer from that confusion. Chalmers accepts that we attend to our qualia. He remarks, 'The clearest cases of direct phenomenal concepts arise when a subject attends to the quality of an experience, and forms a concept wholly based on the attention to the quality, "taking up" the quality into the concept' (2003: 235).

Why shouldn't e-qualists assign the relevant cognitive work to *other* non-physical cognitive states or processes? We know these other states cannot themselves be e-qualia because cognitive states must have effects, while e-qualia are inert; but why shouldn't other non-physical states perform the relevant cognitive functions? A sufficient reason is that it would be incompatible with (E4), according to which 'human beings consist of nothing but functioning bodies and their related e-qualia'. Apart from that, these suggested non-physical items could not be affected by e-qualia, since the latter are inert. That would prevent them from cognitively processing e-qualia, as I shall argue shortly, in the course of exposing the incoherence of the e-qualia story itself.

According to the e-qualia story, the conscious experiences of human beings consist solely of the occurrence of e-qualia suitably related to functioning bodies. Since the cognitive functions we have noted cannot be performed by e-qualia, they must be performed by bodies. That is the main conclusion of this section; and we shall soon see that in fact these cognitive functions cannot be performed by bodies consistently with the e-qualia story. But first let us consider a related objection to the e-qualia story, together with a reply that has been suggested.

4.5   ARE E-QUALIA ALONE ENOUGH FOR EPISTEMIC INTIMACY?

The objection I shall be pressing is that the e-qualia story cannot provide for such things as the conceptualizing, storing, and retrieving of information about e-qualia. The related objection is that we could not think, talk, or know about the qualities of our experiences if they had no effects on the physical events involved in those activities themselves. It seems particularly powerful if one already accepts any sort of causal account of content and reference (cf. Shoemaker 1975: 297). Chalmers has a reply. He accepts that 'consciousness is *explanatorily irrelevant* to our claims and judgments about consciousness' (1996: 177) and regards what I just described as an 'objection' as constituting a paradox: the 'paradox of phenomenal judgment'. (It is only a paradox if you agree with him that zombies are conceivable.) He suggests that the epistemic situations of zombies and ourselves are radically different. He claims:

there is not even a conceptual possibility that a subject could have a red experience like this one without having *any* epistemic contact with it: to have the experience is to be related to it in this way. (1996: 197)

This intimate epistemic relation both ensures that we can refer to and report on our experiences, and justifies our claims to know about them. Since our zombie twins have no experiences, hence no such intimate epistemic relation, their quasi-phenomenal judgements are unjustified. Chalmers is suggesting that even though e-qualia have no causal influence on our judgements, their mere presence in the appropriate physical context partially constitutes the contents of the thoughts involved: it helps to ensure that our thoughts are *about* those e-qualia. It also, he thinks, constitutes justification for our knowledge claims even when our experiences are not explanatorily relevant to making the judgements involved (1996: 172–209; see also his 2003).

There is a serious problem with this response. Certainly it is an essential component of the e-qualia story that e-qualia ensure there is phenomenal experience in the first place, to which, by its nature, we are intimately related. But this important proposition can hardly be taken for granted when that story itself is being challenged. E-qualists owe an explanation of how we *can* stand in an intimate epistemic relation to items which have no effects on our cognitive activities even if (as they typically assume) there is isomorphism between e-qualia and some of the physical processes which constitute those activities (Chalmers 1996: 243). I will argue that the e-qualia story precludes such epistemic intimacy.

4.6 MY ZOMBIE TWIN'S SOLE-PICTURES

By definition my zombie twin Zob is physically just like me, and his life exactly parallels the life of my body; in particular, his physical processes include ones just like those involved in my own cognitive activities. The difference between him and me is that he lacks e-qualia, and so, according to the e-qualia story, lacks consciousness. Now, let us for argument's sake assume that the situation envisaged by the first four clauses (E1)–(E4) of the definition is conceivable: cannot be seen a priori to involve incoherence. Given that assumption, clauses (E2) and (E4) ensure that associating suitable e-qualia with Zob will result in a conscious being. So let us suppose that those natural laws which, according to the e-qualia story, ensure that my own bodily processes cause e-qualia, suddenly come into play in Zob's world, with the result that his bodily processes cause e-qualia.

According to the e-qualia conception, some individual is thereby made conscious: I don't see how it could be Zob, but that issue does not affect the argument. The question is this. How can this individual possibly have any sort of epistemic intimacy with e-qualia, as (E5) requires? To bring out the point of the question, consider another: why should associating e-qualia with Zob result in an individual who stands in an intimate epistemic relation with his experiences, when the presence of moving pictures on the soles of his feet would not result in anyone's being in such a relation to those pictures? E-qualists will dismiss the question as frivolous, but it is serious.

To elaborate. Since Zob is my zombie twin, all my brain processes are mirrored by his. In particular, those neural processes which cause my visual e-qualia according to the e-qualia story are mirrored in Zob's brain too. But now, by a strange shift in the natural laws of his world, those same visual processes in Zob cause sequences of constantly changing pictures to appear on the soles of his feet. The changing coloured patterns on his soles are isomorphic to those neural processes in the same way as my e-qualia are isomorphic (or at least are typically supposed to be isomorphic) to similar processes in my brain. So if (per impossibile) I were transported to Zob's world and managed to view his sole-pictures, I would find them an acceptable record of my own evolving visual experiences. The question is: could the causation of these sole-pictures by processes in Zob's body make his continuing cognitive processes at all *epistemically relevant* to them?

The answer is obvious. The story has it that he never even notices his sole-pictures, so we can deduce from it a priori that his cognitive processes are not epistemically relevant to them in any way. They are not about them; and they obviously don't ensure that he notices, attends to, thinks about them or compares them. They do not result in his being in any relation of epistemic intimacy to them.

How can we be so sure? Because there is nothing about Zob which could provide for him to know anything about his sole-pictures, or for them to play any part in his thinking. Things would have been different if he had noticed them; but the story rules that out—it is the main point of the story. The story has it that his sole-pictures have no effects on his perceptual and cognitive processes, which, remember, mirror my own. (And I have no sole-pictures: I have checked.) Given that information, to insist that Zob knew or thought about his sole-pictures, or attended to them, would conflict with any normal understanding of aboutness, intentionality, and attention. When we are completely ignorant of a certain matter, and no beliefs or hypotheses concerning it figure in our thoughts, it makes no sense to say we are thinking about it, still less that we are attending to it. No doubt there are unconscious thoughts. But they are hypothesized in the first place only because of their supposed *causal* role: they are taken to play some active part in our reasoning. Zob's sole-pictures have no such causal role.[3]

If Zob and his sole-pictures strike you as too far-fetched even in the context of the zombie debate, here is something a little less so. Suppose the complex electro-chemical processes inside our brains which constitute perceptual processing induce, without themselves being affected by, isomorphically patterned electric currents in their vicinity. If that were the case, would our cognitive processing be about those patterned electric currents? Would we notice or attend to them? Would we be able to compare them, or stand in any sort of epistemically intimate relation to them? Obviously not, given we know nothing about such currents and they have no effects on our cognitive processing. There is nothing to make it the case that our thoughts would be epistemically relevant to such electrical activity.

I hope it is now clear that the fact that certain items are caused by and even iso-morphic to certain cognitive processes is not sufficient to ensure that the latter are about the former, or that they involve attention being paid to them, or that they are in any other way epistemically relevant to them. If those conditions had been suf-ficient, then Zob's cognitive processes would have been epistemically relevant to his sole-pictures, and mine would have been epistemically relevant to the patterns of electrical activity imagined. Since they are not, those are counter-examples—given we can see there is nothing else around which could do the job.[4]

4.7   THE E-QUALIA STORY IS NOT CONCEIVABLE

Back now to the scenario where the laws of nature in Zob's world change, and he is provided with e-qualia rather than sole-pictures. According to the e-qualia story the result ought to be that he becomes epistemically intimate with them. Might that be correct? If it is, there must be some relevant difference between e-qualia and sole-pictures.

---

[3] Balog argues that zombie philosophers' seeming talk about their qualia would really be about the neural processes which zombists think cause them (1999: 514–21). But there is a vital difference from the present case: the processes in her story have *effects* on zombies' utterances purportedly about them. In the case of Zob's sole-pictures there is no such reciprocal causation.

[4] See also Objection A in section 4.9 below.

Certainly there are striking differences. One is that sole-pictures are physical while e-qualia are non-physical. But that couldn't make Zob's cognitive processing epistemically relevant to his e-qualia. Consider: instead of physical pictures on the soles of Zob's feet, the story might have been that some of his perceptual processes caused *non-physical* processes that were, like the sole-pictures, isomorphic to those perceptual processes. E-qualists might argue that such non-physical processes would immediately result in consciousness: might actually be e-qualia. But they could not argue that it was *the mere fact of their being non-physical* that made Zob's cognitive processing epistemically relevant to them. Their being physical or non-physical would obviously be beside the point.

Another difference is that Zob's sole-pictures are visible while e-qualia are supposedly invisible—except perhaps with the Cartesian eye of the soul. But that difference too is obviously irrelevant to epistemic intimacy: to aboutness, attention, and so on. If anything, invisibility would make e-qualia even less accessible epistemically.

Are there any other relevant differences between sole-pictures and patterns of electrical activity on the one hand, and e-qualia on the other? Here we bump up against the fact that the e-qualia story has very little to say about e-qualia. Apart from being supposed to ensure there is consciousness, all that can be said about them is that they are non-physical, caused by, and perhaps also isomorphic with certain physical processes involved in perception. There is simply no basis for claiming that there are or might be other relevant differences.

Or is it perhaps relevant that e-qualia may be said to *represent* aspects of the world of which we are conscious? Consider what might ensure that they represented those aspects. Being isomorphic to them? Being caused by them? I know of no other half-way plausible candidates. But there seems to be no basis for saying that e-qualia could perform representational functions that would not equally be performed by sole-pictures and patterns of electric currents. If e-qualia represent aspects of the world, then so do they; so there is no relevant difference between them here. In any case, whether or not certain processes p, caused by an individual's (physical) perceptual processes, represent aspects of the world, seems on reflection irrelevant to the question whether that individual's cognitive processing puts some entity into an intimate epistemic relation with p. After all, p might have been patterns of electrical activity without any systematic relation to aspects of the world, which could not plausibly have been claimed to represent anything.

So there seem to be no relevant differences between the two cases. The only relevant features of e-qualia are that they are *caused by* and *isomorphic with* certain perceptual processes. But those features are shared by Zob's sole-pictures and my patterns of electrical activity. It follows that, since Zob's cognitive processing cannot produce epistemic intimacy with his sole-pictures, and mine cannot produce epistemic intimacy with my electric currents, such cognitive processing cannot produce epistemic intimacy with e-qualia either. If that is right, we can see a priori that the conception of consciousness envisaged in the first four clauses (E1)–(E4) of the e-qualia story precludes conscious subjects from being able to think about, notice, attend to or compare the qualities of their experiences. The story allows individuals no more epistemic access to their e-qualia than Zob has to his sole-pictures, or I have to the electric currents in my brain: that is, none.

Thus the e-qualia conception of consciousness is not just odd or empirically improbable but incoherent: clauses (E1)–(E4) could be true only if (E5) were false. Since we discovered that fact by a priori reflection, the e-qualia story is inconceivable in the relevant sense.

That gives us:

(I) The e-qualia story is not conceivable.

I now have to establish (II): if zombies were conceivable, the e-qualia story would be conceivable.

4.8   IF ZOMBIES WERE CONCEIVABLE, THE E-QUALIA STORY WOULD BE CONCEIVABLE

We need to distinguish two claims. One is that the conceivability of zombies entails that the e-qualia story is true of the actual world. That is obviously false. Zombists are not forced to take up epiphenomenalism. Indeed, the conceivability of zombies is even compatible with interactionism. Zombists can maintain that although zombie worlds are by definition subject to the causal closure of the physical, the actual world is not. (That is why Chalmers can say the conclusion of his anti-materialist argument is not epiphenomenalism, but 'the disjunction of panprotopsychism, epiphenomenalism, and interactionism' (1999: 493. See also his 1996: 150–60). Here he seems implicitly to accept that the e-qualia story is at least conceivable.)

The claim I am defending is different. It is that the *conceivability* of zombies would entail the *conceivability* of the e-qualia story. To recall: a proposition or situation is conceivable only if no amount of a priori reflection on it would reveal incoherence (3.3). I have to show that so long as zombists stick to their thesis, its implications force them to maintain that no amount of a priori reflection on the e-qualia story would reveal incoherence. I suspect that most zombists, not only those who already believe the e-qualia story is true of our world, but those who maintain there is dualistic interaction in our world, would accept that the e-qualia story was at least conceivable—or rather, would have been inclined to accept it if they had not been put on their guard. I will argue that all zombists are committed to the conceivability of the e-qualia story, like it or not.

The broad idea is simple: if zombies were conceivable, then conceivably a zombie world could be transformed into a world where the e-qualia story held. If that is right, the conceivability of zombies would entail the conceivability of the e-qualia story. If that approach strikes you as promising, you are probably not a zombist. A lot hinges on this argument, and I must make clear that it goes through cleanly, and that some apparently available escape routes for zombists are blocked.

The first step is to recall that by definition, a zombie world would be subject to causal closure: all effects in it would be caused physically (3.1). So the conceivability of zombies would entail the conceivability of a world z such that:

(A1) z is a purely physical, causally closed system;

(A2) Physically, z is as far as possible exactly like the actual world;

(A3) The human-like inhabitants of z lack phenomenal consciousness.

(Some zombists believe the actual world is not physically causally closed because certain neural events are caused by non-physical events. However, I assume neuroscience proves it is at least conceivable that what these zombists believe to be caused non-physically should be caused physically. That legitimizes (A2), which ensures the resulting causal gaps are filled by physical events and processes, so that there is causal closure, and the zombies in z behave, and are disposed to behave, like us.)

Now, assuming z is conceivable, what sort of metaphysical upheaval would be needed to provide its inhabitants with the kind of phenomenal consciousness we enjoy? Obviously something would have to be added to z, and this something must be non-physical. (If anything purely physical could do the trick, purely physical organisms could be conscious, contrary to what the alleged zombie possibility is supposed to show.)

Assuming a zombie world is conceivable, then, is it also conceivable that there should be a non-physical item or items x ('item' from now on) which, when appropriately associated with z, would ensure that its inhabitants acquired our kind of phenomenal consciousness? I will argue that zombists cannot consistently resist this crucial step in the argument.

Either the non-physical item they think provides for consciousness in the actual world—call it y—has no physical effects, or it has some. If it has none, then on reasonable assumptions (for example, that we are not the puppets of some superior being) our behaviour is caused purely physically. But in that case the physical component of our world is essentially like z, and these zombists are already committed to the view that if something like y were associated with z, its human-like inhabitants would acquire our kind of phenomenal consciousness: which is what I am claiming.

To resist this claim, therefore, they must maintain that in the actual world y has physical effects. Now, causal relations are contingent; anything which actually has certain effects could conceivably have failed to have them even if they and all other processes and events were held constant. So if these zombists' theory about the actual world is conceivable, it is also conceivable that y should have failed to have physical effects, and that its actual effects should have been caused purely physically (as neuroscience shows is conceivable). Again, that is what I am claiming they are committed to.

If they still wish to resist this claim, then, they must take the line that although *y* is necessary for phenomenal consciousness, it is not also sufficient. They must say it is an a priori (or conceptual) matter that whatever non-physical item is involved in making us conscious, it only succeeds in doing so if it has physical effects. But they cannot consistently say any such thing. (I had better add that so far as I know, no zombists do say such a thing: it would be a desperate attempt to defend what I am arguing is an untenable position.)

The reason zombists (unlike some behaviourists and functionalists) cannot consistently take that line is that they all agree that we have a special kind of access to our phenomenal consciousness: to there being 'something it is like' for us. It is only because we have this access that, according to them, we can know we ourselves are not zombies. Further, having this sort of access is what enables us to tell what our experiences are like without having to check whether they have physical effects. When I am asked about the flavour of the wine, I may grope for suitable words; but I don't have to grope for the experience itself. Nor do I have to check whether the experience itself (unlike the alcohol which accompanies it) has any physical effects before I can tell I am having it. Such effects cannot therefore be necessary for having the experience.

Whichever way they turn, it seems zombists cannot deny that the conceivability of zombies would entail that conceivably, a non-physical item *x* could be associated with the zombie world *z* so as to transform it into a world *z** whose ex-zombie inhabitants enjoyed our kind of phenomenal consciousness.

Is there any other way for zombists to escape that conclusion? It would be futile to try to anticipate all possible responses, but I will mention one I have met in discussion. It fastens on the fact that our kind of phenomenal consciousness includes epistemic intimacy with the qualities of our conscious experiences: noticing, attending to, thinking about, and comparing them. The suggestion is that zombists might concede that *z* might conceivably be transformed into a world whose inhabitants were phenomenally conscious, yet not epistemically intimate with their experiences.

Now this suggestion conflicts with something Chalmers implies in the passage quoted earlier, where he says there is 'not even a conceptual possibility' that a subject should have a red experience 'without epistemic contact with it' (1996: 197). If he is right, being epistemically intimate with one's experiences is not even conceptually detachable from being phenomenally conscious: it is part of it. However, although Chalmers's assumption is plausible, it is not needed for this argument. Perhaps it isn't *inconceivable* that the phenomenally conscious ex-zombies in the transformed world should have epistemic intimacy; but all the argument needs is that zombists should concede that it is conceivable. We can quickly see that they must concede this.

If these zombists were to maintain that the non-physical item *y* which they think produces phenomenal consciousness in the actual world is also what produces epistemic intimacy in our world, then they would be conceding the point at issue: if it does so in our world, then conceivably something like it does so in z. These zombists must therefore deny that, although *y* produces consciousness in our world, it is also what produces epistemic intimacy. However, on their account there is nothing else in our world beyond its purely physical component on the one hand, and *y* on the other. (Of course they might say there were other items present; but equally, conceivably those items might be absent. See also Objections D and E in the next section.) So they must suppose that, given that *y* produces our consciousness, our epistemic intimacy is supplied by purely physical items. But that is a dead end too, since by (A1) and (A2) the necessary physical processes are already present in z^*, so that (on the present suggestion) epistemic intimacy is already provided for, and must be conceded to be conceivably present in z^* together with phenomenal consciousness. (Or is there a third alternative: that the alleged non-physical component should provide only for epistemic intimacy, while phenomenal consciousness itself was provided for by purely physical events and processes? No: by hypothesis all the relevant physical items would already be present in the zombies in z, who would therefore not have been zombies after all.)

Zombists therefore cannot object that it is inconceivable that *x* should provide for epistemic intimacy as well as consciousness. So the earlier conclusion stands. Even those zombists who hold that there is non-physical interaction in the actual world must concede that conceivably, a non-physical item could be associated with a zombie world so as to transform it into a world z^* where the ex-zombies enjoyed phenomenal consciousness and epistemic intimacy with their experiences.

To summarize the results of this section so far: the conceivability of zombies would entail the conceivability of a world z^* satisfying the following conditions:

(Z1) z^* is partly physical, and its whole physical component is closed under causation: every physical effect in z^* has a physical cause.

(Z2) The human-like organisms in z^* are related to a special kind of non-physical item *x*. *x* makes it the case that they are phenomenally conscious.

(Z3) *x* is caused by physical processes but has no physical effects: it could be stripped off without disturbing the physical component of z^*.

(Z4) The human-like inhabitants of z^* consist of nothing but functioning bodies and their related *x*. (Although I have not explicitly shown this, it is clear that even if there might have been other items in such a world, conceivably they might have been absent.)

(Z5) The human-like inhabitants of z^* are able to notice, attend to, think about, and compare the qualities of their experiences.

(Z1)–(Z5) mirror the wording of (E1)–(E5) with just three differences: 'z^*' occurs instead of 'the world'; 'human-like inhabitants' occurs in place of 'human beings'; 'a special kind of non-physical item *x*' occurs in place of 'e-qualia'. None of these differences is significant. Taking the first two together: (E1)–(E5) is a story about how the actual world and its human inhabitants might conceivably be or have been, while (Z1)–(Z5) is a story about a special kind of world and its human-like inhabitants, which is, however, also how the actual world and its human inhabitants might conceivably be or have been on the assumption that zombies are conceivable. So the first two differences are not significant. As for the third: even if x were some kind of unitary substrate rather than a collection of properties, it would still have to underlie, realize, or otherwise provide for a plurality of properties. For the inhabitants of z^* must still, in conformity with (Z2) and (Z5), have experiences with phenomenal qualities which they could notice, attend to, and so on. So far as the e-qualia story is concerned, therefore, those qualities might just as well be called 'e-qualia'.

There is an important point to be noted about the dialectical role of (Z1)–(Z5) compared with (E1)–(E5). When arguing earlier that the e-qualia story ((E1)–(E5)) was incoherent, I appealed to the causal inertia of e-qualia. This ruled out the possibility of e-qualia doing their own cognitive processing. But why shouldn't the non-physical x in z^* include items themselves capable of such processing? In that case (Z1)–(Z5) would not after all be equivalent to the e-qualia story. However, there is a straightforward reply. The question is not whether some metaphysical story or other could be told by which non-physical items were capable of cognitive processing. It is whether the conceivability of zombies entails the conceivability of the e-qualia story. Hence all I have to do is to show that if zombies are conceivable, then so is a version of (Z1)–(Z5) according to which x is inert. And this is a consequence of the fact that causation is a contingent matter. Suppose it were conceivable that there should be an x conforming to (Z1)–(Z5) but including causally active items. By the same token it must also be conceivable that those same items should be inert.

The differences between the e-qualia story and (Z1)–(Z5) are therefore not significant. It follows that the conceivability of (E1)–(E5) (the e-qualia story) would be guaranteed by the conformity of z^* to (Z1)–(Z5). So we have:

(II) If zombies were conceivable, the e-qualia story would be conceivable.

We already have (I): the e-qualia story is not conceivable. By contraposition, therefore:

(III) Zombies are not conceivable.[5]

4.9 OBJECTIONS

Objection A: 'In your argument for premiss (I) you presuppose a causal theory of aboutness and content, so you just beg the question.'
Reply A: No. All the sole-pictures argument presupposes is that there must be *something* to account for the 'intimate epistemic relation' that conscious subjects

---

[5] See Objection D below.

have to the qualities of their experiences. It does not depend on a causal theory; only on the fact that e-qualists have no resources to account for that relation. At most they have only isomorphism and physical-to-e-qualia causation; and the stories of sole-pictures and patterns of electric currents are counter-examples to the assumption that those factors are sufficient for such an account. There is nothing to make it intelligible that Zob's cognitive processing is epistemically relevant to his sole-pictures. By the same token there is nothing to make it intelligible that Zob's cognitive processing—or anyone else's—would be epistemically relevant to any e-qualia he might acquire. Certainly part of the reason for this unintelligibility is that e-qualia are causally inert; so the argument provides support for the view that the qualities of our experiences contribute to causing behaviour. But the argument does not presuppose a causal theory.

Objection B: 'This whole dispute remains a battle of competing intuitions. All you have to set against the intuition that zombies are possible are your intuitions about aboutness and epistemic intimacy.'

Reply B: Our ordinary understanding of what it takes for cognitive processing to be relevant to, or about, or in any other way epistemically intimate with something else is not on the same footing as the zombie intuition. There are at least three reasons for this.

First, unlike the conception of consciousness entailed by the zombie intuition, the intuitions about aboutness and attention appealed to in the argument do not conflict with others. The widespread intuitions about zombies which sustain and are sustained by the jacket fallacy and the e-qualia story are in striking conflict with the widespread intuition that qualia have effects on conscious subjects. But the intuitions (if that is what they are) which lead us to accept that Zob's cognitive processing is not about, directed at, or otherwise epistemically relevant to his sole-pictures, and hence not epistemically relevant to his e-qualia (and which further encourage us to agree that he does not attend to or compare them) are not in conflict with other intuitions.

Second, unlike the zombie intuition, these ordinary intuitions do not concern what is possible, but what it is correct or appropriate to say. They come into play in the same way as the intuitions (better: the conceptual and verbal understanding) on the basis of which we ordinarily decide whether or not a given description applies to a confronted state of affairs.

Third, current non-epiphenomenalistic *theories* of content, aboutness, and intentionality do nothing to support the view that the mere fact that something is isomorphic to and caused by certain processes is sufficient to ensure that those processes provide for there to be thoughts about it, or for attention to be paid to it, or for any subject to be epistemically intimate with it. We noted earlier that any broadly causal approach to these matters rules out such intimacy—and such approaches are of course widely accepted. The other main broad approach would have it that thoughts, utterances, and other behaviour refer to or are directed at the item in question if the overall pattern of relationships in which they figure provides a slot which, on balance, it seems to fit best. ('Inventor of bifocals' fits Benjamin Franklin; the cat's stalking behaviour forms a pattern which suggests it is directed at the mouse.) But we have seen that in the case of Zob, the overall pattern of relationships implies that his cognitive activities are *not* about or directed at his e-qualia any more than they are directed at his sole-pictures. Isomorphism and one-way causation won't do the trick even on the 'overall pattern' basis. I leave it to the reader to consider whether there are other theoretical approaches to intentionality which might help the e-qualia model.

Objection C: 'The argument proves nothing more than our epistemic incapacity: we can't imagine how the e-qualia story could be true—rather as Thomas Nagel suggested that his argument in "What is it Like to Be a Bat?" did not actually disprove physicalism, but only showed we have no conception of how it might be true.'

Reply C: That misses the point of the sole-pictures example. We know Zob is not thinking about his sole-pictures because we know everything relevant that there is to know, and can see there is nothing to make him epistemically intimate with them. The same goes for the case of e-qualia. It is not that there may still be some way, if only we could hit upon it, in which the story could provide for e-qualia as defined by (E1)–(E5) to be accessible to Zob's cognitive processing. It is that we can see there is no way for such accessibility to be provided for.

Objection D: '*Interactionist* dualists could resist the argument for (II) by simply rejecting the e-qualia story. Why should it matter if that story is not conceivable, so long as non-physical qualia might interact with bodily processes in the *actual* world (which might be in physical respects not entirely closed under causation, or might include overdetermination)?'

Reply D: There may indeed be a coherent alternative story to be told about qualia—as contrasted with e-qualia. My point is that it had better not entail the conceivability of zombies. Merely pointing out that there is some sense of 'qualia' in which qualia interact in the actual world would not escape the argument if it is so much as conceivable that those qualia should have been inert. Any version of interactionism which entails that qualia could conceivably be stripped off a conscious subject, leaving a zombie as residue, entails that the e-qualia story is conceivable when it isn't. It is guilty of the jacket fallacy.

Objection E: 'You seem to assume that zombists who reject epiphenomenalism and parallelism have no alternative but a simple variety of interactionism. But there are other non-idealist alternatives: panpsychism is one; what Chalmers calls 'panprotopsychism' is another. It's not clear that your argument works against zombists who adopt such views.' (Panprotopsychism seems to be like panpsychism except that it does not entail that every object has full-blown phenomenal properties. Instead, only things with the right kinds of organisation have such properties; other things have only 'protophenomenal' properties, which are a

special kind of non-physical properties whose combination results in full phenomenality. Chalmers concedes that these ideas are not as clear as they might be:
1996: 293–301; 2003.)

Reply E: If the exponents of such views allow it to be *conceivable* that the non-
physical components of the universe should be removed, leaving a zombie world
subject to causal closure—and they certainly seem to allow that—then their view
offers no resistance to my argument. They may resist the actuality of the e-qualia
story, but they concede its conceivability. If on the other hand their view entails
that such a world is inconceivable, then it entails that a zombie world is inconceivable, which is my conclusion.

4.10 SOLE-PICTURES VERSUS SOUL-PICTURES

The jacket fallacy has been under attack for decades, for example by Wittgenstein,
Ryle, and Dennett. I would argue that those particular attacks have been too behaviouristic; but they contain much pertinent material. Dennett nicely highlights the
trouble with the e-qualia model by means of a comparison. Consciousness, he points
out, is 'not a single wonderful separable thing ... but a huge complex of many different informational capacities that individually arise for a wide variety of reasons. . . . It
is not a separate organ or a separate medium or a separate talent' (1995: 324). He
compares *health*:

Supposing that by an act of stipulative imagination you can remove consciousness while leaving all cognitive systems intact—a quite standard but entirely bogus feat of imagination—is
like supposing that by an act of stipulative imagination, you can remove health while leaving
all bodily functions and powers intact. ... Health isn't that sort of thing, and neither is
consciousness. (1995: 325)

He has said he 'cannot prove' that there is no such consciousness as the zombist
conception implies (1991: 406). My hope is that this chapter fills that gap.

   No doubt the e-qualia story is encouraged by half-conscious thoughts on the
lines of the traditional sense-datum or Cartesian Theatre model of perception: an
ethereal picture-show. It is ironic that the e-qualia story actually rules out the
Cartesian Theatre. If e-qualia could have functioned like pictures, then the idea of
seeing such pictures with the eye of the soul would have appeared to make sense,
neatly explaining how we might attend to and compare them: how we might
be epistemically intimate with them. But as the examples of sole-pictures and
induced electrical activity show, the conception of consciousness entailed by the
zombie idea cannot account for cognitive activity being directed at such 'soul-
pictures': no one could have stood in a relation of epistemic intimacy with them.
While the sense datum model at least envisages a spectator of the internal show,
the e-qualia story rules that out.

4.11 COROLLARIES

The argument of this chapter engages with more than the zombie idea. It exposes a fundamentally misconceived way of thinking about consciousness. Among other things, it therefore demolishes any views which entail the conceivability of the e-qualia story. We already know that epiphenomenalism is among these. Parallelism obviously entails the conceivability of the e-qualia story too, since the latter differs from parallelism only by having physical processes cause non-physical qualia rather than merely running parallel to them; and it cannot be inconceivable that such qualia should be actually caused by those physical processes.[6]

Dualistic interactionism is another matter, as I hinted in replying to objection D. Certainly I know of no good reasons to adopt this view, and regard it as incompatible with the scientific evidence. But I know of no a priori refutation of it either. In particular, I see no reason why it should be so formulated as to entail the conceivability of zombies or the e-qualia story. However, there may be versions of dualistic interactionism according to which the physical world is *as if* closed under causation, while actually being subject to causal overdetermination (assuming that were conceivable): some neural events being caused not only by physical events but by qualia as well. Any such variety of interactionism would obviously entail the conceivability of zombies and the e-qualia story, and would therefore be exposed to the argument of this chapter. To rub it in: if dualistic overdetermination is conceivable, then so is the e-qualia story; the e-qualia story is not conceivable, therefore dualistic overdetermination is not conceivable either.

A further corollary bears on the idea of the inverted spectrum: that the qualia I have when I see a ripe tomato might have been the ones I would have had if the tomato had been unripe, and vice versa, and similarly throughout the colour solid—while the physical set-up remained exactly the same in all its details. (If the physical set-up is different it is arguable that there are no significant problems: see for example Kirk 1994.) Chalmers says that although both the inverted spectrum possibility and the zombie possibility establish 'that consciousness fails to supervene logically', the conclusion established by the first is 'strictly weaker' than the conclusion established by the second (1996: 101; cf. his 1999: 476). This seems to be strictly correct, but only, I think, because someone might perversely maintain that although *colour* qualia do not supervene logically, some other qualia do.

---

[6] The following objection was suggested to an earlier version of this chapter: What if our neural states, together with the behaviour they cause, were all 'meaningless', 'mere physical happenings, while all meaning resides in the attendant epiphenomenal stream of conscious states'? If that admittedly absurd state of affairs is possible, so are zombies—and according to this objection I haven't shown that it is an impossible state of affairs. Well, that state of affairs may be prima facie conceivable. If it is, then so are zombies. But my argument shows that, contrary to what appeared prima facie to be possible, zombies are not conceivable in the relevant sense. I conclude that the state of affairs just envisaged is not conceivable either. At least it cannot just be assumed possible without explaining what is wrong with my argument to the contrary.

Assume for argument's sake that the inverted spectrum without physical differences is conceivable. In that case, nothing stronger than natural necessity can ensure that a given physical set-up is associated with a particular distribution of colour qualia. But what mere natural necessity has joined together could conceivably come apart. Given our assumption, therefore, conceivably there are individuals with that same physical set-up but no colour qualia at all. It follows that conceivably an individual without hearing, touch, smell, or taste—someone whose sole operative sense modality was visual—should have had no qualia of any kind, and would have been a kind of zombie, albeit a perceptually limited one. That poses essentially the same problems for physicalism and the understanding of consciousness as the standard kind. If you maintain that such a purely visual zombie is conceivable, then you commit yourself to the e-qualia story for the special case of persons whose only operative sense modality is visual. But if my earlier reasoning is sound, that model is inconceivable. Therefore the purely visual zombie is inconceivable too, in which case the inverted spectrum without physical differences is also inconceivable. The inconceivability of the inverted spectrum without physical differences is thus a corollary of the inconceivability of zombies.

The inconceivability of zombies does not have implications only for dualistic views. As you will have noticed, it also has implications for any purported versions of physicalism which leave open the c-possibility of zombies. Recall the 'weak thesis', according to which phenomenal truths are not necessitated a priori by physical truths, but are necessitated a posteriori by physical truths. If the argument of this chapter is sound, it demolishes that 'weak thesis', physicalistic or not—unless perhaps a significant distinction is made between a priori necessitation and c-necessity, in which case the weak thesis is not what it seems.

4.12 LOOKING AHEAD

In the last three chapters we have seen how the zombie idea, fantastic though it is, leads straight to the heart of the problems of phenomenal consciousness. If I am right, it also leads straight to an incoherent conception of the nature of a human being. I hope the sole-pictures argument, in particular, has sufficient intuitive appeal to break the spell of the zombies. Perhaps it will also nudge us towards a better way of conceiving of phenomenal consciousness.

As noted earlier, Joseph Levine regards the conceivability of zombies as 'the principal manifestation of the explanatory gap' (2001: 79). If zombies are in fact not conceivable in the sense that matters, does that entail there is no explanatory gap? I am not sure whether it entails there is no explanatory gap in Levine's sense (10.11 below). But I am sure there is still a lot of explaining to do.[7]

---

[7] Levine accepts the impossibility of zombies while insisting on the persistence of the explanatory gap (1993: 2001). Nagel at first assumed zombies were possible; he is now inclined to concede the contrary: the problem is to make 'transparent' why that is so (1998: see also 5.5 and 5.10 below).

5

What Has To Be Done

I believe the sole-pictures argument is conclusive, and shows not only that zombies are impossible but that the whole idea betrays a fundamentally mistaken conception of consciousness. But what sort of thing would the right conception be? We have to get reasonably clear about *what it is* for an object to be a phenomenally conscious subject; but what illumination can we realistically hope to achieve? In this chapter I will consider the general character of the project of explaining what phenomenal consciousness is, noting what has to be done—and what need not be attempted.

5.1 VARIETIES OF CONSCIOUSNESS

What I am most concerned to explain is 'phenomenal' consciousness, especially when involved in perception. First let us note some differences between it and other sorts of consciousness.

(a) There may be kinds of perceptual consciousness which do not necessarily involve there being *something it is like* for the subject; if so, I am not primarily concerned with them.[1] When it becomes necessary to make this focus explicit I will use the (regrettably clumsy) expression 'perceptual-phenomenal consciousness'. This kind of consciousness typically involves consciousness *of* something out there in the world. With this we can link perceptual *awareness*; I see no point in trying to distinguish these. As I write this (in a park, as it happens) I am conscious of the breeze on the back of my neck and the cooing of wood pigeons in the distance. I see leaves moving in the trees, blown and made to rustle by the breeze; I hear voices and the sound of cars on the distant road; I detect a whiff of cigarette smoke; I feel the pen in my hand. I am perceptually conscious (and aware) of all those things. As with all other uses of the word, this sort of consciousness comes (I think) in degrees. But in all cases of perceptual consciousness—at least in the sense that concerns me—there is something it is like for the subject; it is a variety of *phenomenal* consciousness. If zombies were possible, they might be said to have

---

[1] Peter Carruthers argues that there are non-conscious perceptual experiences (1996: 2000). To those who would object that experiences are conscious by definition, he replies that that only puts off the real problems. I discuss his views later: 10.11, 10.12, 11.9.

a kind of perceptual consciousness which was not necessarily also phenomenal. But by definition they would lack phenomenal consciousness.

For each of the various sorts of things I am conscious of as I sit in the park, *what it is like* for me is different: phenomenally different. The feel of the breeze on my skin is different from hearing the sound of the pigeons, which are both different from the smell of cigarette smoke. As well as those phenomenal differences between different sense modalities, there are, within each sense modality, differences in what the different experiences are like, in how they strike us subjectively: the experience of hearing the pigeons is subjectively (that is, as far as the subject could judge) different from that of hearing the voices; feeling the breeze on my neck is subjectively different from feeling the pen in my hand.

Some philosophers distinguish between what I am calling perceptual consciousness and an organism's being *conscious rather than unconscious* of events in its environment. (Armstrong 1968; Carruthers 1996: 149. Chalmers makes a similar distinction, though for different reasons.) Carruthers maintains that animals may be conscious of such events without what he calls '*conscious* awareness of these things' (1996: 149). These are subtle ideas; I note them here without being sure what is intended. A standard example in this context is Armstrong's absent-minded driver, who after driving perfectly competently for some time suddenly comes to, and realizes he has no recollection of any conscious experiences of where he has been or what has been happening. To clarify my use of 'perceptual consciousness' let me repeat that I see no point in distinguishing between perceptual *consciousness* of things and perceptual *awareness* of things.

We can contrast consciousness (or awareness) *of* things and consciousness *that* so-and-so is occurring. Consciousness *of* something is very common even when the subject lacks the most appropriate concept for whatever they are conscious of. I may be conscious of an odd smell without knowing it is acetone. Being conscious *that p*, however, requires the subject to have whatever concepts are introduced in the belief or proposition that *p*. This is a distinct case, as follows.

(b) I am conscious/aware *that* I am writing on a dull white sheet of paper. So I am also aware or conscious *of* what I am doing. However, it seems that sometimes I can be conscious of something without also being conscious *that* I am conscious of it. I may be conscious of the sound of the pigeons, for example, without being conscious that I am hearing it. Being conscious that I am experiencing something is a variety of self-consciousness; and it seems we can be conscious of things without being self-conscious in that sense (see Dretske 1993).

(c) Many cases of conscious experience are subjectively more or less *like* perceptual experience. The closest is hallucination. Other examples include after-images; bodily sensations such as tingles, pains, nausea, sexual pleasure; dream experiences; and the wide range of feelings and sensations typically involved in emotion.

What we sometimes refer to as our consciousness of some of our thoughts may come under this heading, although perhaps it should be described as consciousness

of activities involved in thinking rather than consciousness of the thoughts themselves. When thinking we often formulate bits of sentences; that doesn't seem quite
the same as having the thoughts. Knowing what our thoughts are, in contrast,
doesn't seem to be a matter of experience at all; more a matter of being able to say or
otherwise indicate what they are.

A further set of examples includes the sensation you get when you know you
have to do something but can't recall what it is.

(d) A substantially different sense of being conscious shows up in the difference
between being conscious and being unconscious. We are conscious when awake
and (in this sense) unconscious when asleep, even when dreaming, and even
though, as I suggested at (b) above, dreaming appears to be one kind of conscious
state. Being conscious in this sense (sometimes referred to as 'creature consciousness') is necessary for conscious perceptual experience but not also sufficient: a
creature may be conscious in this sense without even being capable of perceptual
consciousness or any other kind of phenomenal consciousness: see the next two
chapters. For that reason alone it would be wrong to say there is necessarily something it's like to be conscious in this sense.[2]

(e) Being *self-conscious* is not straightforward. In ordinary talk we tend to
restrict the expression to situations where someone gets embarrassed on realizing
they have become the object of attention by others. However, the expression can
also be used for our ability to think of ourselves as beings with a history and a
future, and as thinkers and agents in the world—roughly, as persons. It appears to
be a more sophisticated ability than perceptual consciousness.

(f) 'Consciousness' is also sometimes used to cover the whole range of mental
activities, with particular reference to beliefs, desires, hopes, wishes, fears, and all
the other so-called 'intentional' states—states that have 'content' or are directed at
'objects'.

(g) Relatedly, we may be conscious *of* our intentional states: our beliefs, desires,
intentions, and so on; in which case they are said to be, at the time, 'conscious'. If
Descartes was wrong, and Jane Austen, Dostoyevsky, Freud, and others were right,
we are not *necessarily* conscious of them, or not in that sense. In fact it seems a
truism that at any time a person has masses of beliefs, desires, intentions and so on
which are not all at that time conscious. It is an interesting question how far consciousness of beliefs, desires, and the rest involves there being something it is like,
but I shall not discuss it.[3]

---

[2] David Rosenthal contrasts 'creature consciousness' with 'state consciousness': the subject's being
conscious with the subject's states being conscious (e.g. his 1997: 729–31). That seems unproblematic; but note that my approach is to consider what it is for a system as a whole to be a subject of
perceptual consciousness. Thinking in terms of a state's being conscious can prompt misleading
expectations: see the last paragraph of 10.11 below.
[3] Carruthers says it is 'highly counter-intuitive to claim that what makes a conscious experience to
be conscious is quite different from what makes a conscious thought to be conscious', and regards it as
'a legitimate constraint on accounts of mental state consciousness that they should be univocal across

I am concentrating on (a): the sort of perceptual-phenomenal consciousness I am enjoying now, as I experience the sound of voices and of leaves moving and rustling in the breeze, the smell of grass, and so on. Now, if the zombie idea is as radically mistaken as I have argued, those descriptions are in all probability ways of talking about physical processes. Explaining what phenomenal consciousness is therefore requires an explanation of how that can be so when experiences and underlying physical processes appear utterly different, and fall under different concepts. How can such different concepts apply to the same reality?

5.2 NAGEL'S TWO KINDS OF CONCEPTS

In 'What Is It Like to Be a Bat?' Thomas Nagel puts his finger on a highly relevant difference between the concepts involved in specifying physical facts and those used to specify the facts of consciousness. He reasonably assumes that bats, like us, have conscious perceptual experiences. In that sense there is 'something it is like' to be a bat. (If he is mistaken about bats his argument can be stated in terms of whichever other species have them. If you think no non-human creatures have conscious experiences, keep reading.) We know that certain species of bats rely on echolocation much more than on vision. A succession of high-pitched squeaks enables them to find their way about even in the dark. The squeaks are bounced off objects around the flying animal, enabling it to track small insects, avoid wires, and generally keep up to date with the passing scene.

Suppose we have finally acquired a complete understanding of how a certain species of bat works, purely as a complex physical system. Nagel asks whether that enables us to know what it is like to be a bat. Regardless of whether you are inclined to reply 'Yes' or 'No' to this question, you have to admit that the answer is not obvious. His own reflections lead him to conclude that the answer is 'No'. Even if we had all the relevant scientific information at our disposal, we still wouldn't be able to tell what it's like to be a bat. I happen to agree over that, and think he has done us a service by raising the question so vividly, and supplying a good reason for accepting his own answer. But we need to be clear about this reason, and about where its implications stop.

He begins by distinguishing what are in effect two broad categories of concepts. The distinction is based on the fact that some concepts are accessible to any suffi-ciently intelligent creature—human, Martian, robot—regardless of the specific nature of their perceptual systems: whether or not they have our type of colour vision, for example. These concepts include all the ones traditionally used in con-nection with the so-called 'primary qualities' of things: shape, distance, relative size, relative motion, mass. If there were sufficiently intelligent language-using

different categories of mental state' (1996: 151). I find nothing counter-intuitive in the claim he challenges; at the same time I need not defend it.

bats, they would be just as capable of using these concepts as any other kind of creature. The same goes for all the other concepts that figure in physical theory, including not only the general concepts of logic and mathematics but such special ones as *electron* and *quark*. These and similar concepts could in principle be grasped by creatures with very different sensory equipment, because grasping them doesn't depend on any particular kind of access to the items in question. For example, you can understand the point and nature of physics without being able to see or hear. I am not saying that a creature without *any* means of perception could use those concepts or even grasp them. The point is that their possession and use does not call for any particular type of sensory equipment. We can call these concepts *viewpoint-neutral*.[4]

All other concepts are *viewpoint-relative*. They cannot be fully grasped except by creatures with the appropriate 'point of view'. Just what counts as a point of view in the relevant sense is a question we can put off for the moment. It will be enough that part of it involves having a particular type of sensory equipment. Straightforward examples of concepts which cannot be fully grasped except by individuals with the right types of sensory capacity are *red, sweet, headache, squeak*. To use a venerable illustration: blind people can know a great deal about colour concepts—they can use the words appropriately in many contexts, for example— but it is at least disputable that they grasp them fully. (Are the very general concepts of *experience, feeling*, and *sensation* also viewpoint-relative? The question is interesting; but I will ignore it because what matters is that the examples just mentioned call for some particular type of perceptual capacity.) On Nagel's view, only creatures with appropriate sensory capacities are capable of acquiring a full grasp of those concepts. That view is widely shared; I need not defend it here. I think that in addition to having the right sensory capacities, grasping the concepts in question also requires actual experiences in the right sensory modalities, perhaps even, in some cases, experiences of the specific kinds to which the concepts apply. At least it requires the ability to create in imagination something akin to the experiences in question.

Nagel's point, as I understand it, is this. The full scientific story of bat perception is assumed to be in viewpoint-neutral terms. But viewpoint-neutral concepts cannot yield translations or even logical equivalents of statements in viewpoint-relative terms. That is implicit in there being a distinction between the two categories of concepts. There is no way to convey a full grasp of viewpoint-relative concepts in viewpoint-neutral terms. Now, suppose bats with sufficient intelligence were to have concepts in terms of which they could describe their own characteristic experiences of things perceived by their distinctive system of echolocation. They would be able to say what their own battish (or micropteric) experiences were like. But because *we* lack such concepts we cannot describe those experiences. We cannot say

---

[4] Although these terms are not Nagel's, I believe this does justice to his approach. See also Kirk 1994: 223–38.

what it is like for them; we cannot even understand what it is like for them. For that reason alone the full viewpoint-neutral scientific account of how these bats function cannot equip us to proceed to a knowledge of what their experiences are like.

I am not saying Nagel's argument is complete in every detail, or even that it is entirely sound, although I think it is (as far as it goes: of course I reject the anti-physicalist conclusion he proceeds to base on it). The two points I want to make about it don't require it to be absolutely solid. The first is just that the case Nagel makes is at least persuasive; and I shall presuppose it in what follows. If he is wrong, that won't damage my overall project. The other point is more relevant, since I am committed to a philosophical investigation of perceptual-phenomenal consciousness even though some people are sceptical about such approaches. It is that Nagel and many others have overlooked a vital distinction.

Nagel argues that the point I have expressed in terms of the difference between viewpoint-neutral and viewpoint-relative concepts exposes a serious problem for physicalism. I think he has bundled together two problems which must be kept apart. One is the problem he has emphasized: whether we can get from a knowledge of relevant viewpoint-neutral facts to a knowledge of the character of the bat's conscious experiences: a knowledge of what it is like (for the bat). That is the *what-is-it-like* problem. The other problem is whether we can get from a knowledge of those same viewpoint-neutral facts to a knowledge of whether the bat is phenomenally conscious at all. That is the *is-it-like-anything* problem.

5.3 THREE PROBLEMS: (I) WHAT IS IT LIKE? (II) IS IT LIKE ANYTHING? (III) WHAT IS IT?

Suppose Nagel is right about the problem of what it is like. That is, suppose it is impossible to acquire a knowledge of what a creature's perceptual experiences are like purely from a knowledge of the relevant viewpoint-neutral facts. That doesn't seem to rule out a solution to the other problem: whether it is like anything. In order to deal with the is-it-like-anything problem we have to deal with the really fundamental problem in this area, the one I am focusing on from now on: what does it take—or *what is it*—for something to be perceptually conscious?

A solution to this what-is-it problem would presumably enable us, given ingenuity and persistence, to move from scientific or other viewpoint-neutral information to an answer to the is-it-like-anything problem. In the case of bats, solving the what-is-it problem would enable us (or at least suitably informed and equipped scientists) to tell whether there was *something* it was like for the bat to perceive the world by means of its echolocatory system. Our solution would spell out what conditions must be satisfied for something to be perceptually conscious, and we should be able to tell, at any rate in favourable cases, whether they were satisfied (presumably not in all cases because of complexity, inaccessibility, alienness, and so on). If, as I happen to think, there is no reason why a system working on ordinary physical principles should not satisfy those conditions, then we should have cracked a major component of the mind-body problem. We should also have largely vindicated physicalism (although that is not my aim: I don't think the conditions for perceptual-phenomenal consciousness have to imply that it is possible only for purely physical systems, though they had better not rule it out).

However, solving the problem of *what it is* would seem to give no reasons to expect we could solve the general problem of *what it's like*. There is an enormous difference between discovering that a creature satisfies the conditions for being a subject of perceptual consciousness, and discovering what its experiences are like. It is unfortunate that the what-is-it-like problem tends to get conflated with the is-it-like-anything problem. As we have seen, Nagel's reasons why the former cannot be solved are not reasons why the latter should not be solved. The main reason the what-is-it-like problem cannot be solved in general is that there is no general procedure for acquiring a full grasp of the perceptual concepts associated with the various different possibly sensory systems. If I don't perceive the world as a bat does, then I can't acquire a full understanding of the sorts of concepts that would be needed in order to characterize battish experiences. (Just saying 'the sort of experience a bat has when it echolocates a telephone wire', for example, wouldn't help us if we lacked bat-like perceptual consciousness.) But that is no reason to conclude that I can't tell *what it is* for a creature to have conscious perceptual experiences, and on that basis move on to discovering whether it is like anything for the bat.

For those reasons I don't think the what-is-it-like problem is fundamental or even particularly important—though it is certainly interesting. I shall come back to it briefly in the next section. What is really fundamental is the what-is-it problem.

5.4   DO WE HAVE TO GET A PRIORI FROM PHYSICAL FACTS TO WHAT IT IS LIKE?

I have accepted Nagel's reasons for concluding there is no general solution to the what-is-it-like problem, but you may wonder whether that conclusion does not undermine my project. I maintain that even a minimal physicalism is committed to the strict implication thesis, according to which truths about consciousness are strictly implied by P; and later I shall be arguing that the sorts of physical and functional facts that P provides for are capable of fully accounting for phenomenal consciousness. But if we cannot get a priori from P to a knowledge of what it is like for any given organism, how can P *necessitate* phenomenal consciousness? What would prevent the character of each organism's experiences from floating free of the physical and functional facts, just as Chalmers and others maintain?

If we look more closely we can see that the inference is not correct; but there are two potential sources of confusion. One is the general slipperiness of the vocabulary of modality, already noted. A special symptom of this slipperiness is that some philosophers write as if 'a priori' were a species of necessity: which is why, earlier, it seemed not unreasonable to assume provisionally that what is 'a priori possible' coincided with what is 'c-possible'. Now, the expressions 'a priori' and 'a posteriori' (alternatively 'empirical') have traditionally been used for epistemic notions rather than metaphysical ones. I follow Kripke (1972) and many others in thinking they are too useful in that role to be allowed to be assimilated to varieties of modality. I will use them only in connection with possible ways of coming to know things. On that understanding something is knowable a priori just in case we can come to know it without having to investigate how the world is; otherwise it is knowable only empirically/a posteriori.

That leaves theoretical room for truths to be *strictly implied* by P without automatically being *a priori knowable* on the basis of a knowledge of P, in which case the a priori possible does not coincide with the c-possible. I think that is actually the case for certain truths about phenomenal consciousness. But here we encounter the second main source of confusion. It is that in many cases understanding and knowledge come in degrees; they are not all-or-nothing. Connectedly, grasping concepts is in many cases a matter of degree. Concepts which bear on the character of experience are an important example. Nagel's reasoning is attractive because it is at least plausible that we are not capable of a *full* understanding of statements involving viewpoint-relative concepts unless we have either had the relevant kinds of experience or can somehow construct them in imagination.

This does not mean that people without the necessary experiences or imaginative capacities cannot have any understanding at all of the statements in question. Locke's 'studious blind man', who suggested that scarlet was 'like the sound of a trumpet', clearly had an excellent grasp of some facts about the colour red.[5] Red is salient among colours in a way analogous to the way the sound of a trumpet is salient among sounds. No doubt he also realized that colours are properties of objects which people with normal eyesight usually detect easily in normal light; that every visible object has some colour; that each of us can arrange the colours in a scheme where some are more similar in colour than others; and so on. If you know all that, you cannot be described as having no grasp whatever of colour concepts. Still, as Locke emphasized, and as Jackson's story of Mary brings out so sharply, the blind man is far from knowing *what it is like* to see red things.

It seems that Jackson's Mary could not get a priori from knowledge of P to knowledge of what it is like to see colours: that she could not acquire the full grasp of colour concepts that seems to be available only to those who can actually see colours. Conceivably Mary might have the pretty extraordinary capacity to construct the right sorts of experiences in imagination. But even if she could, she could not also tell *a priori* which type of experience goes with which physical processes.

---

[5] 'A studious blind Man, who had mightily beat his Head about visible Objects, and made use of the explication of his Books and Friends, to understand those names of Light, and Colours, which often came in his way; bragg'd one day, That he now understood what *Scarlet* signified. Upon which his Friend demanding, what *Scarlet* was? the blind Man answered, It was like the Sound of a Trumpet' (Locke 1689/1975, III.iv.11).

She must first have the experiences in question, and then match them to the various underlying physical processes. So in any case, as long as she is in her grey prison, Mary cannot acquire a full understanding of truths about colour experiences.

However, because her knowledge of P would enable her to acquire an excellent understanding of the physical and functional facts involved in the human use of colour concepts, she could still acquire a high level of understanding of the workings of those concepts, including the 'phenomenal' concepts which are supposed to apply to the actual characters of our experiences. That understanding would of course include the argument of the last chapter. And here is a crucial point. Together with a knowledge of P, that understanding would enable her to work out which statements ascribing colour experiences were *true*. For among the physical and functional facts at her disposal are facts about people's verbal dispositions, for example facts concerning the patterns of sound that individuals are disposed to utter, or give signs of assent to, when faced with, say, something red. Certainly Mary in her prison (assuming she couldn't perform the necessary imaginative work) would lack the full understanding of those truths that is possessed by people with normal colour vision; but she would still have the sort of grasp that is possessed by Locke's blind man.

To summarize: Mary in her prison could not get a priori from P to full knowledge-with-understanding of truths about people's phenomenal experiences—for example full knowledge-with-understanding of 'On 1st January 1800, Napoleon had a greenish after-image'. But she could get to know a priori from P which statements of that kind were true, and in general, *that* certain statements about phenomenal experience in Q were true. (This presupposes, of course, that the zombie possibility is not open—as Mary, being a brilliant scientist, knows.)

This means that what I called the 'strong thesis', according to which phenomenal truths are 'necessitated a priori' by physical truths, needs to be construed with some care. The phrase 'necessitated a priori' comes from Chalmers (1999); but in a later article Chalmers and Jackson (2001) define 'a priori entailment', which they also refer to as 'implication', as holding 'when it is possible to know that P entails Q with justification independent of experience' (2001: 316). Now, we have just seen that Mary is able to know *that* P implies Q (or at least the phenomenal truths in Q) independently of experience. For she can get a priori from P to the conclusion that such and such phenomenal and other non-physical statements are true. Therefore the story of Mary need not be an embarrassment to those who maintain the strong thesis in Chalmers and Jackson's sense. However, we have also seen that Mary cannot get a priori from P to a full knowledge-with-understanding of the truth of those statements. If the strong thesis is to be construed in that sense rather than in Chalmers and Jackson's sense, then the story of Mary does indeed seem to show that it is false. But that need not bother physicalists: they have no need to maintain the strong thesis so construed.

Those complications over the interpretation of the strong thesis suggest that physicalists would be better to stick to the strict implication thesis, which, it is now clear, must be distinguished from the strong thesis however the latter is to be construed. For the strict implication thesis is neutral as to whether it is possible to get a priori from P to Q.

There is a further complication. Consider the situation after Mary has been released from her grey prison and has acquired the same full grasp of colour concepts that others have. Can we say she is now in a position to move a priori from P to Q? We know that even before her release she could tell which statements about people's visual experiences were true—via her knowledge of the relevant physical and functional facts. For example, she could learn that it is true that Napoleon had a greenish after-image on 1st January 1800. Now that she is freely enjoying her colour experiences, she fully understands the content of that statement. Doesn't it follow that she can move *a priori* to a full knowledge of it and similar statements? If that is correct, doesn't it follow that the rest of us can do the same, in which case the strict implication thesis and the 'strong thesis' are equivalent after all?

There is a flaw in that reasoning. What equipped Mary with her present full grasp of the relevant concepts was not her knowledge of P alone: it was actually seeing coloured things. As a result of her experiences of colours she was able to say things like, 'So *this* is what it's like to see ripe tomatoes!' She could only acquire that knowledge a posteriori. Therefore she is still not able to move a priori from P to Q. Since she is now essentially in the same position as the rest of us, it follows that no one is able to move a priori from P to Q. (Interestingly, that makes the conditional from P to Q c-necessary but a posteriori: but we need not pursue that point.) Thus the strict implication thesis remains distinct from the strong thesis. Of course, if the strong thesis holds, so does the strict implication thesis. The point is that the converse is not true.

To return briefly to our bats. If Nagel is right to hold that we cannot know what it is like to be a bat, then language-using bats could describe the character of their echolocatory experiences in terms we could not fully understand. With respect to a grasp of the nature of bat experience, we are all in a position analogous to Mary's before her release. Certainly we could discover a great deal about micropteric experiences. We could acquire the relevant physical, neurobiological, and functional information. Rather like Mary, and more like Locke's blind man, we could reach some understanding of what language-using bats were saying. But we could not reach a full understanding of their descriptions. (And unlike imprisoned Mary with respect to human colour experiences, we could never come to do so—at least, not without prosthetic implants and brain modifications.)

You might suspect that the original problem remains. If we cannot move a priori from P to full knowledge-with-understanding of Q, how can the character of experiences be fixed to these particular physical arrangements? Let p be my present physical state as I look at the red cover of this book and have the particular experience r that I do, and let g be the experience I should have had if the book had been green instead of red. You might be willing to concede that some kind of *natural* necessity ensures that p is associated with r rather than with g. But natural necessity is not enough for strict implication. How can incoherence be involved in the idea that *p* might have been associated with *g*? Surely the claim that P strictly implies that the experience is *g* is excessively strong?

Well, no, it isn't. The examples of mountains and digital images helped to show that the incoherence involved in denying cases of strict implication does not depend on obvious or direct conceptual links; and the only reason why it seems as if the physical set-up *p* might have been associated with *g* rather than *r* is that there are indeed no obvious or direct conceptual links from one to the other. But we can contrapose: if the strict implication thesis is true, then truths ascribing particular experiences to individuals are strictly implied by P. We can go further. If in the course of this book I succeed in explaining what it takes for something to be a subject of phenomenal consciousness, then my account can be used to explain how it is that P strictly implies such truths as 'human beings are phenomenally conscious'.

From that it will follow that what it is like for each individual human being is strictly implied by P. For obviously it isn't possible that there should be something it is like for a given individual without there being something it is like in particular. If, as I am momentarily assuming, P fixes that it's like *something*, it fixes *what* it's like. So if the strict implication thesis holds, P fixes what each experience is like even if we can't work out what it's like a priori from P alone. Those considerations help to explain how the strict implication thesis can be true even if there is no general solution to the what-is-it-like problem.

You may perhaps concede that the truth of statements such as the one about Napoleon's greenish after-image can be worked out a priori from P, but deny that truths involving what Chalmers calls 'direct phenomenal concepts' can also be worked out a priori from P. As we saw, he says that 'The clearest cases of direct phenomenal concepts arise when a subject attends to the quality of the experience, and forms a concept wholly based on the attention to the quality' (2003: 235). An example is the sort of concept he takes it that Mary uses when she sees something red for the first time. If there are such concepts, our account of phenomenal consciousness must provide for their applicability. And if it is not possible to get a priori from P to truths expressible in terms of such concepts, still our account must provide for there being such truths. I suggest that if the account works at all, it will do that too. The reader must judge whether the account to be developed in later chapters is successful in this.

5.5 MUST THERE BE A THIRD TYPE OF EVENT?

In work subsequent to 'What Is It Like to Be a Bat?' Nagel has urged that

if there were a necessary connection between the phenomenology and the physiology of tasting a cigar, it would not be evident *a priori* on the basis of the ordinary concept of that experience, since the possession of that concept involves no awareness of anything about the brain. . . . The relation (to the brain) is completely absent from the concept, and cannot be retrieved by philosophical analysis. (1998: 349)

He goes on to conclude that 'these two ways of referring—by the phenomenological concept and the physiological concept—pick out a single referent', but 'that the logical link cannot be discovered by inspecting the concepts directly: rather it goes only through their common link to the referent itself.' So he suggests that in order for us to be able to understand the necessity of the connection between the mental and the physical, we need a theory of a 'third type of events that admits these two types of access, internal and external'. This theory would 'render transparent the relation between mental and physical'. The mental will not do this 'because it simply leaves out the physiology, and has no room for it'. But neither will the physical, 'because while it includes the behavioral and functional manifestations of the mental, this doesn't, in view of the falsity of conceptual reductionism, enable it to reach to the mental concepts themselves' (1998: 351).

For Nagel's reasoning to succeed, 'conceptual reductionism' (whatever exactly it is) must require obvious or direct conceptual links from the physical to the mental. For reasons noted earlier I am inclined to agree that there are no such links, and that conceptual reductionism in that sense is false. However, I think the arguments in the last section show that that does not block the strict implication thesis. The falsity of conceptual reductionism in Nagel's sense does not entail that there must be a 'third type of event'. If the strict implication thesis is true, then incoherence of the sort explained in Chapter 2 would be involved in the denial of 'If P then Q'. Hence if I manage to find acceptably clear and non-circular necessary and sufficient conditions for perceptual-phenomenal consciousness, conditions which could be satisfied by purely physical systems, the main work of justifying the strict implication thesis will have been done and there will be no need for a new science to introduce a third type of event. True, we cannot construct physical/functional *definitions* of phenomenal concepts. Nagel is right if that is what he means by saying that the physical cannot 'reach to the mental concepts themselves'. But I have argued that there is no reason to require it to do so. The assumption that it is necessary seems to be a consequence of conflating the what-is-it problem with the what-is-it-like problem.

5.6 BLOCK'S TWO CONCEPTS OF CONSCIOUSNESS

It will be useful to consider another case of what is claimed to be the illegitimate conflation of concepts. Ned Block has urged that 'The concept of consciousness is a hybrid, or better, a mongrel concept.' He thinks 'there are a number of very different "consciousnesses"', and concentrates on two, which he calls 'phenomenal consciousness' and 'access consciousness'. 'Phenomenal consciousness', he says, 'is experience; the phenomenally conscious aspect of a state is what it is like to be in that state. The mark of access-consciousness, by contrast, is availability for use in reasoning and rationally guiding speech and action. These concepts are often partly or totally conflated, with bad results' (1995: 227). A closely similar distinction is made by David Chalmers, who writes of 'the phenomenal and the psychological concepts of mind' (1996: 11–32).

Block's concept of 'phenomenal consciousness' is close to mine, and covers aspects of what I am calling 'perceptual-phenomenal consciousness' as well as such phenomena as having after-images and bodily sensations. His concept of 'access consciousness' is very different. We need not pursue the details of Block's distinction at this stage, but it will be helpful to note how he uses it.

He applies it in connection with certain claims based on empirical results. Notably he picks out blindsight. As is widely known, blindsight patients acquire, via their eyes, information about stimuli in the blind part of their visual field. This is clear from their success rate in answering questions about the nature of those stimuli, in spite of their denials that they see anything in their blind fields (Weiskrantz 1986; 1997). Typically the patient is presented with a 'forced choice'. For example they are asked to guess between two alternative descriptions of the stimulus, and it turns out that their performance is substantially better than chance. They cannot, however, easily 'harness this information in the service of action', as Block puts it. So it has been argued that 'a function of phenomenal consciousness is somehow to enable information represented in the brain to guide action'. Block objects that the stimuli in the blind field are *both* access-unconscious and phenomenally unconscious, and concludes that the experimenters are guilty of a fallacy. They have 'illicitly transferred' to phenomenal consciousness what is a function of the machinery of access-consciousness (227). (There seems to be a question about how the information could be 'access *un*conscious' if it enables the patient to 'guess' successfully; but that is not what concerns me just now.)

Surely the concepts Block distinguishes are indeed distinct. If the scientists he criticizes have assumed that what goes for access consciousness automatically goes for phenomenal consciousness too, they are guilty, as charged, of a methodological error. However, it obviously doesn't follow from the fact that the concepts are distinct that they apply to distinct components of reality; it doesn't even follow that they apply to *logically* distinct items. *The cube root of 216* is one concept; *6* is a different one, yet necessarily they apply to the same number. So if it turns out that truths about phenomenal consciousness are strictly implied by truths about access consciousness (analogously to the way truths about mountains are strictly implied by narrowly physical truths) the error is not as significant as he makes out. Admittedly it has not been proved that truths about phenomenal consciousness *are* strictly implied by truths about access consciousness. But the assumption that they do is not obviously wrong; and if my proposed solution to the what-is-it problem is right, they could well be strictly implied by truths about something which, though significantly different from Block's 'access consciousness', is related to it. If that is right, his discussion, in spite of having a legitimate target in the fallacious reasoning he describes, is misleading. For he hints that the difference between his two concepts of consciousness implies that the facts of phenomenal consciousness are *not* strictly implied by the facts of access consciousness.

Comparably, Chalmers distinguishes two 'quite distinct concepts of mind' as follows:

The first is the *phenomenal* concept of mind. This is the concept of mind as conscious experience, and of a mental state as a consciously experienced mental state .... The second is the *psychological* concept of mind. This is the concept of mind as the causal or explanatory basis for behaviour. ...

On the phenomenal concept, mind is characterized by the way it *feels;* on the psychological concept, mind is characterized by what it does. ... Neither of them is the correct analysis of mind. They cover different phenomena, both of which are quite real. (1996: 11)

Unlike Block, Chalmers is explicitly concerned to show that the phenomenal facts do not 'logically supervene' on what he calls the 'psychological' facts any more than, according to him, they supervene on the purely physical facts. When he introduces the above distinction he has already offered the arguments for non-supervenience that we examined in Chapter 3, so he needs to prepare the way for a conception of the mind that will be compatible with his claim. Later in his book he draws a further distinction, connected to the one made in the quoted passage: between consciousness and what he calls 'awareness'. Awareness in his sense is the 'psychological' correlate of consciousness (in the sense of 'psychological' explained in the quotation). Zombies have full awareness, he says, and share all our other 'psychological' properties. All they lack is phenomenal properties.

In contrast to Chalmers I shall argue that the phenomenal facts of perceptual consciousness are strictly implied by certain psychological truths. In contrast to Block I shall argue that the conceptual difference he points to doesn't amount to an objection to the necessary and sufficient conditions for perceptual-phenomenal consciousness that I shall be proposing.

5.7 DO WE NEED A NEW SCIENCE?

Impressed by what they see as the failure of attempted solutions to the philosophical problem of consciousness, some philosophers have concluded that it is insoluble. Colin McGinn believes there is a solution: a wholly adequate theory of relations between the mental and the physical. Unfortunately, he thinks, human beings will never be able to formulate it or even understand it because of our innate cognitive kinks (1991).

Nagel is less pessimistic. As we have seen, he thinks that in order to render the relation between mental and physical 'transparent' we need a new theory, which provides for a 'third type of event' (1998: 351). So he thinks we are challenged 'to develop a new form of understanding' (1994: 67). Galen Strawson takes a similar line. He suggests that 'Our existing notions of the physical and the mental or experiential cannot be reconciled or theoretically integrated as they stand' (1994*b*: 84).

Like Nagel and Strawson, I have no idea how a radically new form of understanding might be developed to meet the challenge they discern. But I see no reason to suppose that radically new forms or theories are needed. As far as the physical facts about our universe are concerned, I see no reason to look for types of understanding and theorizing other than those supplied by natural science, philosophy, and psychology (both everyday and scientific)—which is not to say I envisage no possibility of radical changes *in* physics or the other sciences. It is a challenge to explain how, assuming the universe is a purely physical system, the purely physical facts about us can *necessitate* phenomenal consciousness. But I think that can be done by means of philosophical explanations.

5.8 DOES THIS PROJECT INVOLVE 'CONCEPTUAL ANALYSIS'? DOES IT INVOLVE ARMCHAIR SCIENCE?

Some readers might suspect I face a dilemma: either the project of finding necessary and sufficient conditions for phenomenal consciousness is 'conceptual analysis' or it is armchair science. Conceptual analysis in general is widely believed to have been discredited by Quine (in spite of Jackson's (1998) vigorous defence of it; see also Chalmers and Jackson 2001). In this particular context it is found objectionable for the further reason that, as we have seen, there seem to be no relevant conceptual links between the physical and the phenomenal. This is indeed the core of the alleged 'explanatory gap'. As to the other horn of this dilemma, armchair science is regarded as, if possible, even more disreputable than conceptual analysis.

I suggest the dilemma is false. We don't have to choose between those alternatives. I accept a broadly Quinean holistic view of our various cognitive projects, and see no sharp dividing lines between science and philosophy. For that reason I see no objections to something that might be called 'armchair science', or better, 'armchair pre-science', although obviously it cannot be purely a priori: we must be allowed to bring basic empirical knowledge to the armchair. For the same reason I reject the assumption of sharp dividing lines between what might be described as conceptual analysis and what might be described as empirical work. The task of explaining how everyday descriptions involving consciousness relate to descriptions of the world in objective terms has to be done somehow, no matter how it is labelled. It had better take account of empirical work; but purely empirical work will not be enough because it leaves the field open to zombists and other e-qualists. Keep in mind the lessons of Chapter 2: the project of explaining how P strictly implies Q does not require a derivation of Q from P in logical or semantic terms; nor does it require semantic reductions or conceptual analysis in any tight sense. It requires only (only!) an explanation of *what it is* about the world whose existence is provided for by P that also provides for the truths in Q.

Certainly my project includes that of making it intelligible how a purely physical system could be phenomenally conscious, hence how the physical facts could necessitate the phenomenal facts. ('Could': although I am not setting out to prove physicalism, we do need an explanation of how it *could* be true.) But carrying this project forward does not commit me to any particular doctrines about analyticity. Readers must judge how far, if at all, this minimal commitment damages the prospects of success in the overall project.

5.9 MORE ON THE WHAT-IS-IT PROBLEM

The what-is-it problem is about the *nature* of phenomenal consciousness. Investigating things' natures is typically a matter of discovering what underlies their obvious superficial properties. In many cases such investigations are purely scientific; water is an example. An acceptable answer to the question 'What is water?' will have a certain character because the stuff we pick out by its liquidity, colourlessness, transparency, and so on is assumed to be a natural kind and to have a scientifically identifiable inner nature. With consciousness and other everyday-psychological mental states, however, the situation is different. What reason is there to assume that mental concepts pick out scientifically identifiable natural kinds? Our everyday psychological concepts were developed among communities with virtually no scientific knowledge, for purposes quite unlike those of modern physicists and chemists. There is no reason to suppose that their concepts were intended to pick out scientifically identifiable inner natures. Recall the landscape case: the vocabulary we use to talk about landscape features was also built up over ages by people without scientific motivation. Quite generally, what is salient and seems worth taking account of in ordinary life tends not to coincide with what is salient and seems worth taking account of to scientists. These differences in focus bring with them differences in what is picked out as relevant for purposes of classification. When we are focusing on landscape features, what matters is things like large-scale contour patterns or concentrations of liquid; minute details of the underlying fine structure don't count. In that sense, landscape concepts deal with different properties from those of interest to physical science—even though no more is involved in things having those properties than is covered by facts about fine structural details. Analogous points hold for psychological concepts. I know of no good reason for assuming that a given structure of psychological states could only be realized by a physical system satisfying some very tight constraint, for example that it must be in neural terms. Something more widely applicable is needed.

Of course the what-is-it problem is only a problem for us because we conceptualize in certain ways. Imagine a Martian population had evolved whose concepts were all viewpoint-neutral and included nothing like *believing, desiring, wanting, hoping*. Could they find themselves puzzled by the what-is-it problem? It is hard to see how. We, in contrast, have those everyday psychological concepts, and they do raise problems for us. So I believe that solving the what-is-it problem requires us to attend to, and to some extent use, the everyday psychological concepts in terms of which it is posed. (Everyday psychology got us into this, and everyday psychology is gonna have to get us out.[6])

Unfortunately we seem unlikely to reach a crisp and clear set of necessary and sufficient conditions for perceptual consciousness in terms of everyday psychological concepts because of their vagueness. They are blunt implements for dealing with the sorts of situation we actually find ourselves in, not cognitive scalpels. Since the what-is-it problem is inevitably specified in everyday psychological language, we shouldn't expect to be able to reach an ideally clear statement.[7] Still, it is not the vagueness of our consciousness-involving concepts that causes all the trouble so much as the difficulty of understanding how they relate to other concepts, ones we find less problematic. We have a reasonably firm grasp of how some of our everyday psychological concepts work. Perhaps, then, we should follow the example of David Armstrong (1968) and use the concepts we have a better understanding of to improve our grasp of the ones that perplex us. I aim to produce necessary and sufficient conditions for perceptual-phenomenal consciousness in terms which we can understand pretty well, even though they fall short of the clarity we would ideally like.

5.10 THE MODERATE REALISM OF EVERYDAY PSYCHOLOGY

Before moving on, let us acknowledge that psychology is not empirically neutral. That is a truism for the case of scientific psychology; but it ought also to be considered a truism for everyday psychology. By 'everyday psychology' (or 'folk psychology') I mean the powerful, flexible, vague, complex, but practically indispensable complex of concepts, assumptions, prejudices, tendencies, and patterns of description, explanation, and much else that we constantly use to describe, predict, understand, and explain the thoughts, words, and other behaviour of ourselves and other people. The only reason it is not universally considered a truism that everyday psychology has empirical implications is that some philosophers have been misled by its abstractness and wide applicability into taking it to be as empirically neutral as mathematics or logic. True, its empirical implications, such as they are, are characterizable only at high levels of abstraction. Nevertheless

---

6 The harassed central character in Philip Roth's *My Life as a Man* remarks, 'Literature got me into this, and literature is gonna have to get me out' (1976: 195).

7 Papineau is so impressed by the vagueness of viewpoint-relative concepts that he despairs of a theory of consciousness. He thinks the general notion of consciousness may be 'too thin to pick out any real kind' (2003: 380; cf. his 2002). However, his target is a particular variety of physicalist account, which seeks a kind specifiable in scientific terms: it is not my project.

I suggest that everyday psychology does have implications about how things actually are, implications that show up in some facts about our dispositions to accept or reject psychological descriptions in context.

These dispositions relate especially to the moderate realism of everyday psychology. One example is that if a certain behaving system's behaviour and behavioural capacities all turn out to be the result of a vast look-up table, then even if it seemed highly intelligent, most of us would refuse to call it so. That is because most of us, at least according to my own admittedly limited sociological investigations, on reflection refuse to allow that something is really intelligent unless it works out its own behaviour on the basis of its own assessment of its situation. The realism which that seems to reflect is only moderate, however, requiring no more than that there be *some* processes going on which constitute the system's working out its own response to the situation as it assesses it. There seems no basis for going further and requiring that the processes in question be those of a language of thought, for example. Nor, I must add, does everyday psychology seem to require that those processes be physical rather than non-physical.

A few other examples of that sort of moderate realism in everyday psychology will appear later. Because it has empirical implications, it is exposed in principle to scientific refutation. For example it is exposed to refutation by the conceivable but not very likely discovery that a lot of otherwise normal people are controlled by teams of homunculi. But its implications seem no more likely to be overthrown in practice than the implications of folk physics, such as that stones break ordinary glass windows, or that it takes more strength to push a car than a pram. For all that, the fact that everyday psychology has implications such as the one mentioned in the last paragraph will be useful in what follows.

5.11 SUMMARY

I am focusing on the problem of the nature of perceptual-phenomenal consciousness: the what-is-it problem. I accept Nagel's argument for the view that there is no possibility of finding a general solution to the 'what-is-it-like' problem; but that does not prevent us looking for what we need above all: a solution to the what-is-it problem (hence to the is-it-like-anything problem). Jackson's Mary could not get a priori from the physical and functional truths to a full knowledge-with-understanding of phenomenal truths; but she could get a priori from the physical truths to a knowledge of *which* phenomenal statements were true. Given the inconceivability of zombies, that blocks an inference to the view that phenomenal consciousness is logically independent of physical or functional facts. The 'falsity of conceptual reductionism' does not entail that explaining consciousness will depend on a 'third' type of event that is neither physical nor phenomenal. The difference between what Block calls 'access consciousness' and 'phenomenal consciousness' does not amount to a difficulty for my project; nor does Chalmers's comparable distinction. Contrary to what some philosophers maintain, we do not need a new science. Nor is it necessary to choose between conceptual analysis in some tight sense, and armchair science.

Understanding the nature of perceptual-phenomenal consciousness does not require us to look for some scientifically based condition comparable to the scientific formulas of chemical compounds. We have reasons to expect that there are no such conditions. Instead, we can look for broad necessary and sufficient conditions in terms of everyday psychology, using concepts that we understand reasonably well (5.9). A feature of everyday psychology that will be useful in what follows is its *moderate realism*.

6

Deciders

Perception, I believe, is, in some degree, *in all sorts of Animals*; ... We may, I think, from the Make of an *Oyster*, or *Cockle*, reasonably conclude, that it has not so many, nor so quick Senses, as a Man, or several other Animals; ... But yet, I cannot but think, there is some small dull Perception, whereby they are distinguished from perfect Insensibility.

(John Locke, *Essay*, 1689/1975, II.ix.12)

It is easy to agree with Locke in ascribing conscious perceptual experience to at least some non-human animals, even if not to bivalves. By following his example and considering animals less complicated than ourselves, I think we shall have a better chance of uncovering what really matters for perceptual consciousness and avoiding the confusions that can result from too close attention to the complexities of specifically human consciousness. In particular, we shall be able to consider how much cognitive sophistication is needed before we have a plausible candidate for perceptual consciousness. In this chapter, after considering some broad classes of behaving systems, I shall eventually argue that only those with what I call the 'basic package' (equivalently 'deciders') are serious candidates.

6.1   WHAT REALLY MATTERS?

As we go back down the phylogenetic scale it becomes less and less appropriate to apply the concepts of everyday psychology. It is natural to view chimps and other apes as sharing a lot of our psychological traits: they have a complex social life; they interact in a range of interesting ways; expressions like 'jealous', or 'protective' are natural ways to characterize their attitudes; they have a range of moods apparently much like ours; they solve problems; they make tools; they even seem able to learn fragments of human language. It doesn't make much sense to ascribe thoughts to them which depend on language for their specific character; on the other hand it seems silly to deny that they can work things out and comprehend fairly complex relationships. With animals like cats and dogs the situation is different. We still tend to talk as if they too had quite complex thoughts, but we don't take that too seriously; in intellectual capacity they are clearly not the equals of chimps. Even so, there seems nothing wrong with ascribing different moods to cats and dogs; they do solve some problems, which implies they are capable of some kinds of thinking; and it is natural to think of them as having experiences. (I don't know whether those points are reinforced by something I learnt recently: that there are 'cat psychologists'—people, not cats.) Similarly for birds, in spite of the fact that they lack a cerebral cortex (something else I learnt only recently, again with surprise).

But what about fish? Lizards and other reptiles? Octopuses? Spiders and insects? Crustacea? Locke's oysters and cockles? What about protozoa or bacteria? I am no zoologist: any information about animal psychology and physiology that I may have is owed to reading and naive observation. But so far as I can tell, most people would refuse to apply any psychological terms to bacteria or protozoa, and would be very hesitant about applying them to crustacea and molluscs, or to insects, and dubious even about reptiles. Broadly speaking the psychological concepts we apply to people can seem appropriate for animals that we think resemble us in significant respects, less appropriate the less close the resemblance.

What really matters from this point of view? What sorts of differences from us are relevant? Obviously not appearance. Suppose that one day large spider-like creatures emerged from a spacecraft and started interacting with us by means of sophisticated technology—perhaps even rounding up humans for what looked like scientific study. Soon enough we would start applying ordinary psychological concepts to them. We would say they were *intelligent*; that they could *plan*; had *intentions, beliefs, desires, objectives*; that they made *decisions; saw* or *heard* or perhaps *echolocated* things; and we should find it hard to doubt that they had *experiences* associated with their perceptual capacities. We would say those things in spite of their physical differences from us.

We would say those things, too, in spite of the fact that our everyday psychological concepts have evolved to deal not with aliens, but with the kind of creatures we take ourselves to be. We are adept at applying those concepts to creatures unlike ourselves: not only to many of the non-human animals we encounter, but (in imagination at least) to science-fictional aliens. Part of the reason is no doubt that our everyday concepts evolved without much knowledge or understanding of the internal processes underlying our behavioural capacities. Denied access to relevant internal processes, we are forced to base our judgements on behaviour and whatever capacities and tendencies we can learn about from observation. But another part of the reason is that our grasp of everyday psychological concepts seems to depend on recognizing patterns of behaviour as they develop over time, rather than, for example, on detecting particular kinds of movement made by particular kinds of limbs. (To know a spider is eating we don't have to see it using a knife and fork.)

None of that implies that we need only consider overt behaviour. It is not true that any kind of internal processing will do provided the system has the right behavioural capacities. If that had been the case behaviourism (of the philosophical kind) would have been the right approach, and the zombie problem would never have seemed puzzling. Our zombie twins would have had the right behavioural capacities; so, by philosophical behaviourism, they would also have had all the mental states we do, including conscious experiences.

6.2 PERCEPTION AND CONTROL

I am focusing on *perceptual* consciousness. Whatever else perception may involve, it certainly involves the individual's learning about the environment. But what does that mean? One thing it seems to mean is that the changes involved must enable the individual to adapt to its environment: to interact with it as it otherwise could not have done. These changes must persist for a while, even if the organism has no long-term memory to speak of: without at least a short period of retention it would not acquire the new capacities the changes enable it to exercise. Here there is an important distinction to be noticed. Individuals may be adaptively affected by their environment in ways other than perception. Sweating, for example, is an automatic response: not something we can decide to do unless, perhaps, we are yogis. But like perception it is adaptive: it helps us avoid something (getting too hot) that does us harm. What distinguishes those kinds of environmentally caused change that count as perception from the rest?

I used to think there was a fairly simple answer: the changes that count as perception enable the individual to control its behaviour; others don't. Certainly that seems to fit the broad definition of perception suggested by the last paragraph: that it is a matter of the organism undergoing changes caused by things in the environment and adaptively related to them in ways that enable it to interact in ways it otherwise could not have done. However, I now think we have to distinguish different strengths or grades of perception. I suggest that the highest grade—perception in the full sense—requires the individual to be able to *monitor and control* its own behaviour on the basis of the perceptual information it acquires. But there are lower grades where, although information gets into the organism and makes a difference to its behaviour, that behaviour cannot be said to be monitored or controlled by the organism as a whole. The point of those remarks will become clearer as we consider a range of different types of behaving systems in this and the next chapter. Consideration of examples will help to develop a framework for thinking about systems simpler than human beings. The definitions of types of systems in the following four sections are artificially schematic, but they bring out some important points about the monitoring, control, and causation of behaviour.

6.3 PURE REFLEX SYSTEMS

To illustrate apparent but not genuine perception, Locke uses the examples of sensitive plants and 'the turning of a wild Oat-beard by the Insinuation of the

Particles of Moisture' (1689/1975 II.ix.11). Both are cases of mere reactivity. Non-living things like litmus paper, smoke-detectors, and camera film also show mere reactivity, in spite of there being a sense in which they discriminate different kinds of things: the sense in which they behave differently when acted upon by those different kinds. The same goes, it seems, for many humble animals.

It appears that bivalves such as Locke's oysters and cockles discriminate broadly between food and other substances that they draw into their shells. And a great deal of insect behaviour can be explained in terms of different hard-wired responses to different stimuli. Given a stimulus (for example certain molecules striking specialized receptors) a particular response (for example the activation of mouthparts) automatically ensues. It seems that flies are hard-wired so that if their feet break contact with a surface, their wings are automatically caused to buzz; and if their feet make contact with a surface, their wings automatically stop buzzing.

I had better add that by no means all insects, if any, function entirely on that pattern, since typically they are capable of a kind of learning. The much studied fruit fly, for one, learns to find its way home. But suppose for argument's sake that a creature's entire behavioural repertoire is explicable on the simple reflex pattern: there is a set of possible stimuli and a set of possible responses, and by listing which stimulus causes which response we can encapsulate the creature's whole behavioural repertoire:

S0 causes R0
S1 causes R1
...
Sn causes Rn.

Nature does not force us to declare any particular event a stimulus or a response. How we classify it will depend on our interests, which for the moment are centred on the explanation of behaviour. For that purpose we will tend to think in terms of the patterns of behaviour that will help the organism survive. Flies, for example, sometimes fly, sometimes walk about, sometimes eat. A fly not in contact with any surface had better start flying; hence evolution has hard-wired it so that it does. A fly in contact with a surface is on a potential source of food, so had better stop buzzing; hence nature has provided for such contact to have that effect: contact is the stimulus, buzzing the response. If a creature's whole behaviour is explicable according to such a pattern I will call it a 'pure reflex system'. In its usual environment such a system will survive well. Producing its built-in response to one common stimulus puts it into a position to receive another stimulus, the response to which, in turn, puts it into a position to receive yet another, and so on throughout its existence. In a stable environment a perfectly coherent, if limited, life may be lived on that basis.

This artificial notion of a reflex system makes a clear starting point for consideration of more complicated systems, in particular those that can learn. Note, however, that pure reflex systems are simpler even than systems working according to the behaviourist psychology of conditioned responses. The latter can be said to learn, if only in a limited way, while the striking thing about these pure reflex systems is that they do not learn at all. Learning involves the acquisition of new and better-adapted patterns of behaviour ('better-adapted' because there is such a thing as unlearning). In contrast a pure reflex system has all its reflexes hard-wired from the start. It learns no more than a piano does. Protozoa, such as Amoeba, which consist of a single cell, might be pure reflex systems, but so too might vastly more complicated organisms, even oysters and cockles.[1]

Although in this and the next couple of sections I shall be characterizing systems mainly in terms of stimuli and responses, this by no means implies a commitment to behaviouristic psychology. Charles R. Gallistel (1990) offers numerous illustrations of types of animal behaviour for which behaviouristic psychology seems unable to provide adequate explanations.

Because pure reflex systems cannot learn, they cannot be said to perceive except in an attenuated sense. If oysters are such systems, it is questionable whether they have even 'some small dull Perception'. For perception involves changes which enable the system to do things it would not otherwise have been able to do. Admittedly it is natural to describe creatures such as flies (assuming they are pure reflex systems, which seems unlikely) as seeing and otherwise perceiving things; nor am I saying we should stop doing so. The point is that there is an important difference between a pure reflex system and one that really learns and perceives in the full sense of undergoing environmentally caused changes which enable it to control its own activities in ways it would not otherwise have been able to. From the point of view of our interest in perceptual consciousness, it is clear that even if we describe some pure reflex systems as perceiving, what goes on inside them does not begin to look as if it could amount to perceptual *experience*.

There is huge scope for sophistication in the ways that pure reflex systems detect stimuli. A certain level of salinity in the water around them causes oyster larvae to swim; and perhaps that doesn't require any very complicated arrangements. Ticks, however, seem to have quite complicated receptor systems located in 'Haller's organ' in their legs. This organ 'receives external stimuli in terms of temperature, humidity, carbon dioxide concentration, ammonia, aromatic chemicals, pheromones, and air-borne vibrations' (Hillyard 1996: 20). Another example, which pleasingly reveals how straightforward the internal processing downstream of the stimulus may be, is the cricket. Female crickets have a remarkable ability. They can select the 'song' produced by a male cricket—a succession of bursts of sound—and move towards its source. A female 'can distinguish the song of a male of her own species from any other noise and approach that one

---

[1] In spite of the fact that oysters are much more complicated than protozoa: see later. Interestingly, the evolutionary *ancestors* of the oyster had both a usable foot and a head with sense organs, neither of which has survived in the oyster itself: the only bit of its head that has survived is a mouth. Possibly this ancestral creature was capable of 'some small dull Perception' even if its descendant is not.

male even when other males of her own species are serenading her simultaneously with almost identical songs' (Webb 1996: 62–7). When approaching a male in this way the female cricket makes her way round all sorts of obstacles. Is she as clever as she seems? It is suggested that the reason she can distinguish the song of a particular male is that she has a piece of equipment which just doesn't operate except in response to that particular song. This is a resonating device tuned to respond only to that particular pattern of sound. There is no reason to suppose she has any particular auditory experience when that sound is picked up. What happens, it seems, is that she also has another relatively simple device which ensures that when the selected song is coming from one side, it automatically causes the legs on her other side to go into stronger motion. That brings her body round so that the sound comes more from the other side, and in this way her movements on average take her towards the source of the song, her potential mate. Thus the environment's impact on a creature may be modified by any amount of highly sophisticated processing. Yet even a high degree of complexity in the stimulus-sifting processes at a creature's 'front end' (the part which tests and filters out particular stimuli) leaves the ways its behaviour is caused unaltered. It remains a pure reflex system.

Perception in what I am calling the 'full sense' enables a system to monitor and control its own behaviour: notions that will be explained and developed later in this and the next chapter. In contrast, pure reflex systems do not control their own behaviour.

6.4   PURE REFLEX SYSTEMS WITH ACQUIRED STIMULI

The behaviour of actual organisms which may qualify as reflex systems tends to be produced by more or less complex networks of interconnecting nerve cells. Given some flexibility in how these cells develop, there is scope for new nervous pathways to become established and for new connections to be set up, which makes it possible that a system which starts off as a pure reflex system, with all its reflexes built in, should come to connect new stimuli with existing ones, or even replace them entirely. The creature begins its life with a built-in response R to a stimulus S; but then, somehow or other, a new stimulus comes to elicit R as well as, or instead of, S.

That qualifies as 'classical' conditioning. It is one—very primitive—kind of learning. But is it the kind of learning required for perception in the full sense? No, because it doesn't necessarily involve the organism as a whole being able to monitor and control its behaviour. Indeed, we could say the organism itself still doesn't learn anything, since it can't use the information that is acquired. Certainly information gets into it; but as a whole it doesn't have access to it. An organism whose only learning is of this kind is just a sort of locus for its reflexes or (to take account of more complex arrangements) reflex subsystems. Whatever alterations are produced in its patterns of behaviour, they are no more under its control than our auto-immune responses are.

6.5 BUILT-IN TRIGGERED REFLEX SYSTEMS

The behaviour of a pure reflex system is explicable in terms of a set of paired reflexes. These are permanently 'set', so that whenever any of the specified stimuli hits the organism, invariably its paired response is produced. The same is true even if the system is capable of acquiring new stimuli, as considered in the last section. But in some organisms of a broadly reflex type, certain reflexes are not permanently set: they operate only when certain special stimuli, not provided for by the basic reflexes, occur. These reflexes have to be triggered.

A small lizard might normally have, among its other reflexes, a set of reflexes R, which collectively tend to result in its getting food. R might include for example the following:

Ra: *Visual stimulation by lettuce* causes *movement towards source of stimulation*;
Rb: *Molecules floating off nearby lettuce (and impinging on the animal's olfactory system)* cause *lettuce-eating.*

These reflexes R are a component of the animal's 'default' setting: they are normally active. However, this lizard is so constructed that the onset of certain stimuli (for example the pattern of light typically caused by a hawk flying above it) causes R to be inhibited and a different set of reflexes, T, to be activated. T includes:

Ta: *Visual stimulation by undergrowth* causes *running into the undergrowth*;
Tb: *Visual stimulation by a hole in the ground* causes *running into the hole.*

With luck those reflexes, together with others in this 'take-cover' set, will cause the animal to avoid capture.

This type of system has a capacity to learn different from, and in some ways more significant than, that of the last type noted. In the present type of triggered reflex system, the fact that a predator is about is 'registered' inside it. The creature could be said to have a primitive kind of memory—about states of its environment. (In contrast, pure reflex systems with acquired stimuli could be said only to acquire new behavioural tricks.) However, although that gives a sense in which information is registered, the system does not use that information itself any more than a pure reflex system does. It cannot act on it. It still doesn't *control* its own behaviour, because it doesn't choose one of a range of possible courses of action. In that important respect the built-in triggered reflex system is not much different from the original pure reflex type.

The triggering conditions in this type of system are either environmental or, if internal, then supplied by states of the organism's body, such as low blood-sugar levels. Note that although some internal states in organisms like ourselves typically manifest themselves in feelings as well as tendencies to (for example) seek food, there is no basis for supposing that systems of the built-in triggered reflex type have feelings corresponding to their internal triggering states. Given the definition of these systems, such feelings could only be epiphenomenal: they could make no contribution to behaviour. And given the sole-pictures argument, nothing could take any notice of them.

6.6 TRIGGERED REFLEX SYSTEMS WITH ACQUIRED CONDITIONS

The dragonfly is a useful introduction to the next main points:

With its large eyes and extremely mobile neck the dragonfly can see in all directions ... and it can spot its prey over a radius of 20–40 metres while on the wing .... Most dragonflies seem to show some form of territorial behaviour .... [In the case of the male *Calopteryx*] the territory includes a number of perches ... one of which is particularly favoured and from which the dragonfly hunts and drives away other males ... (D'Aguilar *et al.* 1986: 35 f)

Does this creature really 'see' things in a full-blown sense? Perhaps a lot of the dragonfly's behaviour is explicable in terms of a set of reflex subsystems. However, it cannot have been born with the ability to get back to its own perch: it had to learn to find its way round its actual environment. That means its built-in reflexes are supplemented by more complicated ones, whose formation involves a less primitive kind of learning than that considered two sections back. Nor does it seem that even the type of learning shown by built-in triggered reflex systems would be enough.

What would appear to be enough, though, is that the organism's existing reflex subsystems should come to be triggered by *new conditions*. In a system of this new type some triggering conditions are set innately; but other sorts of event can become new triggering conditions for a given reflex subsystem. Perhaps the creature's 'flight' behaviour, for example, is preset to be activated by a certain built-in triggering condition (by stimulus-patterns typically caused by predatory birds, for example). But perhaps also, in time, other stimulus-patterns come to do what was hitherto done exclusively by the built-in ones. Such new conditions for triggering a given reflex subsystem would reflect the creature's own individual encounters with threats.

I will call such a system a *triggered reflex system with acquired conditions*. The key feature is that a reflex subsystem triggered by a particular condition at one period could come to be triggered by a different condition at a later period. Our dragonfly might have a built-in 'perch' reflex subsystem which works for perches in general, but is flexible enough for the triggering of built-in perching responses to be narrowed down to stimulation from a particular individual twig or stone. This structure's flexibility might provide for a different perch to supersede the one currently favoured.

Such systems are capable of a kind of individual learning unavailable to the other reflex types. It is different in that it enables them to relate in distinctive ways to individual features of their environment. Still, even these more flexible systems cannot sensibly be described as capable of *acting* on the information they register, since they are not capable of choice or decision in anything like the usual sense. Although information about some of the prevailing conditions (for example, presence of a predatory bird) can be registered, the organism's behavioural structure provides nothing that could count as its considering what it might do next—not even in a sketchy rudimentary way.

Of course it is natural to say that such systems perceive. However, although they can properly be said to perceive, their perception is not of a kind that provides a basis for perceptual-phenomenal consciousness. Information gets inside them; but there is no provision for them to receive incoming perceptual information without something being automatically caused to happen, which may or may not help the organism. Once a given reflex subsystem is triggered, the response is simply caused to occur, just as striking middle C on the piano causes a particular tone to be produced. Nor are there any processes which could constitute such organisms' having experiences. The significance of those remarks will become clearer in the course of the rest of this chapter and the next.

I must guard against a possible misunderstanding. In what I am classifying as a reflex system there is no cascading of reflexes, where outputs from one reflex serve as inputs to another. Instead, although any number of different sets of reflexes may be brought into operation, only one set is operative at any one time, so that a given stimulus causes just whatever the fixed response may be. Systems where the outputs of one reflex serve as inputs or conditions for other reflexes are crucially different from what I am calling reflex systems. They are potentially immensely powerful, being equivalent to programmed computers.

6.7 MONITORING AND CONTROLLING THE RESPONSES

Both the built-in and the acquired types of triggered reflex system are capable of registering information, or having 'memories' in that restricted sense. When an internal 'switch' is in one position, it registers that one type of event has occurred; when it is in another it registers that another type of event has occurred. From the standpoint of an interest in how organisms can improve their chances of surviving, that feature is hugely important. While the behaviour of a pure reflex system is determined solely by the stimuli that impinge on it, that of a triggered reflex system depends partly on its internal states. The reflex system with acquired triggering conditions is capable of genuine learning, and for that reason has a chance of developing patterns of behaviour that enable it to do better than its pure reflex rivals: get food and escape predators faster, for example.

However, because even triggered reflex systems with acquired conditions cannot modify their *responses*, they are at a disadvantage compared with organisms which can. Suppose for example that a dragonfly is a triggered reflex system with acquired conditions, and that when a certain pattern of light typically associated with predatory birds hits its eyes it produces a certain type of zigzag downward flight. Suppose that particular pattern of flight behaviour is a built-in response, and usually results in the dragonfly evading its pursuer. But suppose further that certain birds come to learn patterns of pursuit which enable them to anticipate that particular stereotyped dragonfly escape-flight pattern. Any individual dragonflies that were capable of learning to *modify* their escape pattern in mid flight—noticing the bird in hot pursuit and changing course—would improve their chances of avoiding capture. Of course, over time, evolution might produce a revised escape-flight pattern in a whole species; but that would only be after the loss of many individuals. It is obviously advantageous for individuals to be able to learn new responses. How could that happen?

This problem is radically different from that of introducing a new *stimulus* that will evoke a given response, as in the last three types. It is not a matter of originating a new reflex or even a new triggering condition. Stimuli come from the organism's environment: the organism need have nothing to do with their production (although it may on occasion somehow cause the stimulus, as by moving one of its own limbs across its eyes). Suppose an organism is set to produce a response R whenever stimulus S impinges on it. Assuming it is in the first place sensitive to a certain other type of event, T, there seems no great difficulty in understanding how T could come to be associated with R via relatively straightforward associative mechanisms. The organism would have 'learned' to respond to a new stimulus, as in classical conditioning. Acquiring a new response, however, is a different sort of thing altogether.

Responses are a product of the organism, not of the environment alone. How might a new response be introduced? One conceivable way would be by the evolution of a mechanism which just randomly caused any of the organism's built-in patterns of response to be replaced by something different. Suppose an aquatic organism has the fixed response of diving when stimulated by a sudden rise in temperature. A randomizing mechanism might produce a quite different pattern of behaviour in response to the same stimulus: attacking anything that came near it, for example. Clearly that could be disastrous. Producing new responses totally at random would not be evolutionarily good. Evolution would have ensured that on the whole, the organism's built-in responses served it well, while random substitution of different ones could be fatal.

Those considerations suggest that nature will have ensured that if random modifications to an organism's built-in responses occur at all, they are relatively slight. Other things being equal, that will avoid the huge risks of major changes of response; it will also give the responses a reasonable chance of being improvements on the built-in ones. But such random modifications are not at issue now. We are considering an absolutely crucial evolutionary development, in which the organism itself becomes capable of somehow *monitoring* its own responses and *modifying* them on the basis of incoming perceptual data. The imagined dragonfly is able to detect its own response (or at least some relevant aspects of it) and to bring about modifications to it. Only if the modified responses are monitored by the organism itself will its ability to produce modifications give it an advantage. Although evolution could in time equip the species as a whole with new *built-in* responses, the ability of individuals to monitor and modify their own responses is obviously advantageous.

We have reached a highly significant watershed. For a system to monitor and modify its own behaviour involves a major break with the reflex pattern. Monitoring and modifying must involve not only the organism's being able to perceive its own behaviour, or at least the effects of its behaviour on its environment, but also to adjust its behaviour in ways appropriate to its goals. That requires it to be able to control its own behaviour on the basis of its information, in a way that none of the types of system so far considered is capable of.

Before discussing and elaborating these points I had better guard against three possible misconceptions. First, I am not suggesting that the evolutionary transition from a triggered reflex system to a system capable of monitoring and controlling its behaviour is a single step. Second, and relatedly, I am not suggesting that a system's monitoring and modifying its behaviour is a simple matter. Finally, I am not suggesting that that there is only one possible architecture that would enable a system to be capable of monitoring and controlling its own behaviour. On the contrary, it seems probable that what we can conveniently refer to as 'monitoring', 'modifying', and 'controlling' are highly complex processes, capable of being realized to a greater or lesser degree, at different levels of organization in the system as a whole, and in an indefinitely wide range of possible internal structural patterns. A baby in its first few weeks offers persuasive illustrations of the first two points; the point about architecture will be illustrated in the next chapter.

Clearly, in order for a system to control its own behaviour there must be processes which make a relevant difference to its responses. But that is not enough. There are plenty of types of system where that condition is satisfied, while the system as a whole is not in control of its behaviour. One of these would be a system with a fixed set of possible stimuli and a fixed set of possible responses, but where the response to each stimulus-event is allocated by a central randomizer. Another example is the artificial giant to be discussed in the next chapter. What the randomizing system and the artificial giant lack is a certain kind of *integration* of the processes of behavioural control and use of information: another topic to be pursued later.

Thus systems whose behaviour can only be accounted for by reference to some kind of integrated control on the basis of information stand in sharp contrast to all the reflex types, even those capable of a genuine kind of learning. However, there remains a vital contrast within the class of systems that do have some sort of central control. It is between those that I am calling 'deciders'—or systems with the 'basic package'—and the rest.

6.8   DECIDERS

Deciders can choose between alternative courses of action, if only in a rudimentary sense. For reasons I hope to make clear, being a system of this kind is at any rate necessary for being perceptually conscious. In contrast to the other types of system, a decider's behaviour must be arrived at in a way consistent with our ordinary concept of 'deciding'. Just what that amounts to is something I hope to make reasonably clear in what follows, especially in the next chapter—although I cannot make it as crisp and clear as would be desirable.

Being able to make choices, or to decide how to act, is correlated with having goals or objectives, in contrast to a mere tendency to satisfy needs. Even an organism whose entire behavioural repertoire is explicable on the pure reflex model can be said to have needs (food, reproduction, whatever) provided its particular reflex set has evolved. But deciding involves more than needs. Choosing between two alternative courses of action, both available for consideration in however rudimentary a sense, is something that only a system with goals or objectives can do. If it has no goals or objectives it can have no motive for choosing one course of action rather than another. It might have a randomizing subsystem which ensured it always did one or the other rather than getting stuck like Buridan's ass; but that would be the opposite of choosing.

An organism of this type, a decider, can be said to opt for one course of action rather than another. It cannot do that, though, unless it also gathers its own *information* about its environment: this information enables it to guide its behaviour. Associatedly we can say it *represents* things, however primitively, as being a certain way. The cat which hears a mouse squeaking a few feet away and at the same time sees a dog much further away has some sort of conception on the lines of 'Mouse here, dog there'.

The processes of decision-making do not have to be conscious. It is not controversial to say that we ourselves make decisions unconsciously; and I know of no reason why other creatures should be supposed capable of only conscious decision-making.

The capacities mentioned so far bring other capacities along with them. One is that the system must be able to *interpret* incoming information. If a bird sees a pair of gleaming eyes surrounded by fur, for example, just beyond the leaves of the strawberries it is poised to sample, it may classify its situation as not just *food-berried* (or something of the sort), but *cat-threatened*. Such interpretation is a matter of ensuring that the incoming information contributes to its conception of its situation. For if there is to be a sense in which it decides which action to take, it must have some conception of its situation, hence be capable of *assessing its situation*.

Again, this may be in a very rudimentary sense. That leads us to another capacity: it must be able to make use of *stored* information. In any case, since it can guide its behaviour on the basis of its goals, it must for that reason be able to retain information about what it is aiming at. (The bird chooses between flying away from the cat and swallowing the berry. Its deciding to fly away is partly guided by its retaining the information that the cat is dangerous.) All those capacities involve conceptualization, or at least something we might call 'proto-conceptualization' (a topic to which we shall return in Chapter 8).

Now for a crucial point. The descriptions used in specifying the abilities of the different types of systems mentioned so far, especially those of deciders, are to be taken in a 'neutral' or purely 'functional' sense: a sense in which they can legitimately be applied to a system without first requiring it to be conscious. When I say a decider has the capacity to 'interpret' information, for example, I mean it has that capacity to the extent that this does not directly imply it is conscious. This seems unobjectionable, if only because it is widely accepted that we conceptualize unconsciously. Admittedly, saying a system 'represents' situations, 'interprets' information, 'assesses' its situation, and so on, may *indirectly* imply that it is conscious. Indeed, it is one of my central contentions that if a decider has a certain additional feature ('direct activity', to be described in Chapter 9) then that feature together with the basic package does strictly imply that it is a conscious perceiver. But the individual descriptions are to be understood in a non-question-begging sense. In that sense the friends of zombies can happily concede that zombies are deciders even though they supposedly lack consciousness.

6.9 UNITY OF THE BASIC PACKAGE

To summarize, a *decider* has the following capacities—together, of course, with whatever these entail. It can:

(i) *Initiate and control* its own behaviour on the basis of incoming and retained information: information that it can use.

(ii) *Acquire and retain information* about its environment.

(iii) *Interpret* information.

(iv) *Assess its situation.*

(v) *Choose* between alternative courses of action on the basis of retained and incoming information (equivalently, it can *decide* on a particular course of action).

(vi) *Have goals.*

Those capacities form the basic package. This idea is a central component in my framework for explaining perceptual consciousness, and I will try to demonstrate its viability. In the rest of this chapter I shall develop some key points; in the next I shall discuss systems which may appear to have the package but don't, and others which may appear not to have it but do. By the end of the next chapter I hope the idea of the basic package, and its usefulness, will have become reasonably clear.

The capacities in the basic package are closely interrelated; indeed, there are some reasons for thinking that a system cannot have any of them without having the rest. To outline those reasons (sketched in the last section) we can start from the first component of the package.

(i) In order to control its own behaviour the system has to be able to tell what difference, if any, its behaviour is making to its environment. To do that it must be able (ii) to acquire and retain information about its environment, information that it can use for controlling its behaviour.

In order to be able to put stored information to use, a system must be able (iii) to interpret incoming information, and (iv) assess its situation on the basis of stored information. A magpie sighting an egg-shaped object needs to be able to interpret it as a potentially edible egg rather than an inedible pebble; and having done so, on hearing what might be the sound of an approaching human, it needs to assess its situation. That requires it to take account of its current situation and its current objectives. Nothing elaborate is called for: magpies are surely capable of assessing their situation in the sense in question. (In some way they can size up whether it will be best to grab the egg-like object just in front of them, or fly off to escape the man a few yards away.)

Given it can (i) control its behaviour, it must also, having assessed its situation, be able to (v) choose between alternative courses of action (as we just noted). That in turn requires it to (vi) have goals. Thus the first capacity brings the others along with it. That conclusion makes it easy to argue that each of the other capacities also entails the rest.

(ii) If the system can acquire and retain information about its environment, when this is information that it can use, then it must be able to (i) control its own behaviour, which, as we have just seen, entails all the other capacities.

(iii) Similarly if it can interpret information that it can use.

(iv) If it can assess its situation, it must have information (which it can use) about its current situation, from which, again, the other capacities follow.

(v) If it can make decisions on the basis of incoming and stored information it has to be able to acquire information, which also brings with it all the other capacities.

Finally (vi) if a system has goals, it must be capable of (i) controlling its behaviour, so yet again all the other capacities are necessarily involved.

That makes a prima facie case for supposing that capacities (i)–(vi) are so tightly related that they form an unbreakable package: a given system has either all or none of them. Accordingly I used to think it was impossible for a system to have less than all of the capacities involved. However, there are considerations which make it inappropriate to insist on that claim without qualification. For one thing, none of the capacities is all-or-nothing: each may be possessed to a greater or lesser degree. As we shall see, in plenty of cases where for example information gets into a system, it is not clear-cut whether the system itself can sensibly be said to be able to use that information. Similarly for the other capacities. So it is relatively easy to find apparent counter-examples to the claim that the basic package is monolithic. However, there is an important consideration which so far has only been implicit. If these capacities are truly those of the system itself, their exercise must be appropriately *integrated*—convenient shorthand for a complex notion. If it is to make sense to say that a decider can control its own behaviour, then the information it acquires must also be its own, and so must its processes of interpretation, assessment, and decision-making. It is not enough for there to be *some* information getting into the system, some interpretation going on, some assessment, some decision-making: these activities must be interrelated in ways which justify the description of them as the system's own. I do not deny that there are systems in which some but not all of the capacities in the basic package are exercised in some sense or other. What I deny is that such systems are in control of their own behaviour.

The unity of the basic package does not imply that it is a natural kind. It is not. Certainly the evolution of numerous species of organisms with the basic package has been natural enough in the light of the advantages conferred by having it. Nor is the package just a collection of arbitrarily selected components. Given that we have evolved a certain particular system of psychological concepts; given too that perception and choice are crucial in helping species survive even when they are quite primitive compared with human beings, it is not surprising that this particular package is salient for us. But that doesn't make it a natural kind: it is (broadly) a functional kind. (Compare *bipedalism*, a functional feature of many different natural species, but not a natural kind—and also instantiated by some artefacts.)

Although the basic package is defined functionally, it must not be understood in a purely behaviouristic way. That is, it must not be construed so that the nature of a system's inner processing is irrelevant to the question of whether it has the capacities which define the package. The reasons have to do with the moderate realism of everyday psychology: see the next chapter.

At this stage it may be helpful to note some contrasts with Dennett's suggestions about the 'intentional stance'. We adopt the intentional stance towards a system, Dennett says, when we explain its behaviour in terms of beliefs and desires in accordance with the following principles:

First you decide to treat the object whose behaviour is to be predicted as a rational agent; then you figure out what beliefs that agent ought to have, given its place in the world and its purpose. Then you figure out what desires it ought to have, on the same considerations, and finally you predict that this rational agent will act to further its goals in the light of its beliefs. (1987: 17)

One significant difference between Dennett's approach and one based on the basic package is that his ignores the nature of the system's internal processing.

Provided its behaviour is interpretable as indicated, it is an intentional system. Indeed, he asserts that:

> any object . . . whose behaviour is well predicted by this strategy [viz. the 'intentional strategy' outlined in the previous quotation] is in the fullest sense of the word a believer. What it is to be a true believer is to be an *intentional system*, a system whose behaviour is reliably and voluminously predictable via the intentional strategy. (1987: 15)

By aligning itself with the moderate realism of everyday psychology, my approach avoids a view that strikes me as excessively behaviouristic and instrumentalistic. Another difference from Dennett's approach is that, as we shall see, many things are deciders even though they cannot sensibly be ascribed full-blown beliefs or desires. A third difference is that while Dennett's approach requires us to 'decide to treat the object whose behaviour is to be predicted as a rational agent', mine leaves the question of a system's rationality as something that remains open to investigation—though certainly, *if* it turns out to be a decider, then it will be to some extent rational.[2]

6.10 THE BASIC PACKAGE AND PERCEPTION

We were led to the basic package through considering what is involved in an organism being able to monitor and control its own behaviour. We needed to pursue that thought in order to get clear about what is involved in an organism being able in a full-blown sense to *perceive* things in its environment. Let me now state explicitly an assumption I have made about perception:

Perception 'in the full sense' requires the system to acquire and retain information about its environment, information that is for the system because it uses it in initiating, monitoring, or controlling its own behaviour.[3]

I use the expression 'perception in the full sense' as a reminder that there are significant differences in how different types of system can be said to perceive. We find

---

[2] See 8.8 below. The idea of packages of psychological concepts seems to have originated with Aristotle, who remarked that any creature with sense-perception must have the faculty of desire: '. . . for desire comprises wanting, passion, and wishing: all animals have at least one of the senses, touch, and for that which has sense-perception there is both pleasure and pain and both the pleasant and the painful: and where there are these, there is also wanting: for this is a desire for that which is pleasant' (*De An.* II.3). That is at least consistent with the line I am taking over the basic package, and with the common assumption that belief-desire psychology is somehow fundamental. Others have drawn attention to similar packages, for example Armstrong (1968: 253) and Dennett (1969, ch. 3). Peter Unger's (1990) interesting use of the notion of 'core psychology' (the mental capacities that every human being shares with others, as contrasted with those distinctive of an individual's personal history) may appear similar, but involves more sophistication, having been devised in connection with the problems of personal identity.

[3] Kathleen Akins has attacked the assumption that 'the senses function to inform the brain of what is going on "out there" in the external world and in one's own body' (1996: 338). In general, she urges, sensory states are not veridical: they don't record how things really are out there, but only register what matters to the sensory system in question. The assumption just stated is consistent with her position.

it natural to speak of even a simple reflex system like (perhaps) the tick as perceiv-ing, in spite of the fact that it gathers no more information that is for its own use than a piano does. If that is perception at all, it is perception of a very low grade. We find it even more natural to speak of triggered conditional reflex systems with acquired reflexes (such as, perhaps, the dragonfly) as perceiving, since information about their environment gets into them and influences their behaviour. But it is surely most appropriate to describe deciders as perceiving, since only they control their own behaviour on the basis of the information they acquire. That is what I am calling perception in the full sense.

I suggest that perception in the full sense, hence the basic package, is at least neces-sary for perceptual-phenomenal consciousness. Only perception in the full sense enables the system to initiate, monitor, or control its own behaviour; while a system incapable of those things could hardly be described as perceiving at all, except in a strained sense. An example will help to make that clear. Suppose a certain organism perceives things in its environment yet cannot initiate or monitor or control either its overt behaviour or its mental acts on the basis of incoming and retained infor-mation. (An imaginary example is Galen Strawson's 'Weather Watchers': 1994*a*.) In that case it couldn't use the incoming information. It couldn't for example guide its behaviour on the basis of perceptual information. It couldn't even describe what it perceived–even in its head. Nor could it describe what it had perceived at some time in the past, for that would be one way of putting the information to use. In short, it couldn't in any way act on the basis of incoming or stored perceptual informa-tion. Could it nevertheless somehow *think* about its perceptual information? Not if that required it to initiate or control its thinking, or for that matter to decide whether or not to think about some particular item of perceptual information. It seems to me that in that case, if nevertheless perceptual information made some difference to this organism's behaviour, it would be comparable to the way that exposing a photographic film makes a difference to the behaviour of the film, notably by imposing patterns on the light passing through it.

And the point is that the camera perceives nothing. Although it acquires information for us, its users, it acquires no information *for it*, for the camera itself.[4] Information is *for the system* only if it can use it, which means only if it can guide its behaviour on the basis of that information. It therefore seems that if an organism or other kind of system can perceive in the full sense, then it can initiate or monitor or control its behaviour on the basis of some of the perceptual information it acquires; so it must have the first of the capacities in the basic package. But given we are now talking about information which the system itself can use, those capacities tend to form a single complex. In general, therefore, it seems that any system capable of perception in the full sense must be a decider.

A counter-example has been suggested. Many people, for example those suffer-ing from Alzheimer's, can perceive in spite of being victims of extreme memory

---

[4] Dennett introduced this useful phrase (1969: 42).

loss. They are perfectly capable of seeing and hearing, yet they seem incapable of retaining information about their environment (Conee 1995). I think this objection appeals to an excessively narrow conception of memory. If Alzheimer sufferers can still string some coherent sequences of behaviour together—if they can pick up a teacup, for example—then they must be able to retain information, even if only for a short while, otherwise they would not be able to tell whether they were on the way to achieving what they were setting out to do. The basic package doesn't require memories as good as healthy people, only enough for *some* behaviour to be controlled. Alzheimer patients often prove incapable of telling others what they have seen or heard a few moments ago; but that doesn't show they can't retain perceptual information at all. If some are not capable of any coherent behaviour, we need to consider whether they are still really perceiving things rather than reacting automatically. And when we are attempting to decide between those alternatives, behaviour alone is not the sole factor to be taken into account: see also the next chapter.

Another alleged counter-example is that of paralysed people. We accept that they perceive things and have sensations in spite of not being able to move their limbs. They are offered as a counter-example to the claim that capacity (i) (to initiate and control behaviour) is necessary for perception. I agree that paralysed people are usually capable of perception; they do present a difficulty for my account. I suggest dealing with it in two stages. The first is to suggest that there are central and standard cases of perception and peripheral and non-standard ones. The central cases are those who can control their *bodily* behaviour. Paralysed people are not central cases because they lack that capacity; yet I suggest they are sufficiently similar to central cases for it not to be too problematic that they too can perceive. They resemble central cases in that something has interfered with the control of their bodily behaviour—rather like the action of a paralysing drug. The second stage of my reply is that although bodily behaviour is the typical kind involved, it is not their only behaviour: there is also mental behaviour. Paralysed people lack the capacity to initiate and control bodily movements; but they can still initiate and control trains of thought. If there are cases where they are incapable even of that, it is problematic whether they are deciders at all.

Is the basic package also *sufficient* for perception in the full sense? That is hard to deny when we reflect that perception in general is not necessarily conscious. Recall in particular the following capacities from the basic package: (i) to initiate or control behaviour on the basis of incoming and retained information, (ii) to acquire and retain information about the system's environment that it can use, and (iii) to interpret information. It is hard to see how a system with those capacities could fail to perceive in the full sense, although again the decision is complicated by the fact that these capacities are not all-or-nothing.

I therefore suggest that being a decider (having the basic package) is both necessary and sufficient for perception in the full sense (though not also, necessarily, for *conscious* perception).

6.11 USEFULNESS OF THE BASIC PACKAGE IDEA

The idea of the basic package provides a framework for thinking about behaving systems which advances the overall project of understanding perceptual consciousness. This framework helps to bridge the gap between descriptions of systems in purely physical or biomechanical terms, and descriptions in psychological terms. Among its other virtues, it will help us sidestep the tendency to assume that something must be either a full-blown concept- and language-user—perhaps even a person or Kantian subject—or else nothing of the sort. Reflection on the examples to be discussed shortly helps to reveal that there is something like a continuum, stretching from systems which lack it, through vast numbers of indeterminate cases, to those which have it—and plenty of scope for variation and further sophistication among the creatures which have it.

Recall the concepts used to specify the basic package: *acquisition and retention of information, control of behaviour, interpretation, assessment, choice and decision, goals.* Perhaps not all come directly from everyday psychology; but they do fall naturally into the field of everyday psychology when linked together as jointly specifying the basic package. The unity of the package (even though qualified) imposes useful constraints on how we apply its component concepts to candidate deciders. For example, we might notice that a certain computer-controlled car-painting robot stores information about the volume of paint in its container. Is it a decider? It might be—but not just because *we* can use the robot's record of how much paint it has; nor just because its register of paint-volume has potential effects on its behaviour. In order for that information to be *for it*, the robot must be capable of assessing its situation and making decisions on the basis of that information. Conceivably it is an unusually clever robot and really has those capacities, in which case it is a decider; though such robots are not normally deciders. What matters is whether it has all the capacities in the basic package, not whether it seems to have one or two of them considered in isolation. We have to consider the situation holistically.

You might suspect that the unity of the package constrains the application of its component concepts too far; for you might suggest that when these concepts are combined in the package they are not only intentional concepts, but actually presuppose consciousness. But that would be to overlook the proviso that these concepts are to be taken in a 'neutral' or purely functional sense. The observable behavioural, physical, and neutrally conceived non-physical facts (if any) are all that is to be taken into account.

How can we tell whether a given system has the basic package? Clearly there is no algorithm guaranteed to do the trick. Even if we ignore the possibility of systems with non-physical components, the range of purely physical systems that could be deciders is indefinitely large. We can only study the given system, make hypotheses about what it seems to need or want (recalling Anscombe's remark: 'The primitive sign of wanting is *trying to get*': 1959: 67), test our hypotheses by interfering with its environment in various ways, check, try again, and otherwise see how we get on. If to our surprise we open up a likely candidate and find it is controlled by an enormous look-up table, then we must conclude that it doesn't really control its own behaviour and is not a genuine decider. For whatever else a decider must do, it must, in line with the moderate realism of everyday psychology, cobble together its own responses to the situations it finds itself in. Further examples will help to reinforce these points.

7

Decision, Control, and Integration

Some creatures are pretty obviously deciders (chimps and other higher apes for example) others obviously not; and there will be indeterminate cases. In this chapter I will consider some examples that are in various ways not straight-forward. Discussing them will help further to clarify the idea of deciders, and to sharpen the contrasts between them and other behaving systems. It will also prepare the ground for the conclusion that the idea raises no serious philosophical problems. The basic package will then be ready to serve as the chief load-bearing component in my account of perceptual consciousness.

7.1 SIMPLE ORGANISMS

The main point of the abstract and artificial classifications of reflex systems in the last chapter was to narrow our focus to what really matters from the point of view of an interest in perceptual consciousness, and to emphasize important contrasts between those systems and deciders—while keeping in mind that many types of systems are neither reflex nor deciders. When we descend from those abstractions to consider the physical structure and behaviour of actual organisms, the over-idealized character of the reflex models becomes apparent. That is so even for the case of protozoa. These single cells are quite complex structures, and can differ strikingly in behaviour as well as appearance. One important consideration is that it is by no means straightforward to identify stimuli and responses. Many protozoa swim by moving fine tendrils ('flagella') about in the water. The rate and direction of their swimming is influenced by light. In Euglena, for example, the way light falls on a certain light-sensitive swelling

is held to determine flagellar activity. The swimming response is photopositive when the flagellar swelling is periodically shaded by the adjacent red-pigmented stigma, but photo negative when the flagellar swelling is continuously illuminated. (Sleigh 1973: 43)

It might be possible to represent this aspect of Euglena's behaviour as follows:

> Weak light causes positive phototaxis;
> Strong light causes negative phototaxis.

Thus by selecting sufficiently high-level descriptions we could make the creature's swimming behaviour fit the pure reflex scheme. But is it sensible to treat phototaxis as a response? It seems more like a whole reflex. That would make Euglena a 'built-in triggered reflex' type. There are other aspects of protozoan behaviour that it is hard to force into any of my reflex classes, though I am not saying it couldn't be done. Still, protozoa are clearly far from being deciders, and for that reason far from being potential subjects of perceptual consciousness.

With multicellular organisms we find more interesting behaviour. 'The tiny pond-living *Hydra*', for example,

... sits at the bottom of a pond or stream attached to rocks or water plants and waving its tentacles above its mouth. Like a sea anemone, it closes these down and contracts to a blob of tissue if touched .... When a small organism, like a crustacean, brushes past the tentacles, the hydra shoots out poisonous threads ... The paralysed victim is then collected by the tentacles, thrust into the mouth and swallowed ... Sensory mechanisms must exist to indicate the presence of prey or danger and the response of emission of poison or contraction into a blob must be made appropriately, the mouth must open at the right time and the gut muscles must be controlled ... Depending on its internal state, that is, whether it is well fed or starved, the hydra will be quiescent or will wave its tentacles about in a more or less agitated manner. (Rose 1976: 145)

The 'sensory mechanisms' raise the question whether this animal might have 'some small dull Perception'. Here there do seem to be natural candidates for stimuli and responses. Its sensory mechanisms detect when it is touched as by a predator; so we might pick, as one stimulus, a pattern of stimulation typically caused by potential predators. These organisms also detect potential prey, so patterns of stimulation typically caused by their potential prey would be another candidate stimulus. One response is *contraction*; others are *shoot out poisonous threads* and *open mouth*. True, the last sentence in the quoted passage shows that Hydra is not a *pure* reflex system; but it doesn't seem to provide a basis for a higher classification than built-in triggered reflex system. In spite of possessing numerous cells, it seems not to be a decider.

Prawns and shrimps (the difference seems to be purely of size) are a good deal more complex. One species from the Indian Ocean, for example, is said to be 'aggressively territorial, and will generally fight any approaching conspecifics to death with fights lasting minutes to hours'. They also form pair bonds between individuals, and appear to be able to tell the difference between a partner and a stranger (Rufino and Jones 2001: 390 f.) If they are reflex systems at all, therefore, they are of the last type defined: triggered reflex systems with acquired conditions. Whether they are more sophisticated than that, and are even deciders, is left unclear by the evidence I have come across.

7.2 'BEES CAN THINK SAY SCIENTISTS'

Clever little things, bees. Or is that headline (*Guardian*, 19 April 2001) just journalistic hype? It refers to an article in *Nature*, 'The concepts of "sameness" and "difference" in an insect' (Giurfa *et al.* 2001). According to Martin Giurfa and his colleagues, 'not only can bees learn specific objects and their physical parameters, but they can also master abstract interrelationships, such as sameness and difference' (930). The investigators used a Y-shaped maze to train bees to recognize various sorts of stimuli: different colours; different black-and-white grating patterns (parallel lines or concentric circles) on discs; different smells. When a disc of one colour (say blue) was placed at the entrance to the maze, and one of the same colour placed at one of the two turnings, while a disc of a different colour (say yellow) was placed at the other, the bees quickly learned to go down the turning whose colour matched the one at the entrance. So far, then, they could be described as having learned something roughly on the lines of, 'same colour points to something sweet'. They also quickly picked up the same lesson for different grating patterns: 'same grating pattern points to something sweet'.[1] Similarly for smells: lemon and mango. However, the bees didn't just learn, for each of the chosen different sensory modalities, that *the same-smell sign* (for example) *points to something sweet*. They ended up generalizing: to 'transfer the learned rules to new stimuli of the same or a different sensory modality' (930). We might put it by saying that what they learned included a quantifier within its content.

That is pretty remarkable, even for those already impressed by the bees' famous dances, by which scouts convey to colleagues back in the hive information about the direction, distance, and quantity of a food source. Yet do their reported accomplishments show that bees have the basic package? I don't think the answer is straightforward; this is where questions about control and integration are pertinent. Whether bees have the right sorts of control and integration is largely an empirical matter—but not wholly, since what counts as the right sorts is open to philosophical debate. I suggest that in spite of the fact that the investigators have discovered remarkably sophisticated processing by the bees, it doesn't force us to classify them as deciders. Rather, they could be an example of triggered reflex systems with acquired conditions, as dragonflies might be.

Certainly the bees' 'front end' is strikingly sophisticated. But although much complex information gets into these animals, and undergoes complex processing before it affects their behaviour, those facts do not force us to conclude that the stored information is *for the organism* in the relevant sense, enabling it to guide its behaviour on the basis of its own assessment of its situation. Quite possibly the ways the information is processed, and the ways in which it triggers behaviour, do not constitute what we could properly count as interpretation, assessment, and decision-making by the whole organism. Of course it is a puzzle how the bees' processes of abstraction could fail to involve conceptualization, hence the basic package. But there are alternatives. One might be that the system is constantly *testing*: putting questions to the incoming streams of information (Is there an x-pattern? Is there a y-pattern? Is the incoming pattern similar to one of the existing stimuli? . . .). In that

---

[1] Giurfa *et al.* do not use statements like the ones in quotes. I have made them up.

case the system as a whole needn't have concepts any more than we have concepts of, for example, low blood-sugar levels or dangerous bacteria in order for our bodies to take appropriate action. Even simple computer word-processing programs bring about something like abstraction: think of 'joker' characters.[2] However, the idea of information being for the whole organism, and the related ideas of interpretation, assessment, and decision-making as activities of the whole organism, are at the heart of what I mean by 'integration'. They need further consideration in the light of the examples to be discussed in the rest of this chapter.

7.3 INTERPRETATION, ASSESSMENT, AND DECISION-MAKING BY THE WHOLE ORGANISM

By definition a decider's behaviour must be arrived at in a way consistent with our ordinary concept of 'deciding'; but that is unacceptably vague. After all, we sometimes speak of inanimate things like cars and washing machines 'deciding' to do things such as slowing down or squeaking. It is well within our normal practices to describe even such lowly animals as ants or bees 'deciding' to go off in this direction rather than that. My definitions must be qualified: the concepts of deciding, interpreting, and assessing must be our ordinary ones as we use them on informed reflection. I suggest that when we are being careful we will use these notions only in connection with systems with something like the basic package.

It is useful to talk of information being for 'the whole system'—and about decision-making and so on being by the whole system—in order to contrast this sort of decision-making with whatever might occur inside its subsystems, and be relevant only to transactions there, or within groups of subsystems rather than the whole. Reflex systems with acquired triggering conditions, of which bees might be an instance, certainly acquire information that influences their behaviour. But it doesn't influence their behaviour by being interpreted by them in the light of their assessment of their situation, in that way enabling them to decide how to behave.

It may seem worrying that what counts as a 'whole' organism or system rather than a subsystem is relative to our ways of thinking about it. But that is not a problem for my account, which needs no more than that in any given context we can (because we do) think of certain items as being organisms or systems, and of certain other items as being their components or subsystems. From the point of view of our normal ways of thinking of human organisms, digestive systems are subsystems; but that doesn't prevent us from treating the digestive system itself as a 'whole system' on occasion. (John Searle quotes an interesting passage from the journal *Pharmacology*, according to which 'The gastro-intestinal tract is a highly

---

[2] Tye (2000) argues that bees are phenomenally conscious. Although I am sympathetic to much in his broad approach to 'simple minds', the patterns of behaviour he refers to do not seem to compel us to classify bees as deciders rather than sophisticated triggered reflex systems with acquired conditions.

intelligent organ that senses not only the presence of food ... but also its chemical composition, quantity, [and] viscosity .... Due to its highly developed decision-making ability, the gut wall ... is often called the gut brain'. (Searle 1992: 81. Searle evidently finds it obvious that the gut wall could not be correctly and literally described as intelligent, or as making decisions. I don't know enough to assess that assumption, but would not at present rule out the possibility that the gut wall is a decider. On the basis of the quoted words, however, it need be no more than a triggered reflex system.)

The following objection may have occurred to you. If information is for the system at all, it must be either for *some* subsystems, in which case bees qualify; or for *all* subsystems, in which case neither we nor bees qualify; or else for something like a central control, which I and many others do not think exists in evolved organisms. How, then, can bees be ruled out? The reply is that it doesn't matter whether those internal changes which, given their role in the behaviour and other functioning of the whole system, constitute its receipt and processing of information, impinge on one, two, or all subsystems in order for it to be for the system as a whole. What matters is whether it guides the system's behaviour (that is, what we naturally think of as the whole system's behaviour) via processes of interpretation, assessment, and decision-making in the integrated way I am trying to clarify. If, but only if, that condition is satisfied, then the system is a decider, and at least some information is for the whole system. In the bees' case we don't seem to have evidence for that. If those remarks strike you as still unclear, I agree—but invite you to suspend final judgement till the end of the chapter.

Among much other fascinating research concerning animals of all kinds, Gallistel describes evidence that 'bees represent the time of day at which nectar is available at a given source and time their visits to that source accordingly' (1990: 1). He is not implying that the bees say or otherwise represent to themselves things like, 'Ah, eight o'clock. Better be getting along to the terrace where that scientist has his breakfast marmalade.' On the contrary, it seems the information is processed automatically by the animals' nervous system.[3] On that basis, it seems entirely possible that such processing sets up a conditional trigger, so that when the creatures' internal time recorder reaches eight o'clock, appropriate foraging behaviour is set off. However, we are now well into empirical territory. Reluctantly I turn away from the bees.

You might wonder whether a sophisticated triggered reflex system with acquired conditions might not actually *constitute* a decider. If it does, my admittedly rough scheme of classification doesn't partition the field, but permits overlaps. So, could a triggered reflex system be a decider? No. The definition of deciders rules that out. In all types of reflex system a given stimulus, whether innate or acquired, invariably

---

[3] 'That virtually all organisms, *including bacteria*, possess an endogenous twenty-four-hour clock is widely known' (Gallistel 1990: 6, my emphasis). However, if for that reason virtually all organisms can be said to have information, clearly it is not *for* them in the sense that they use it via interpretation and decision-making.

causes its associated response (subject to the relevant conditions). In deciders, in deliberate contrast, although of course some behaviour may have the reflex form—we ourselves still have some reflexes—at least some of it does not. Some of a decider's behaviour results from its own decisions, when these are taken on the basis of its assessment of its situation in the light of its information, not just more or less directly caused by the stimulus, regardless of how sophisticated may be the processing which filters that stimulus.

7.4 THE HUMAN EMBRYO, FOETUS, AND NEONATE

From a single fertilized egg the process of cell division results first in a sort of container of 'external cells' surrounding a bundle of 'internal cells'; then, by further gradual stages, in an embryo; then in a foetus which acquires more and more human features until it is ready to be born. In its early stages the embryo cannot usefully be described as a behaving system at all. Even after several weeks it still seems to be, at most, a pure reflex system. But at some stage in the transition from foetus, through birth, to an infant a few weeks old, we have an organism with the basic package. It will be useful to consider some relevant facts. Here are passages from a couple of textbooks:

During a significant part of the fetal period (from 9 to 26 weeks), the eyes are closed, but toward the end of the fetal period, the fetus can see light and hear sound. The heartbeat is affected by the level of light or the tempo of music to which the mother is exposed. (Dye 2000: 75 f.)

The sensation of taste also seems to be present *in utero*. Experiments in which the rate of swallowing has been measured have shown that the addition of saccharine to the amniotic fluid increases the rate of swallowing, whereas distasteful materials such as opaque media cause almost complete cessation of swallowing. (Austin and Short (eds.) 1972: 83 f.)

It is a sensitive question whether the foetus is perceptually conscious. Does it really see and hear and have sensations of taste? At this stage I am not considering that question, but only whether it is a decider. The quotations show that the foetus is at least differentially sensitive to various stimuli in different sensory modalities; but that is consistent with its being a pure reflex system.

More to the point is evidence that the foetus can learn and remember things. For example, newborn infants have been shown to prefer their mother's voice to that of an unfamiliar female. To rule out the possibility that this learning was post-natal, it has further been shown that the babies studied show 'a preference for their mother's voice as it sounded in the womb', rather than as it sounded after birth. There is also evidence that the foetus can learn to distinguish not just types of sound but soundpatterns. P. G. Hepper found that 'babies, if their mothers had watched the TV soap "Neighbours" when pregnant, preferred this tune after birth to other unfamiliar tunes' (1997: 344. The other information in this paragraph comes from the same article). There is similar evidence relating to other sense modalities. However, even that amount and type of learning is consistent with its being a matter of acquiring new stimuli, or at most, new triggering conditions. It doesn't add up to a demonstration that the foetus has the basic package; the evidence is consistent with its being a triggered reflex system with acquired conditions.

Resistance to the view that the foetus is a decider seems to be reinforced by the information that 'similar (identical?) evidence of prenatal learning and memory abilities can be found throughout the animal kingdom' (Hepper 1997: 345). 'Embryos of birds in the egg are capable of learning the calls of their parents'; 'tadpoles are capable of learning about odours present in their pre-hatch environment'; and 'even invertebrates have been shown to be capable of learning and remembering stimuli in their environment prior to their emergence from the pupae' (345).

There is also some evidence *against* the view that the foetus is capable of learning in anything like the sense in which a decider learns. This shows up in facts about the development of the infant's nervous system after birth. There is for example a reflex that makes the baby's eyes follow any passing object. It takes time for the baby to become capable of overriding this reflex: that happens only with the explosion in brain growth around ten weeks. Then, by inhibiting the reflex, the baby becomes able to attend to something without being distracted. As time passes nervous connections permitting this control are strengthened. That suggests, even if it doesn't imply, that the newborn baby lacks control over its behaviour. Now, we cannot sensibly ascribe to the foetus cognitive capacities not yet possessed by the neonate. So if the baby really can't control its behaviour until after those post-natal developments in its nervous system, only then can it come to possess the basic package, and only then does it perceive the world in what I am calling the full sense.[4] (If that is correct, then, by the reasoning in the last chapter it is only at that stage that the infant is a candidate for genuine perceptual-phenomenal consciousness.) So there is some reason to say that even the foetus ready to be born is not yet a decider.

The foetus is still picking up quantities of information—information that will make a difference to the baby's behaviour. But that is consistent with the newborn baby's being no more than a triggered reflex system with acquired reflexes, in which case its perception is of a low grade. What the foetus acquires is not yet information 'for it': or rather, it is at best information for it as it will become, not for it as it is. Watching a baby develop is an excellent way to see how the terms I am using to define the basic package ('interpretation', 'assessment', 'decision-making',

---

[4] True, the basic package doesn't necessarily require the ability to control *overt* behaviour, as we saw when discussing paralysed people (6.10). Conceivably babies become able to control some of their thinking before they control their behaviour. But the considerations in the text undermine assertions such as the following: '. . . the capacity to feel sensations is innate and certainly present long before birth' (Bermúdez 1998: 192). Since I am not at present focusing on sensations I will leave the topic there.

and the rest) do not pick out unitary all-or-nothing capacities, but complex clusters of capacities and skills which take time to develop. There is a time when the baby cannot sensibly be said to have any control over its behaviour—when it just seems to be a bundle of reflexes—and there is a time when it has clearly acquired at least some degree of control: some control over its voice, for example. But the interval between those times is taken up with the gradual accumulation of those capacities, whose complexity becomes obvious when you observe and reflect on their development.

7.5   THE ARTIFICIAL GIANT

The artificial giant resembles an enormous human being but is controlled by a team of puppeteers inside it who monitor its environment, plan what it will do and say, and ensure that it behaves in all ways much as one might expect a giant to behave. Is it a decider? If we think of it as including the people inside it (and why not?) then so far as observers ignorant of its innards are concerned, it behaves just as if it interprets information, assesses its situation, makes decisions, and controls its behaviour on the basis of incoming and stored information. To such observers it appears to have the basic package. If you happen to be a behaviourist you might say it has the basic package even when you know what's going on inside. Even so, we can see that it need not bother behaviourists, and is not really a decider.

You might suggest that the trouble is simply that there are people inside it who determine its behaviour: Putnam once proposed that a system should not be allowed to qualify as a subject of psychological states if it has components vital to its operations which are themselves capable of such states (1967: 434). But although that does not seem unreasonable, we need to consider what exactly the problem is: mere intuitive plausibility is not enough. One explanation of what prevents the giant from qualifying as a decider is that although information about its environment gets into it and enables appropriate behaviour to be initiated and controlled, the processes constituting its acquisition of information on the one hand, and those constituting the control of its behaviour on the other, are not appropriately related. In my sense they are not integrated.

Suppose the giant's operators say, 'It's done a lot of walking. Let's make it sit down and say it's tired'—and they make it utter 'I feel tired' and sit down on a convenient hillside. Now, they themselves have been comfortably seated inside it all the time: *they* don't feel tired, and the utterance doesn't express any of their thoughts. Yet it was their idea to initiate the behaviour in question; no processes other than those involved in their having that idea did it. So it's just a kind of puppet, not a decider.

Behaviourists might still claim that it doesn't matter how the giant's behaviour is caused: its thinking consists purely in behaving appropriately and having the right capacities and dispositions. That leaves us with two conflicting accounts of what's going on when the giant says 'I feel tired'. According to the first it has no thoughts: the only thoughts in the neighbourhood are those of its operators and it is just a puppet, caused to move about as if it had thoughts and feelings. According to the second (behaviouristic) interpretation it has its own thoughts, which are constituted by its behaviour and dispositions. I suggest reflection on the need for integration of a decider's capacities supports the first account and undermines the second. What turns the balance is the moderate realism of everyday psychology. The giant's behaviour and dispositions do not supply any real events that could be counted as, for example, its making its own decisions about what to do.

A further consideration is how information is used by the giant's operators. To have the basic package, a system must be able to initiate and control its own behaviour on the basis of incoming and stored information: it must be able to take at least some of this information into account. The artificial giant could not have that key capacity because (to take one aspect of this difficulty) some of the information which would have had to be acquired by the giant in order for it to do its own interpreting, assessing, and deciding need not be acquired by anyone—not even by the operators. Suppose the giant is standing in a place from which it can supposedly 'see' through the upper window of a building which its operators already know is empty. Someone on the ground shouts, 'What can you see?'; the operators make it reply 'Just an empty room'. Now, there is normally someone on watch through the giant's 'eyes'; but we can suppose this lookout is taking a break. The purported explanation of the giant's utterance is that it heard and understood the question, looked inside the room, found it was empty, and reported what it had learnt. But that is not correct. The operators heard and understood the question; they caused the giant to move its head; it was their knowledge of the state of the room, together with their determination to make the giant behave appropriately, that made them cause the giant to produce its reply. When the giant's 'eyes' looked into the room, *nobody* acquired visual information about anything relevant. So the giant's behaviour is not initiated or controlled on the basis of information that is for it. It cannot use the information retained by the operators, and thus lacks capacity (i) of the basic package. Again, although information gets inside it and makes a difference to its behaviour, information and behaviour are not appropriately integrated. What is needed is that the acquisition of the information, its interpretation, its assessment, the making of decisions involving it, and its use should all interact in ways that permit them to be described as activities of the whole system, in line with everyday psychology. I doubt if we could force those constraints into a crisp definition; but examples such as the giant show we have a pretty reliable grasp of them.

7.6 BLOCK'S MACHINES

A Block machine is controlled by a computer in which all possible life histories of within a certain fixed duration have been stored (Block 1981). I will follow Block's example and focus on the restricted case of verbal intelligence. We are to consider the *Neo-Turing Conception* of verbal intelligence, according to which it is a matter of having the right capacities. Of course this idea is what Block himself opposes; but it is a good way of putting his opponents' position. According to this behaviourist conception,

Intelligence (or, more accurately, conversational intelligence) is the capacity to produce a sensible sequence of verbal responses to a sequence of verbal stimuli, whatever they may be. (Block 1981: 18)

If Block were defending this behaviouristic conception he would be open to objection for his use of 'sensible'; but he is just leaning over backwards on behalf of his opponents. He argues that behavioural capacities alone are not enough: the nature of the internal processing matters. He sketches a procedure which (if it were practicable, which it isn't) would result in setting up a machine with a very simple program.

First fix a time limit for the test, say an hour. Then establish the maximum number of characters typable in sequence within that modulus on a standard keyboard of, say, 60 characters: pretend the maximum is 1000 characters. Consider now the set of *all* sequences of up to 1000 characters (60^{1000} sequences on our assumptions: a ridiculously large number). Cause all those 'typable' sequences to be ground out, and engage millions of research students to sift out all and only those which satisfy the following condition: they can be regarded as conversations between two people in which the second participant's contributions are sensible in the context of the conversation as a whole.[5] Put all these 'possible conversations' into a computer, marking off the segments supposedly contributed by each of the two participants. Finally program the computer as follows: When a sequence of characters is typed in, search the stored possible conversations for the alphanumerically first one whose initial segment matches what has been typed in so far. Having found it, put out the next segment in that same conversation. And so on. If the research students have done their work properly the machine will have the capacity to produce sensible replies to whatever the interlocutor may type in— including foreign languages and total gibberish—within the allotted time limit.

Block claims that although his machine has the capacity described it has 'the intelligence of a toaster' (1981: 21); in which case it is a genuine counter-example to the Neo-Turing conception of verbal intelligence. I agree with that conclusion, but will emphasize a couple of points that are easily overlooked. First, the machine doesn't necessarily produce the same output for the same input unless, mistakenly, we were to count the human interlocutor's total contributions as a single input. How it responds to a given contribution from a human interlocutor depends on the preceding segment of the conversation. (For that reason alone it is not a pure

---

[5] Block originally said, 'Consider the set of all typable strings *of sentences*' (my emphasis). But restricting the sequences to sentences unnecessarily reduces the system's scope. We could perfectly well test it by typing rubbish. The condition that its contributions should make sense as a whole ensures that it may be programmed to put out rubbish in contexts where that would make sense.

reflex system.) Second, objections based on the machine's admitted ignorance of what is going on around it during the conversation are not valid. The test is not a test of its perceptual powers; so it is in order for it to be treated, for the duration of the test, as lacking all perceptual capacities other than what it needs to receive and put out typed messages.

Block remarks that 'all the intelligence it exhibits is that of its programmers'. That is true but misleading, because it suggests that what demolishes the system's claims to intelligence is that its programmers exercised their own intelligence. That cannot be right. Its program did not have to depend on the work of the research students. Instead, as Block points out in a footnote, it could have resulted from a cosmic freak—a violent electric storm perhaps.

One way to see why the machine lacks intelligence, I suggest, is to see that in spite of appearances it lacks the basic package, given the moderate realism of everyday psychology. What goes on inside a Block machine cannot be counted as its interpreting information, assessing its situation, or making decisions. The only field of action about which it might conceivably have done such things is that of producing responses to what is typed in. Does it really interpret its interlocutor's inputs? No: all that happens is that those inputs cause whatever comes next in the stored 'possible conversation' to be put out. Is there syntactic or semantic analysis of the interlocutor's utterance? No. Is there anything that could be counted as working out how to respond? Again, No. Nor does anything count as its acting on a decision to put out that particular response. Every response it makes was already there in the stored conversation, which is inconsistent with its resulting from some process of considering and deciding what to say. Contrary to what is required of deciders, it does not work out for itself how to behave on the basis of its own assessment of its situation. Finally, could anything be counted as the Block machine's recognizing sensible or nonsensical utterances? Obviously not. It would put out a stream of rubbish as readily as the sensible remarks that have been programmed in. It does indeed have just about the intelligence of a toaster.

Block explains how to extend the idea to cover all kinds of behaviour, not just verbal. As before, we fix a suitable time interval: an hour, a hundred-year lifetime, whatever. We quantize time into sufficiently brief instants for our program to enable the system's behaviour to exhibit the smooth transitions through time that characterize much real human behaviour. Then we consider the total pattern of inputs to all a person's sensory receptors at one of those instants; and similarly the total pattern of outputs from the brain's efferent nerves to the motor nerves. (Each such total pattern of inputs or outputs is analogous to one of the characters that may be typed in or out in the purely verbal case.) The aim is to construct a set of all 'possible life histories' (in terms of sequences of possible sensory inputs and possible outputs to the efferent nerves), corresponding to the set of all possible conversations in the verbal case. The principle is the same, and the implications for the notion of a decider are the same, so I will not pursue the further development of this idea.

Since all the Block machine's behaviour depends on a fixed set of built-in reflex subsystems, each primed to be triggered by the satisfaction of certain conditions embodied in the stored sequences of inputs and outputs, it might be described as a built-in triggered reflex system. However, it is significantly different from the systems to which I applied that name in the last chapter: so different that I think they ought to be kept distinct. The main difference is that in a Block machine the outputs from one lot of reflexes or reflex subsystems serve as inputs to others (or as further triggering conditions). As noted earlier, such systems can be immensely powerful.

The Block machine teaches us that something with behavioural dispositions exactly like those of the most sophisticated deciders we know—human beings— may yet have *no* processes of interpretation, assessment, or decision-making going on inside it, not even ones that are not integrated.

7.7   THE MACHINE-TABLE ROBOT

The next example of something which may seem to have the basic package, but doesn't, is another special kind of computer-controlled robot. Like the general version of Block's machine, the machine-table robot works on the basis of a quantization of time into suitably brief instants, and the specification of a set of possible total instantaneous patterns of sensory input and a set of possible total instantaneous patterns of output (to the robot's 'efferent nerves'). On reasonable assumptions the numbers of these possible inputs and outputs are finite; similarly the number of possible instantaneous states of the machine is finite. But the machine contrasts very significantly with Block's machine in two respects: no time limit is fixed for its working life; and there is no attempt to anticipate and build into its program any sequences of behaviour at all, much less any possible life histories. Instead its behaviour is controlled by a 'machine-table'. This is a very large but finite set of ordered quadruples of numbers. The first member of each quadruple stands for one of the possible total instantaneous patterns of sensory input; each of the second and third members of a quadruple stands for one of the many possible states of the machine; and the fourth member stands for one of the possible total instantaneous patterns of output. (Being a standard von Neumann system, each of its possible instantaneous input and output patterns is *already* interpretable as encoding a number.) It is presupposed that the brain works in such a way that given its current state and input, both its next state and its output are thereby determined. So the machine-table specifies, for each of the system's possible instantaneous current states and total inputs, its next state and output. Assuming the body works properly, then, this table encapsulates a person's whole system of behavioural dispositions and specifies how the system will behave under any possible sequence of sensory stimulation.

If the working of a human brain cannot be captured by such a machine-table, the example fails for that reason. Yet it still has a use in teasing out some implications of the basic package; so let's pretend the brain's workings can indeed be captured in that way. Then the robot will behave, and be disposed to behave, like a normal human being. Each total instantaneous pattern of sensory input causes the relevant number to be registered in the machine at the time it comes in. Also at each instant, the machine's current 'state number' is also being registered. The machine's program consists of (a) a suitably encoded version of the machine-table; (b) the following instruction: Given the current input and state numbers, search for the line of the machine-table which starts with those two numbers, change the state number to the one specified by the third number, and put out the output specified by the fourth number. (There is further discussion in Kirk 1986.)

Does the machine-table robot have the basic package? Given our assumptions, it has the right behavioural capacities and dispositions. But the Block machine showed that that was not enough. In addition the system's internal workings must be consistent with its interpreting information, assessing its situation, and deciding what to do. These processes and their interactions must be integrated with the causation of the whole system's behaviour in ways consistent with their being the activities of the whole system, not just of its individual components. Clearly the machine-table robot is much closer to being a genuine decider than the Block machine. Even when we know how it operates, we may still feel inclined to say that, unlike a Block machine, it works out its own responses to the situations it finds itself in. For that reason alone it is a serious candidate decider; yet I think you will eventually agree that it too fails to qualify.

Of course a vast amount is built into the machine-table (the set of ordered quadruples, or rather its physical instantiation) since it represents the hugely complex workings of a mature human brain. But that by itself would not prevent this robot from qualifying as a decider. We could say the machine-table performs some of the functions of the brain's structure, together with the laws of nature that govern its workings. Seen in that light, what is built in is shared with systems that indisputably have the basic package: the mere fact of having so much built in cannot disqualify this robot. But now, we saw that the artificial giant lacked the right sort of integration of (to put it roughly) information flow and the causation of behaviour. The trouble with the machine-table robot, we might say, is that it suffers from too much integration. There is indeed a sense in which the machine-table represents the workings of a brain. But it does so very abstractly, by means of a set of quadruples of numbers. The transitions from one machine state to the next result from the fact that the two numbers corresponding to those states occur one after the other in the machine-table. They do not result from anything like the various different kinds of features that cause one state to follow another in a central nervous system.

Take for example the reception of inputs from the retinas in a normal human being, where those inputs are distinct from inputs from other sense receptors, and are processed distinctly and differently. In the machine-table robot a single number represents total sensory input at an instant. There is no way in which that number incorporates distinctions between inputs from eyes, ears, tongue, or other receptors. It is just an arbitrary number standing for the lot. That by itself would seem enough to show that no internal processes correspond adequately to the processing of visual information as distinct from other sensory information. But even if we ignore that fact, the next stage in the system's processing leads to the same conclusion. For we now have two numbers, one representing the current total instantaneous sensory input, the other the 'state number'. These two numbers determine a particular quadruple of the machine-table: the one starting with precisely those two numbers. The remaining two numbers in that quadruple fix what the output and next state number shall be. But nothing in this transition to the next state number provides for distinct components corresponding to the processing of information from distinct sensory channels. In strong contrast, there are in us distinct sequences of events corresponding to the distinct kinds of perceptual awareness. For example the events that constitute my awareness of changes to the blue characters on my computer screen as I type this are distinct from those which constitute my concurrent awareness of the monotonous whirring of the machine's cooling fan; and those again are distinct from my hearing the sound of footsteps outside the room and smelling freshly ground coffee. No distinct processes inside the machine-table robot could be counted as its interpreting specifically visual information, or auditory information, or olfactory information. Thus a vital component of the basic package is missing. It has only the net residual effect of those distinct processes.

You might object that the machine-table robot *does* interpret incoming sensory information; it just happens to benefit from a great simplification in its functioning compared with us. We laboriously interpret different kinds of sensory information separately; it interprets everything together. But that overlooks a crucial fact. It still behaves just like one of us, appearing to attend to *specific distinct sources* of incoming information. Notably it utters what we should ordinarily count as descriptions of different kinds of perceptual experience. It says for example 'I like the hint of gooseberry in this wine.' Yet nothing can be counted as its receiving or interpreting or being affected specifically by the *taste* of anything, rather than by its total sensory input at the time. It doesn't taste the wine, so nothing counts as its reflecting on the taste of the wine, hence nothing counts as its deciding to comment on some particular aspect of that taste.

Certainly its overall behaviour is affected by specific features of the world it interacts with. The trouble is that there are no distinct events which could constitute its acquiring distinct packets of information on the basis of which it could assign descriptions to any of those specific features. When it produces utterances like the one about the flavour of the wine, therefore, either it is deliberately lying, or it doesn't know what it is doing. But to lie it must know the truth, which we have seen it cannot—just because it cannot separate in thought the different aspects of its experience which nevertheless it appears to attend to and describe. So *it doesn't really know what it's doing*. All of that follows, I suggest, from the moderate realism of everyday psychology.

Am I imputing too much detail to everyday psychology? I don't think so. It seems to be a pretty broad requirement that in order to be counted as genuinely talking about a certain type of experience, an individual must be capable of separating, in thought, that particular experience from others. That doesn't seem like a dangerous venture into armchair neuroscience.

So no distinctively olfactory experiences can be involved in the machine-table robot's apparent comment on the flavour of the wine: it lacks anything that could be counted as either experiencing or attending to flavours. When it seems to be commenting on its experiences it doesn't know what it is doing—which entails it is not in control of its own behaviour. Yet its behaviour and behavioural capacities are just like our own. Nor, in contrast to the artificial giant, is there anything else which could be said to be in control of its behaviour. Nor, again, in contrast to the Block machine, has its behaviour been prepared in advance and triggered when the right inputs strike it. We can hardly deny that its behaviour *is* controlled on the basis of information that it acquires. And processes of interpretation, assessment, and decision-making do go on inside it. The trouble is that the mediation of its machine-table prevents those processes from being integrated in ways that finally qualify it as a system which does its *own* interpretation, assessment, and decision-making.

The above reasoning is not intended to show more than that a robot constructed as explained would not be a decider. It does not purport to show anything so general as, for example, that no computer-controlled robots could be deciders, or that only parallel processors could be deciders. As is well known, any functions performable by a parallel processor can be performed by a serial processor, and vice versa. But a parallel processor controlled by a machine-table as described would still lack the right sort of integration of its activities.

7.8 UNTYPICAL DECIDERS

The three artificial examples considered above all turn out not to have the basic package in spite of appearances. Here are a few equally artificial cases which have it in spite of expectations to the contrary.

(a) Computers Instead of Neurones

Suppose each neurone in someone's head has been replaced by a suitably small computer, programmed to reproduce the original neurone's input-output functions. We can suppose the functions of neurotransmitters and neuroinhibitors are also taken care of, either by their being made to interact with specially made transducers at the connections now replacing the original synapses, or by means of a program with the same effects on the ersatz neurones as the original neurotransmitters had on their originals. The original person was certainly a decider. Would the resulting individual still be one?

The fact that the ersatz neurones would be interconnected in ways exactly matching their originals' interconnections would ensure that the same patterns of internal causation and processing were reproduced in the resulting individual. In particular, and in contrast with the machine-table robot, there would be distinct processes associated with distinct patterns of experience and thought; and the causal interactions of these processes with other processes would mirror those in our own brains. In respect of all processes involved in interpretation, assessment, and decision-making, therefore, there would be isomorphism between the workings of the original person's brain and that of the ersatz brain. So the ersatz individual would remain a decider.

(b) The Homunculus-Head

Recall the example referred to in Chapter 3: each member of a population of many millions of homunculi follows rules for replicating the causal functions of a particular neurone; together they perform the functions of a brain controlling a living human body. Does this system, unlike the artificial giant, qualify as a decider?

At first one might think that because the operators are themselves deciders, the system as a whole cannot be. But why should that be an objection? (See Block 1976: 290 ff.). Certainly the homunculus-head is a bizarre system; but then so are many things we find in reality. From the point of view of classifying something as a decider, all that matters is whether the functions involved in the basic package are performed in a way consistent with the moderate realism of everyday psychology; the system is not also required to conform to our ordinary expectations and preju-dices. Now, in respect of basic-package functions, the homunculus-head is iso-morphic with a normally functioning human organism. In this respect it resembles the computers-for-neurones system. Notably, the component corresponding to the brain (the homunculi who perform the functions of neurones) incorporates processes corresponding one-one with those in a normal brain. Because the human brain has processes of interpretation, assessment, and decision-making going on inside it, and these processes are integrated among themselves and appropriately connected to sensory inputs and motor outputs in accordance with the moderate realism of everyday psychology, the same goes for the homuncular brain. It there-fore has the basic package. (Chalmers's use of the homunculus-head as a putative counter-example to functionalist claims about consciousness may be distracting attention. The present question is not whether the homunculus-head is conscious, only whether it is a decider.)

I must admit I have wavered on the question whether the homunculus-head is a decider. The following objection seemed once to have some force. That the homunculus brain continues to perform its functions, and that the homunculus-headed system continues to have its behavioural dispositions, depends on whether or not a sufficient number of homunculi continue to behave according to the rules. What if they started to disobey the rules, or to take breaks from their tedious labours? In either case the functions involved in the basic package would no longer be performed. It would stop having the right dispositions and it would cease to be a decider. Can we still say that even when it was running properly, its behaviour would be controlled by itself? If its being a decider is at the mercy of decisions by other individuals, does it really 'control its own behaviour'?

But the question is not whether the homunculus-head is a normal or natural sort of system, or likely to be stable for any great length of time. So long as the homunculi behave themselves, the relevant functions actually are performed, and the relevant dispositions are possessed—in the integrated way I have been trying to get clear about. That the homunculi might revolt seems no more of a difficulty than that people's neurones might start malfunctioning: something all too common. Consider also such things as prostheses for the inner ear, which can play a useful part in overcoming deafness. As things are, they are constructed from inanimate materials. But imagine that one such prosthesis was controlled by tiny people inside it. It seems reasonable to suppose that so long as they did their jobs, the person concerned would continue to hear satisfactorily; while if they packed up, deafness would return. This person's hearing would certainly be at the mercy of the little people's goodwill. Does it follow that the person would not really hear even when they were working properly? Surely not. It seems to me that the homunculus-head is comparable. I conclude that so long as the homunculi continue to follow the rules, the system is a decider.[6]

(c) Split Brains

As is well known, in patients whose cerebral commissure has been severed there are certain situations—ones where information from one sense (say, vision) is kept apart from information from another (say, touch)—where each half-brain controls a certain type of behaviour independently of the other. In effect the touch-informed half-brain may produce the response 'Yes' to a question to which the vision-informed other half-brain replies 'No'. (That there is controversy over the interpretation of the empirical findings—on which see for example Shallice 1988, Gazzaniga 1988—is beside the point of this discussion.) Let's agree that in most situations the individual functions as a single person, who is a decider. The question arises whether either of that person's half-brain-based components is also a decider.

Here there are different candidates for being deciders. One pair is the two half-brains themselves. But when we reflect that psychological experiments on such cases typically involve overt behaviour, we are likely to consider that more appropriate candidates are the left half-brain together with the whole of the rest of the

[6] Thanks to one of the anonymous readers for OUP, whose comments prodded me back to the right approach.

body, and the right half-brain together with the whole of the rest of the body. If we were to choose the two half-brains alone as behaving systems, the behaviour in question could only be mental, and at best difficult to discover. By choosing the two composites in which each half-brain is taken together with the rest of the body, we have two systems that are each capable of overt behaviour.

Whichever we choose, it seems clear that each member of each pair is a decider. Each is capable, in its own characteristic way, of initiating and guiding intelligent behaviour on the basis of perceptual and stored information. (At least we may assume that is so, since the point of discussing these cases is not to do a priori neuroscience, but to see how the concept of a decider works.)

(d) Zombies

By definition a zombie exactly duplicates all the physical workings of a human body and central nervous system under the assumption of the causal closure of the physical. So physicalists at least (unless they are eliminativists, according to whom this whole book is off-target) will agree that my zombie twin—again, if he had been possible—would have been a decider. That seems a reasonable position regardless of one's metaphysics. Even the friends of zombies are bound to concede that explanations of behaviour in terms of the concepts used in the basic package work just as well for zombies as for us.

Some dualists may claim that we cannot properly describe any processes in our zombie twins as ones of interpretation, assessment, and decision-making precisely because they would have no qualia. Yet even they must concede that our zombie twins would have everything else that is required for the basic package, since by definition that would be the only difference between zombies and ourselves. It was partly in order to deal with their position that I have *defined* the basic package so that something qualifies as having it even if, according to them, it may still lack qualia. In the end, everyone must concede that zombies would be deciders.

(e) Commander Data

Ned Block adapts a character from Star Trek to make some pertinent claims. His version of Commander Data is 'functionally the same as us but physically different'. More accurately, he is a 'superficial isomorph' of us, which means he is functionally isomorphic to us 'with respect to folk psychology and whatever is logically or nomologically entailed by folk psychological isomorphism, but that is all' (2002: 401). In still more detail, he is a 'merely superficial isomorph', so that 'we have no reason to suppose there are any shared physical properties between our conscious states and Commander Data's functional analogs of them that could be the physical basis of any phenomenal overlap between the two, since we have no reason to think that such shared properties are required by the superficial overlap.' There are no significant overlaps of brain mechanisms either; and 'Commander

Data does not have any part which itself is a functional isomorph of us and whose activities are crucial to maintaining the functional organization of the whole.' Block suggests we might suppose for the sake of example 'that the physical basis of Commander Data's brain is to be found in etched silicon chips rather than the organic carbon basis of our brains' (404).

In spite of those radical physical differences I hope it is clear that Commander Data, like the last two examples, is at any rate a decider. That is guaranteed by the facts that we are deciders and that he is functionally isomorphic with us in respect of whatever is logically or nomologically entailed by folk psychological isomorphism. Block goes on to defend the striking claim that 'We have no conception of a ground of rational belief to the effect that a realization of our superficial functional organization that is physically fundamentally different along the lines I have specified for Commander Data is or is not conscious' (405). If I succeed in my main project I shall refute that claim; the first step is to note that Commander Data has the basic package.

7.9 OTHER ROBOTS

Recall a famous remark of Wittgenstein's: 'only of a living human being and what resembles (behaves like) a living human being can one say: it has sensations; it sees; is blind; hears; is deaf; is conscious or unconscious' (Wittgenstein 1953, sect. 281. See also sects. 283, 360). I have argued that behavioural resemblance is not enough—even when we are considering only the concepts involved in the basic package and not also those further concepts which involve consciousness. Wittgenstein does not say explicitly that behavioural resemblance *is* enough, however: just that it is necessary. Yet his remark remains unclear. What sorts of behavioural resemblance is he thinking of? He seems to have been working at a pretty high level of generality. It makes no sense to ascribe pain to stone, he suggests. 'How could one so much as get the idea of ascribing a *sensation* to a *thing*? One might as well ascribe it to a number!' But 'now look at a wriggling fly and at once these difficulties vanish and pain seems able to get a foothold here ...' (sect. 284). So he thought creatures unlike us in physical structure could still resemble us behaviourally in the relevant sense. That is in line with ordinary assumptions. We don't rule out the possibility that creatures with different structures from ours should have thoughts and feelings. Certainly we acquired our grasp of those very general notions from their application to human beings; but that doesn't stop us applying them to radically different kinds of system.

Including robots? I will take 'robot' to mean any system whose behaviour is controlled by a single suitably programmed computer with standard sequential (von Neumann) architecture. (The point here is to make an explicit contrast with parallel processors, since we have already noted that some parallel systems, such as the computers-for-neurones one, are deciders.) Now, both the robots of that kind so far considered—Block's machine and the machine-table robot—lack the basic package in spite of passing all behavioural tests. But that doesn't prevent other types of robot from qualifying. Why shouldn't a suitable program endow a robot with not only the right behavioural capacities, but the right relations between internal processes, including those of interpretation, assessment, and decision-making? Before pursuing the question, we need to refine it by distinguishing two versions:

(Q1) Could we eventually *devise* a suitable program to give a single-computer-controlled robot the basic package?

(Q2) Could there possibly *be* a suitable program to give a single-computer-controlled robot the basic package?

As we noted when discussing Block's machine, a robot's program does not have to be put in by human agency: a random cosmic freak might do the trick. That is relevant now, since we don't actually know how to produce a program to endow the robot with the basic package. However, for my purposes it wouldn't matter if we could never devise such a program; all that matters is whether there could be one. Question (Q2) is the one for us.

The realism of everyday psychology requires there to be, in some acceptable sense, distinct processes constituting an individual's distinct kinds of perceptual processes. For example the processes constituting an organism's seeing a fox must be distinct from those constituting its catching the scent of lettuce. Not that these processes need involve different hardware components—distinct processes can perfectly well use the same hardware—the point is that they must be distinct causal chains. That point is sharpened when we consider utterances purporting to describe experiences. Suppose the robot produces one sentence to the effect that it's enjoying the smell of a rose, and another to the effect that it dislikes the rose's colour. We shall still have to count it as merely an imitation perceiver, like the machine-table robot, unless not only are the rose's smell and its colour respectively different causal factors in the production of those utterances, but there are two distinct rose-initiated causal chains inside it, one from molecular bombardment of its olfactory system, the other from retinal stimulation of its colour-detecting and processing system. Those causal chains in turn would have to be appropriately linked with interpretation, assessment, and decision-making processes. Could a standard computer provide for such causal chains in a robot with suitable sense receptors and motor control systems?

Evidently the system's program could include different subroutines for processing information from those two different sources. Nor does there seem to be any difficulty in principle over mirroring other causal chains in a human brain by means of subroutines performing similar functions, particularly when it is recognized that these subroutines don't have to perform exactly the same functions as their neural originals. Our robot doesn't have to be an imitation human, just a decider. That being so, it looks as if we may conclude that the answer to question

(Q2) is 'Yes'. The moderate realism of everyday psychology seems to impose no constraints which rule out suitable programs.[7]

7.10   AN INDETERMINATE CASE

Now for type of system, very far from being a robot, which I think neither determinately has the basic package nor determinately lacks it. A nation state receives information about events in its international environment and also about its internal situation. It interprets that information, assesses its situation, and makes decisions on the basis of stored and incoming information. On the face of it, then, it qualifies as a decider. However, those who do the interpreting, assessing, and deciding are in some respects performing functions analogous to those of the controllers of the artificial giant. The giant doesn't have the basic package because its behaviour isn't initiated or controlled on the basis of its own information. It might be argued that, similarly, France has no information of its own, and therefore does not qualify as having the basic package. I see no basis for a sharp decision in this case, but no reason for concern about its indeterminacy.

7.11   SOME LESSONS

Examples have helped to make explicit some of the implications of the idea of the basic package. I suggest this idea has proved solider than might at first have appeared. I suppose the difficulty of articulating the relevant notion of *integration* more sharply than I have managed to do is connected with the complex manner in which everyday psychological concepts are interrelated: attempting to spell out the details would resemble the unmanageable project of assembling all the 'platitudes' or 'principles' of commonsense psychology (Lewis 1966; 1994).

The artificial giant, Block's machine, and the machine-table robot contrast usefully with genuine deciders, and that in different ways. The artificial giant forced us to take note of how, in a genuine decider, the acquisition, interpretation, and assessment of perceptual information are causally linked. Block's machines helped to bring out an important implication of the moderate realism of everyday psychology: to count as intelligent, a system must put together its own interpretation and assessment of its situation. The machine-table robot helped to bring out a further aspect of that realism, also illustrating what is needed for integration: to control its own descriptions of its experiences, the system must be capable of separating, in thought, different sequences of experience.

---

[7] You might wonder whether Searle's (1980) Chinese Room argument has anything to teach us here. I think not, because the 'Systems Reply' refutes it (see e.g. Dennett 1991: 435–40). However, that Reply only refutes Searle's argument *against* the view that a suitably programmed computer would be intelligent. It goes no way to prove that view.

7.12   BASICNESS OF THE BASIC PACKAGE

Saying that relatively humble creatures such as cats, birds, dogs, and sheep have the basic package does not imply they also have 'minds'—whatever exactly that may be taken to mean. Typically it is assumed that having a mind, or (to avoid risking Cartesian assumptions) *mindedness*, involves the capacity for full-blown intentional states such as belief, desire, and intention, and also the capacity to deliberate and make decisions consciously. Mindedness in this sense is a sophisticated property which doesn't seem to be possessed by many of the creatures that I assume have the basic package. It is plausible to say the basic package is a necessary condition for mindedness, provided we make allowance for non-standard cases such as paralysed people. It is not plausible to say the converse is also true: surely it is not. I will develop those claims in the next chapter.

8

De-sophisticating the Framework

You may suspect that only language users could have the basic package. I think this idea rests on heavy framework assumptions which are inappropriate when applied to cognition in general rather than to the special case of language users. Sophisticated conceptions of *concept possession, belief, representation,* and *content* are presupposed. In this chapter I aim to show that the basic package does not need those conceptions. We have to de-sophisticate the conceptual framework in terms of which the basic package is to be understood. Ideas about 'representation' and 'content' are hotly debated; we need to cool down a bit when considering humbler creatures than ourselves.

8.1 THE OBJECTION

Recall the capacities and abilities included in the basic package. The system must be able to (i) initiate and control its behaviour on the basis of incoming and retained information; (ii) acquire and retain information about its environment; (iii) interpret information; (iv) assess its situation; (v) choose between alternative courses of action on the basis of retained and incoming information. It must also (vi) have goals. The system's exercise of these capacities must be integrated in the sense I have been explaining. This means roughly that the internal changes which constitute its acquisition and use of information enable it to monitor and control its own behaviour. Further, at least some of those changes must affect its interpretation, assessment, and decision-making in ways that allow us to say those activities are guided by the information, not just somehow influenced by it. The objection we have to consider turns on what it takes to have these capacities.

The objection is this. If being a decider requires not only the capacity to acquire and use information, but to do so in a sense which involves the ability to represent the world and to have concepts, and in some sense to think about what it is doing, then a decider is a sophisticated system. Indeed, representing, thinking, and the ability to operate with concepts, are such sophisticated accomplishments that it is difficult to understand how they could be possessed without language.[1] If that is

[1] Some philosophers assume it is impossible to have concepts without language. For example John Skorupski asserts that 'grasping a concept is understanding an expression in a language ...' (1997: 33).

right, then contrary to what I maintain, either perceptual consciousness does not require the basic package, or else only creatures with language can be perceptually conscious.

We should reject both alternatives. I know of no good reasons to adopt sufficiently strong assumptions about the relations between information, belief, concepts, and language. Certainly there are contexts where it is helpful to construe 'information', 'belief', 'concept possession', and related expressions so narrowly that they entail language. But the basic package is not such a context. There is no reason why the capacities to process information in the ways it requires should be construed on that basis. Typically, those who adopt strong construals of believing and concept possession are willing to concede that languageless creatures may have belief-like states and concept-like capacities, though less sophisticated than ours. If such states and capacities are enough for the basic package, the objection fails immediately. However, all these ideas are rather elusive. We need a reasonably firm basis for moving on; though providing it will be more a matter of clearing away weeds than laying down much in the way of positive foundations. We can usefully start with a look at some suggestions of Gareth Evans in his posthumous book *The Varieties of Reference*. Though not developed in any detail, they are interesting in themselves and highly pertinent. They have also influenced others; and their key features appear in later and more highly developed accounts.

8.2 THE 'CONCEPT-EXERCISING AND REASONING SYSTEM'

Evans starts by noting:

People are … gatherers, transmitters and storers of information. These platitudes locate perception, communication, and memory in a system—the informational system—which constitutes the substratum of our cognitive lives. (1982: 122)

Any creature with an informational system is capable of being in an 'informational state'. Although we share two of the operations of our informational system (perception and memory) with animals, and although languageless creatures have informational states, they lack something vital that we have: 'a *thinking, concept-applying, and reasoning system*' (158). This means they cannot apply concepts, cannot think, and cannot have beliefs, at any rate in the sense he favours:

It is as well to reserve 'belief' for the notion of a far more sophisticated cognitive state: one that is connected with … the notion of *judgement*, and so, also, connected with the notion of *reasons*. (124)

If that is right, how can animals have informational states? Evans suggests that the explanation of these states' being informational and having content lies in their being 'linked with behavioural output in … an advantageous way' (156). In 'concept-exercising and reasoning organisms', 'the internal states which have a content by virtue of their phylogenetically more ancient connections with the motor system also serve as input to the concept-exercising and reasoning system' (227). But because languageless creatures lack a concept-exercising and reasoning system, the contents of their informational states are 'non-conceptual'. I will come back to that last idea later; just now let us examine the role Evans assigns to the concept-exercising and reasoning system.

It looks as if he simply assumes that thinking, reasoning, concept-using, and judgement-making all require language, and that none of these activities is a matter of degree. Given those assumptions it is unproblematic that animals don't have concepts or beliefs in his preferred full-strength sense. I think the framework for thinking about cognition that he bases on those assumptions is too sophisticated. It obstructs an understanding of how language users could have evolved from languageless creatures, and, indeed, of how human infants can acquire language. Evans's key assumptions are quite widely shared; I will explain why I think they should be rejected. Two key points can be noted straight away.

One is that Evans does not distinguish between reflex systems and other languageless systems, including deciders: he lumps all languageless creatures together. I have suggested there is a vital difference between the various types of reflex systems on the one hand, and deciders on the other, and that only deciders are potential subjects of perceptual consciousness. Suitably complex reflex systems may simulate genuine deciders but are still essentially different, as some of the examples showed. One crucial difference is that there is no good sense in which any sort of reflex system can be said to work out how to behave on the basis of its assessment of its own current situation; while that is a distinguishing feature of deciders.

The other key point is that Evans assumes a sophisticated conception of thoughts and judgements to go with his sophisticated conception of beliefs and concepts. Certainly it is plausible that *conscious* thoughts and judgements should involve language, especially since they often involve the conscious formulation of sentences. But consider the background to such events. Verbal formulas expressing thoughts don't just pop up at random. That may be how it seems to us; but often, what precedes their popping up is itself a kind of thinking. Some of those preceding cognitive events may be conscious; but it is hard to see how they could all be conscious, since they consist of processes we are typically incapable of recognizing or reconstructing. Some such episodes of thinking may be possible for creatures without language. No doubt many of our own thoughts depend on language even when not verbally expressed. But that doesn't rule out the possibility that languageless creatures may engage in forms of relatively unsophisticated unconscious thinking—which precedes and causes not the verbal expression of thoughts, but intelligent behaviour: non-verbal manifestation of intelligence. Not even that occurs in reflex systems; but no reason has been given why it should not occur in languageless deciders. This suggests that Evans's scheme distorts our conception of the cognitive potentialities of creatures without language.

8.3   CONCEPT POSSESSION IS NOT ALL-OR-NOTHING

Cats, babies, and many much less sophisticated organisms perceive, learn about, and represent their environments. To be accessible for use the information they acquire must be organized, if only in rudimentary ways. That organization involves, among other things, their tending to group different items together, so that they can treat them similarly. And that starts to seem like conceptualization, at least in a rudimentary sense, although, as the example of the bees suggests, even very complex systems of classification may fail to involve genuine interpretation, assessment, and decision-making by the system as a whole.

However, Evans is not alone in refusing to allow any system to count as having concepts unless it also has complex and demanding other abilities. John Campbell claims that concept possession is 'defined by' a certain 'core set of abilities' which among other things includes self-consciousness in a strong sense.[2] José Bermúdez requires possession of language: according to his 'Priority Principle', 'Conceptual abilities are constitutively linked with linguistic abilities in such a way that conceptual abilities cannot be possessed by non-linguistic creatures' (1998: 42). Those certainly appear to be strong claims. But it turns out that these philosophers are mostly legislating for the use of 'concept', 'belief', and related words rather than making substantive claims about the limits of thought. They find it helpful for their purposes to impose strong conditions on concept possession and believing, without denying that languageless creatures can have something like beliefs and concepts.

Bermúdez, for example, appeals persuasively to animal studies to support the view that non-linguistic creatures may be aware of themselves. Self-aware psychological subjects will be 'aware of themselves as perceivers, as agents, and as having reactive psychological states' (247). He brings evidence from developmental psychology in support of his view that non-linguistic infants acquire this sort of awareness between 9 and 10 months. However, because he insists that genuine beliefs must have 'conceptual' contents, he refuses to admit that languageless creatures also have beliefs: they have only 'proto-beliefs'. His Priority Principle would do powerful work indeed if we had good reason to accept it. His main justification seems to be that having genuine beliefs and concepts requires the ability to *justify* inferences; and he cannot see how a creature without language could do that. He leads up to this point via consideration of empirical evidence which seems on the face of it to show that languageless infants have the

---

[2] J. Campbell (1994: 3). John McDowell says, 'Creatures without conceptual capacities [sc. in the demanding sense he favours] lack self-consciousness and ... experience of objective reality' (1994: 114). Susan Hurley says that 'if the information that a given object has a certain property is conceptualized, ... it has a structure that enables the person ... [to] quantify and make inferences that depend on such decompositional structure and context-freedom' (1997: 207).

elements of the concept of an *object* (roughly: of something bounded, more or less impenetrable, and spatiotemporally continuous). But then, developing an Evans-type approach, he urges that 'Identifying something as an object is something that one does for *reasons*'—which requires the subject to make a judgement 'that can be justified or unjustified, rational or irrational' (1998: 69). He argues that infants cannot make justified judgements because they are incapable of 'providing any justifications at all for any inferential transitions. . . . It is because prelinguistic creatures are in principle incapable of providing such justifications that the priority thesis is true' (71). There seems to be an unjustified leap here. Why must drawing justified inferences require one to be capable of actually providing justifications? Drawing inferences is a far more basic accomplishment than stating them, and much more basic than being able to grasp 'general rules of inference'. Consider the following possibility: that there are creatures which (a) make inferences; (b) are sometimes justified in the inferences they draw; (c) cannot produce what we would count as justifications for those inferences. According to Bermúdez' principles, (c) entails that these creatures lack genuine beliefs and concepts, although it leaves room for them to have what he calls proto-beliefs. I suggest that for our purposes proto-beliefs would be sufficiently like beliefs for the differences to be negligible. On Bermúdez' preferred construal of beliefs and concepts, languageless creatures necessarily lack them. That gives us no reason to doubt that languageless creatures can have the abilities involved in the basic package.

The behaviour of many languageless creatures suggests they have something like concepts. You only have to watch a blackbird repeatedly coming back to a worm that it is eating bit by bit, or a cat chasing a mouse, to be forced to acknowledge that these animals have at least a considerable subset of the abilities involved in full-blown possession of the concept of an object. A striking example is the famous New Caledonian crows, which construct tools in the wild. In captivity the crow Betty bends a straight piece of wire to form a hook which she then uses to extract a food bucket from a vertical tube (Weir *et al.* 2002). If these creatures don't have the full-blown concept of an object, they have something close to it.

I suspect that part of the trouble is a widespread tendency, prevalent especially among Kant-inspired philosophers, to presuppose that concept possession is unitary: a creature either has full-blown concepts or none at all. If that is taken as a substantive claim it is implausible; even if it is merely a recommendation to restrict the use of the word 'concept' it seems unwarranted. We have excellent reasons to suppose that having concepts, far from being all-or-nothing, involves several related but not necessarily conjoined capacities, themselves subject to variations in degree of strength or practical effect. The assumption that concept possession is unitary plays down continuities between the primitive reasoning of non-linguistic creatures with 'proto-beliefs', and the full-blown beliefs and explicit reasoning of mature language users.

8.4 MORE ON HAVING CONCEPTS

Having a concept cannot be just a matter of reacting distinctively when stimulated in a certain way. If it had been, smoke detectors, pianos, weighing machines, and for that matter pretty well every concrete object whatever would have had concepts. What *is* required for concept possession? In order to count as having concepts, the system must at least acquire information which it can use to control its own behaviour; if it cannot use the information it cannot exercise its concepts, in which case to say it has concepts at all seems misleading: in that sense even pianos have concepts. I conclude that the system must be a decider. That gets us some way, but not far.

Michael Dummett has remarked that, 'for any but the simplest concepts, we cannot explain what it is to grasp them independently of the ability to express them in language' (1993: 97). Nothing I have said commits me to the contrary; but it is vital to notice the difference between Dummett's point and the view that languageless creatures cannot have any concepts at all, even 'the simplest'. I am challenging only the latter view. Dummett suggests what it might be to grasp the concept *square*:

At the very least, it is to be able to discriminate between things that are square and those that are not. Such an ability can be ascribed only to one who will, on occasion, treat square things differently from things that are not square; one way, among many other possible ways, of doing this is to apply the word 'square' to square things and not to others. (1993: 98)

The ability to discriminate square things from others is only one possible component of having the concept *square* among several. The scientists who conducted the bee experiments noted in the last chapter seem to use a concept of concept according to which discriminatory ability is taken to be almost *sufficient* for concept possession.[3] It is worth noting that although this ability is important, and often present, strictly it is neither necessary nor sufficient for having the concept.

It is not sufficient because, as we saw in the last chapter, something with sophisticated discriminatory capacities may still be a reflex system, and such systems lack even the basics of intellectual ability—so much so that they cannot even store information, much less have beliefs or even proto-beliefs. For that reason we can hardly say they have concepts. What we can say they have is certain special capacities which may also come into play in creatures that do have concepts.

The ability to discriminate square things is not necessary for having the concept either. One counter-example to the general claim is Putnam's example of *elm* and *beech*. Even though he cannot discriminate them, he still understands the words because he belongs to a community at least some of whose members

---

[3] Almost. It would not be fair to say they take it to be sufficient, since they demonstrate certain other abilities in the bees. Still, they do claim their experiments show that the bees 'can form and use a concept of sameness . . . and difference . . .' (Giurfa *et al.* 2001: 932). Behavioural psychologists tend to treat this condition as sufficient.

have the necessary expertise (the 'division of linguistic labour': Putnam 1975*b*). But we can go further. It doesn't seem necessary for there to be *anyone* capable of discriminating squares from other things. We might perfectly well have grasped the nature of regular polygons in general, and that a square is a polygon with four equal sides, yet still for some reason have lacked the ability to discriminate between actual squares and other polygons. Another sort of example is concepts introduced in scientific theories, such as *atom, strong force, boson,* where the only way—if any—to discriminate instances may be by means of sophisticated apparatus. In such cases possession of the concept has to include some knowledge of the relevant theory; and perhaps that is all there is to it. I will not pursue this aspect of the topic because I am focusing on simple kinds of deciders. For our purposes we can leave highly theoretical concepts on one side and consider only relatively simple ones.

Take the concept *rabbit,* and consider what is typically involved in its possession by, first, a language-user. As well as (i) the ability to use the word and react appropriately when it is used, there are such capacities as the following: (ii) being able, in normal circumstances, to discriminate rabbits from other things; (iii) being able to recognize rabbits as rabbits; (iv) being able to treat rabbits in whatever way may be appropriate for the concept-user. There is also (v) a set of beliefs about rabbits: where they typically live, how they behave, and so on; and (vi) a set of expectations. We expect rabbits to be furry, with prominent front teeth and long ears; we expect them to lollop about, eat lettuces, and keep away from foxes, and we don't expect them to fly at our throats, attack dogs, or make a roaring noise (which is not to imply that no rabbit could ever do any of those things or lack the properties mentioned).

Reflection on those and related tendencies, abilities, and expectations helps to bring out the point that they may be present in more or less strength and effectiveness. For example, we may be pretty ignorant of the habits of rabbits while still managing to use the word effectively. Reflection also brings out that the absence of (i) (the ability to use a certain bit of language) is compatible with the presence of much else of what constitutes having the concept in question. For that reason alone it seems mistaken to insist on a significant difference in kind between the full-blown concepts possessed by language-users and the concept-like capacities possessed by non-linguistic creatures. This point is reinforced by the fact that the ability to use the bit of language in question seems to depend on possession of most if not all of the other tendencies, abilities, and expectations listed, while the converse does not hold.

This is not to say that behaviour resembling concept-using behaviour implies that the system really has concept-like capacities. Recall the coelenterate hydra, which waves its tentacles above its mouth and shoots out poisonous threads when touched by passing prey. Its behaviour is reminiscent of a more intelligent predatory animal; but even to describe it as having concept-like capacities seems misleading, at least if it is just a built-in triggered reflex system. Such systems hardly qualify as engaging in cognition at all. Contrast shrimps and prawns, which might (so far as I know) be deciders. Fighting other prawns of the same species, but forming pair bonds with individuals, are capacities that call for something approaching conceptualization. As a rough guide, the appropriateness of ascribing to a system the abilities, capacities, and expectations we tend to think of as conceptual seems to go along with the appropriateness of ascribing the basic package to it—not surprisingly, given that the package includes the capacities to interpret, assess, and decide.

There is no need to labour the extremely familiar point that language makes a vast difference. It still doesn't establish a significant difference in kind—a sharp break—between the concepts possessed by language-users and the concept-like capacities of non-linguistic deciders.

Although the six concept-relevant capacities and expectations just noted are distinct, they are closely related. We tend to feel that *having the concept rabbit* is a single something, connecting and explaining possession of all those capacities. I don't need to attempt to decide whether that is right. It is at least partly an empirical matter, and, to repeat, I am not in the business of a priori neuroscience.

8.5 REPRESENTATION

As with the concept of concept, so with the concept of representation, some contexts make it seem desirable to impose strong conditions on what qualifies. My project is not such a context, and the notion of representation is a candidate for de-sophistication.

Given the empirical evidence, there is no point disputing that very humble creatures, even some reflex systems, *do* represent their environments, though in ways that fall short even of the relatively unsophisticated conceptualizing and believing found in languageless deciders. Gallistel (1990) offers numerous examples. Aiming to 'understand learning as a neuronal phenomenon' (1990: 24), he describes the brain as 'representing' an aspect of the environment 'when there is a functioning isomorphism between some aspect of the environment and a brain process that adapts the animal's behavior to it' (15). This conception enables him to describe bees, ants, and other insects, together with more complex animals, as representing aspects of their environments. However, the word 'representation' is also sometimes reserved for more sophisticated states. It will be useful to mention some key points.

A familiar thought about the belief-independence of informational states is this: an experience may represent the world as being a certain way, but we need not believe it is really that way (cf. Evans 1982: 123). My experience of a mirage may represent the presence of water, but I may realize it is only a mirage and not believe there is water there. If in that situation I am right, my experience *mis*represents the world and my belief represents it *truly*; so those are two different types of representation. We might call them respectively 'everyday psychological representation' and 'experiential representation'. They need to be distinguished from a third way of using 'representation', as follows.

(i) Everyday psychological representations

We may be said to represent the world mentally just by having beliefs, desires, hopes, fears, and other 'intentional states' or 'propositional attitudes'. In that sense we can also be said, trivially, to 'have mental representations' of how things are, or how we'd like them to be, or how we fear they might be, and so on. If, like me, you accept that beliefs and other intentional states contribute causally to our behaviour, you are one kind of 'intentional realist', and so not an eliminativist, instrumentalist, or philosophical behaviourist. In that sense only, I am assuming intentional realism throughout this work, believing it to be part of everyday psychology's moderate realism. Many animals represent the world in something like that sense.

Note that in order to be a subject of everyday psychological representations, a system needs something approaching a psychology in the first place. I take it this means it has the basic package: notably the capacities to acquire, store, retrieve, and interpret information, and to initiate and control its behaviour on the basis of information, all in an integrated way.

(ii) Experiential representations

Perceptual experiences represent to us how the world is or might be. For example, my visual experience of the ceiling may represent to me that there's a crack in it. I assume this type of representation too depends on possessing the basic package. But it cannot be assimilated to the first type. We have already noticed one reason: we may not actually believe that the world is the way our perceptual experience represents it as being. Another reason is that experiences are typically transitory, while beliefs and other attitudes may endure. A further reason is that *our* representing the world is a different kind of thing from our *experiences'* doing so. That is so even if, as it happens, both we and our experiences agree in representing the presence of water. Apart from those considerations, beliefs, desires, and other everyday kinds of representation do not necessarily involve experience.

(iii) Realizing representations

Given the minimal intentional realism implied by everyday and experiential representation, our internal states must have *some* properties which provide for it. Other things being equal, it may be on account of brain state b that I believe there are whales in the North Sea. If so, brain state b may be said (other things being equal) to represent—for me—that there are whales in the North Sea. Or again, it may be on account of brain state c that my perceptual experience represents to me that the top line in the Müller-Lyer diagram is longer than the bottom line, so we could say that brain state c represents that feature of my experience. Those are just ways of talking about the 'substrates' or 'realizers' of our intentional states.

Neuropsychologists often talk of representations in that way. A special case of this use of 'representation' is the one noted in Gallistel.

Talk of realizing representations makes no commitments about the form of the realizers: whether for example the information is represented by means of some kind of syntactic structures, as the Language of Thought hypothesis has it; or in some distributed fashion, as connectionism typically holds; or is a matter of adaptive neuronal isomorphism; or just somehow provided for by whatever underlies behavioural dispositions. That there are realizing representations of some kind seems unproblematic.

Although research brings fresh finds almost daily, we still do not know as much as we would like about the nature of realizing representations. That has not prevented philosophers from speculating. A suggestion from Bermúdez invites comment. He says that representations 'should be compositionally structured in such a way that their elements can be constituents of other representational states' (1998: 94). Now, perhaps that condition can be applied to type (i) and type (ii) representations, although if so, it seems to be in a rather strained way. The idea that beliefs or experiences are literally composed from elements is puzzling; but I need not pursue that worry. The point to notice is that Bermúdez' condition implies a very strong claim about the nature and structure of type (iii): realizing representations. It presupposes that at least some realizing representations actually are 'compositionally structured': a strong empirical hypothesis. That is of course an important constituent of Fodor's Language of Thought doctrine, but I find it at best problematic. It seems to rest on the assumption that in order for there to be underlying processes capable of realizing a belief of a certain form (say of the form S is P) those processes must themselves mirror that form. True, we can construct *sentences* of that form; and those sentences may be uttered aloud or written, or privately imaged. When we produce sentences in those ways we may well be having thoughts of that form. But the fact that we can construct sentences of that form doesn't entail that there are parallel items inside our heads. I would argue that it doesn't even amount to empirical support for that hypothesis (*pace* Fodor 1987). (Does the fact that we can construct spiral or other systematically developed patterns from seashells or bricks amount to a good reason to suppose there are such patterns inside our heads?) That hypothesis seems more like a primitive superstition. At one time—before connectionism came along—it seemed plausible. But at one time it seemed plausible that sperms were just tiny human beings. There is no need to pursue the debate over whether the empirical hypothesis that nevertheless there are parallel composite structures in the head is true. For the purpose of explaining deciders, I have no need of that hypothesis.[4]

---

[4] The hypothesis takes us a good way towards the LOT—although substantial further argument would be needed to justify the hefty additional chunk of doctrine that the LOT thesis requires: that the components of the allegedly structured realizing representations actually *stand for*, or are *about*, things. It seems to me that Fodor's (1987) defence of the hypothesis (and Fodor and Pylyshyn's (1988)) presuppose that realizing representations both have compositional structure and stand for things.

8.6 CONCEPTS AND THEORIES

For a decider to be capable of acquiring and storing information, it must in general be able to *combine* concepts. If that is right, a system couldn't have just one concept: it must have either none or several. We might at first have assumed that only one concept was involved in the information conveyed by a simple utterance such as 'Fire', 'Wolf', 'It's raining'. But the point of such utterances is to inform hearers of the *presence* of fire, a wolf, or rain at the place and time in question, rather than, for example, of their existence somewhere or other, somewhen or other. If a cat can have a thought on the lines of 'Dog!', the cat's thought is similarly linked to its here and now. We might—perhaps stretching the point—say it was exploiting something like demonstrative concepts. Related to this requirement (that the item picked out must be assigned to some location in space and time) is the more important requirement that a decider must generally be capable of fitting particular items of information into a broader conception of its field of action and using them to guide its behaviour. Any such conception, however rudimentary, must involve several concepts or concept-like capacities. For one thing, the field of action itself must be capable of displaying different features at different times, so that a conception of it must depend on the decider's having the means to distinguish those different features. (That is so even for the sort of representation commonly described as a 'cognitive map': Gallistel 103–72.) For another, a decider's behaviour has to be capable of being guided by its information, which entails that it must have some sort of conception of what it is doing. (Contrast a smoke alarm. It simply registers that certain chemicals are affecting it when they are, and registers nothing when they aren't. It is not a decider because the information would not be *for it*: could not be used by it.)[5]

Notice by the way that this is one of several places where we can see a significant difference between reflex systems, however sophisticated they may be, and deciders, however primitive. We noticed that dragonflies have favoured perches, which they may change over time. In some sense, therefore, a dragonfly might perhaps be said to have some sort of rudimentary 'conception of its field of action'. But if, as I tentatively suggested, dragonflies are only triggered reflex systems, that description would be misleading. It would imply that the organism as a whole had some grasp of its position in its environment, when, if it really is just an advanced kind of reflex system, that cannot be so. It is a key fact about reflex systems that they provide no basis for the system as a whole to have a grasp of anything.

---

[5] For the general point compare Wittgenstein, 'When we first begin to *believe* anything, what we believe is not a single proposition, it is a whole system of propositions. (Light dawns gradually over the whole.)' (1969: 21, sect.141); also Davidson: 'There are good reasons for not insisting on any particular list of beliefs that are needed if a creature is to wonder whether a gun is loaded. Nevertheless, it is necessary that there be endless interlocked beliefs' (1984: 157).

They are just bundles of reflexes—complicated perhaps, and possibly subject to reconfiguration over time, but no more than reflexes. Keep in mind that the front end of the organism may be extremely sophisticated, as with bees, and that detecting what is in fact the dragonfly's currently favoured perch could be no more than a matter of its being currently apt to have a certain response or fixed action-pattern triggered by distinctive features of the perch. In such cases there need be no processes that could qualify as the creature's own recognition of its position in its environment. With deciders the situation is radically different. In them, given the moderate realism of everyday psychology, there are processes which constitute their assessment of their position in their environment, as well as processes constituting their deciding how to act.

All of that suggests another apparent difficulty for my approach. If every decider must have a 'conception of its field of action', that seems to imply it must have something like a theory of how things are in the world around it. But theories are typically thought of as consisting of *sentences*. Relatedly, having any sort of concept of, for example, *dogs,* seems necessarily to imply having some beliefs or belief-like information about dogs, which in turn starts to approach having a mini-theory of dogs. (Recall the capacities, beliefs and expectations involved in having the concept *rabbit.*) If that is right, languageless creatures cannot be deciders, and my attempt to de-sophisticate the concepts involved in specifying the basic package is misconceived.

Or is there a way out via the Language of Thought hypothesis? Since the only arguments in its favour appear to be philosophical, and to depend on what I regard as the unwarranted assumption that moderate intentional realism commits us to the view that our realizing representations themselves have contents and stand for or refer to things, I would argue against the LOT hypothesis. If my position had to depend on it, it would be shaky.

We can do better: we can appeal to connectionist and neural network models. These offer promising suggestions about how information can be acquired, stored, and processed so as to provide for a system's controlling its own behaviour. According to these models, information storage and processing need not involve anything like formulas or sentences. There is a respectable kind of realism about beliefs and other intentional states which does not require *either* that the sentences by means of which we, the observers, report the contents of such states be mirrored in their internal realizers, *or* that whatever their internal realizers may be, they include items which themselves 'stand for' or 'symbolize' things. Connectionist models are consistent with that moderate, non-Fodorian realism. Although we are no doubt far from having convincing connectionist or neural network models of how a decider might work, those approaches seem at least as capable of doing the necessary work as approaches based on the LOT. Nor is there any special problem about the acquisition, storage, and retrieval of the kind of information about its field of action that a languageless decider might have. We might say it has a *sort* of theory because it has information about a range of different parts of its environment, and (in some sense) about how those items are likely to behave, whether they are good to eat, dangerous, and so on. Connectionist modelling suggests how such information can be processed without sentences.[6]

This is a convenient place to stress another point: the information acquired by languageless creatures—its contents—need not be determinately specifiable in our terms. When we ascribe thoughts, beliefs, and other attitudes to other people, and also when we do so for the case of dumb animals, we perforce do it by means of that-clauses in our own language, hence in terms of our own concepts. In the case of languageless creatures it is doubtful that any such specification could be adequate. Intentional notions like *believing* are tailor-made for their contents to be specified by that-clauses. Anna believes *that there are tigers in India*, Bill hopes *that it won't rain*. Such specifications are most effective if they use only such concepts as their subjects possess. With languageless creatures that project becomes problematic. Even if it is acceptable to say they have concepts at all, their concepts seem unlikely to match ours at all closely. 'If a lion could talk, we could not understand his language' (Wittgenstein 1953: 223). Another familiar remark from Wittgenstein is: 'We say a dog is afraid his master will beat him; but not, he is afraid his master will beat him tomorrow. Why not?' (1953: 166, sect. 650). The concepts *master* and *beat* are not too far removed from concepts a dumb animal might have, while *tomorrow* is. That is no reason to suppose languageless creatures have nothing like concepts. Dogs don't have concepts like *calcium* or *skeletal structure*, but they do seem to recognise other salient features of the sort of bones they actually deal with. This suggests they have something like a concept that we (but not they) might pick out by a concept *quasi-bone*. Perhaps, recalling Gibson's ideas on 'affordances', *gnawable thing* might be more appropriate. At the same time, the fact of treating bones in certain typical ways connects their *quasi-bone* concept with other concepts, such as their *quasi-bury* concept or their *quasi-dig up* concept, and also relates their concepts into simple quasi-theories, such as one roughly to the effect that buried bones tend to stay buried until they are dug up.

Davidson has offered two reasons for the thesis that languageless creatures can't think. One is based on the assumption that 'without speech we cannot make the fine distinctions between thoughts that are essential to the explanations we can sometimes confidently supply' (1984: 163). The last paragraph suggests that, in the case of languageless creatures, we have no right confidently to offer *any* explanations of their behaviour in terms of finely distinguished beliefs or other attitudes. At best such explanations of animal behaviour will be rough. It is therefore no objection to my project that they cannot be made precise.

---

[6] In spite of the fact that some connectionists seem to assume it is up to them to show how connectionism can provide for realizing representations to be symbolic: something attempted by Horgan and Tienson (1996).

8.7 MISTAKEN BELIEFS AND 'PUBLIC NORMS'

Davidson also offers a more elaborate defence of a subtler thesis: that 'a creature cannot have thoughts unless it is an interpreter of the speech of another' (1984: 157). Now, he shows no signs of fudging over the extension of 'thoughts': he doesn't, for example, talk of allowing languageless creatures to have 'proto-thoughts' but not thoughts. So if his argument works it reinstates the dilemma that originally seemed to present such a challenge to my approach: either perceptual consciousness does not require the basic package, or only creatures with language are perceptually conscious.

His argument is not straightforward and he states it compactly. I think (1)–(4) below give a fair impression of its overall shape, though we shall have to consider some further vital ingredients.

(1) For a creature to have thoughts it must have beliefs;
(2) For a creature to have beliefs it must have the concept of belief;
(3) For a creature to have the concept of belief it must belong to a speech community;
(4) Therefore, for a creature to have thoughts it must belong to a speech community (hence be 'an interpreter of the speech of another').

Of course that argument is valid, and premiss (1) seems unexceptionable. On the other hand neither (2) nor (3) is at all obvious; taken together they come close to begging the question. Davidson's grounds for them are epitomized in a couple of brief paragraphs. The first (which I have numbered [i]) chiefly supports (3), the second, [ii], chiefly supports (2):

[i] We have the idea of belief only from the role of belief in the interpretation of language, for as a private attitude it is not intelligible except as an adjustment to the public norm provided by language. It follows that a creature must be a member of a speech community if it is to have the concept of belief. . . .

[ii] Can a creature have a belief if it does not have the concept of belief? It seems to me it cannot, and for this reason. Someone cannot have a belief unless he understands the possibility of being mistaken, and this requires grasping the contrast between truth and error—true belief and false belief. But this contrast, I have argued, can emerge only in the context of interpretation, which alone forces us to the idea of an objective, public truth. (1984: 170; see also his 1982: 480)

The assumption that it was through the use of language that we acquired the concept of belief has some appeal, and I won't challenge it here. But the second clause of the first sentence in [i] comes as a surprise. Why should belief be intelligible only 'as an adjustment to the public norm provided by language'? Once we have acquired the concept of belief we have little difficulty applying it to languageless creatures. And clearly, even if we *acquired* that concept via language, that doesn't warrant the claim that only creatures with language can *have* beliefs, any more than the fact that we acquired the concept of languagelessness through language entails that only creatures with language can be languageless. Not that Davidson commits that fallacy. He seems to regard his assertion that belief is intelligible only as an adjustment to the public norms of language as a *reason* for asserting that we acquire the concept only through interpreting language. Which is strange, since it puts almost the whole weight of his argument on that assertion—when it is unacceptably close to its conclusion.

What I find most problematic about Davidson's argument is premiss (2). I concede immediately that if believing entails the ability to *consider* one's beliefs, then it entails having the concept of belief. If believing necessarily involves conscious belief-formation and belief-revision, it involves the ability to think of beliefs as beliefs, hence possession of the concept. But conscious belief-formation and the ability to consider one's beliefs seem to be abilities that can be developed only by a creature that already has beliefs, very likely only when it has acquired some language. It is at least plausible that human infants acquire beliefs before they have acquired language, becoming able to consider and consciously revise their beliefs only after they have been having them for some time.

Davidson insists that 'someone cannot have a belief unless he understands the possibility of being mistaken'. I suggest that goes too far. Understanding the *possibility* of being mistaken seems inseparable from being able to *consider* one's beliefs, as if one could survey various possibilities and choose among them. As I have said, that capacity seems to be acquired, if ever, only after having acquired the bare capacity to have beliefs. If that is right, Davidson has not justified premiss (2).

But he has a point. It would seem too strong to say that a creature had beliefs if it could not on occasions, and in some sense however limited, *tell* that it was mistaken, or at least that there was a lack of fit between its expectations or (proto) beliefs and the way things actually were.[7] A decider surely needs to be able in some way or other to tell when it has got things wrong—even if it cannot conceptualize the situation in that sophisticated way. A cat waiting for a mouse outside the hole it has driven it into has something like a belief about where the mouse is; and when the mouse shows up somewhere else, the cat recognizes, however dimly, that it has failed. Or consider a dog which on its own initiative has fetched its master's walking boots and then finds its master settling down to watch TV. In such situations an animal's behaviour tends to show it distinguishes between how the world actually is and how it had thought it was. I am not saying such behaviour alone could clinch our characterization of a creature as a decider. Conceivably cats and dogs are just complex reflex systems, though I doubt it.[8] The point is that genuine deciders do need to be able to recognize something like a failure of fit between the world and their expectations or beliefs.

[7] Lowe says that 'at the very least' the subject must be 'capable of taking a critical stance towards' its presumed beliefs, and that '. . . to qualify as genuine beliefs the deliverances [of the faculty concerned] must be open to *correction* by the subject'. He concedes animals have 'informational states' falling short of belief (1996: 120).

[8] Keep in mind that cascaded systems, where the outputs of one reflex feed into other reflexes, do not qualify as reflex systems in my sense (6.6). Perhaps not only dogs and cats, but we ourselves, are such systems.

To say that is not to concede the heavy assumptions Davidson needs. Being able to detect a lack of fit between its expectations or beliefs and the way things turn out does not seem to require the creature to belong to a speech community, or to be subject to any 'public norms' at all. The world is perfectly capable of forcing a languageless creature to notice that it has got things wrong, even when it cannot express its situation in those terms.

8.8   THE BASIC PACKAGE AND RATIONALITY

One consideration which seems to have influenced the view that animals can't have beliefs is that believing, as Evans puts it, 'is connected with ... the notion of *judgement*, and so, also, connected with the notion of *reasons*' (1982: 124). I argued earlier that his approach does not do justice to the fact that having concepts—hence beliefs—is not a unitary all-or-nothing matter but complex, with scope for variations in degree along different dimensions. Allowing for those points about concepts and beliefs, what about judgement and rationality? Have they been overlooked in my account of the basic package so far? What sort of rationality, if any, does the basic package involve?

The package includes the system's capacity to choose or decide how to behave, and to control its own behaviour, given its current goals. If we think first of naturally evolved organisms, those capacities will have tended to preserve the species, and in general to have preserved the lives of individuals. Prawns capture passing larvae and hide from predatory fish; cats catch mice and avoid dogs. In general an evolved organism's behaviour will tend to help it achieve its goals. If a creature's behaviour is controlled by itself on the basis of its information, and tends to help it achieve its goals, then that gives a minimal sense in which it may be said to be rational. The basic package does not demand more rationality than that.

If rationality is taken to require the ability to reason explicitly, or to express reasons, it requires language. But our earlier considerations suggest that nothing in the basic package imposes that requirement, in spite of the influence of Evans's suggestions to the contrary. If indeed 'rational sensitivity comes only with language mastery', as Bermúdez has asserted (1998: 71), then deciders can do without it. Again, McDowell is right to say that 'A mere animal does not weigh reasons and decide what to do' (1994: 115); but the basic package does not entail rationality and conscious decision of that sort. It demands no more by way of rationality than is inevitably involved in being able to acquire and use information about the environment.

8.9   DECIDERS MIGHT BE SUBJECTS OF
EXPERIENCE WITHOUT BEING PERSONS

A decider is a subject of various relatively undemanding psychological descriptions, such as 'aims to catch that mouse', 'controls its behaviour on the basis of stored and incoming information'. Further, I am inclined to think that such animals as cats, dogs, birds, and mice are subjects of conscious perceptual experience even though they lack beliefs and concepts of the sophisticated kind possessed only by language users. For reasons to be discussed in the next chapter I don't think deciders are *necessarily* conscious subjects; but I see no reason why they should not be so in fact. That may suggest a further line of objection.

This would be that only persons can be subjects of such descriptions. Jonathan Lowe in his book *Subjects of Experience* states that he takes '*persons* or *selves* . . . to be subjects of experience . . .'; and that by a 'self' he means 'a possible subject of first-person reference and subject of first-person thoughts: a being which can think that *it itself* is thus and so and can identify itself as the unique subject of certain thoughts and experiences and as the unique agent of certain actions' (1996: 5). Clearly not all deciders are persons in that sense.

Although Lowe appears to leave logical room for subjects of experience that are not persons, and concentrates on human subjects, the idea that only persons in something like the strong sense he explains can be subjects of experience is at least suggested, if not explicitly defended, in some recent literature.[9] I suggest the considerations in this chapter undermine that assumption. I suspect it is only a preference for reserving the words 'belief', 'concept', and their relatives for the strong senses noted earlier that leads to insistence on a correspondingly strong sense of 'experience'.

For similar reasons there is a sense, if still only a minimal one, in which any decider also qualifies as having its own perspective or point of view on the world. By that I mean that, at any moment when it is interpreting incoming sensory information, assessing its situation, or making decisions, it is doing so (a) from a particular spatiotemporal location; (b) in such a way that its sensory information bears on it as it is in that location; (c) it is at least capable of retaining for some time, however short, memories of its spatiotemporal track through its environment. (a) and (b) are obvious implications of the basic package. (c) is also an implication of the basic package (though perhaps less obvious) since the ability to guide one's behaviour depends on the ability to compare one's current situation with one's situation in the recent past.[10]

8.10 THE BASIC PACKAGE AND 'NON-CONCEPTUAL CONTENT'

According to Evans, the fact that languageless creatures lack a concept-exercising and reasoning system (CERS) entails that the contents of their informational

---

[9] See for example J. Campbell 1994; McDowell 1994; Hurley 1997.
[10] This minimal construal of 'perspective' and 'point of view' contrasts strongly with the Kantian conception offered by Peter Strawson (1966) and usefully developed by Bermúdez (1998: 163–92).

states are 'non-conceptual'. He applies this notion to the informational states they acquire through perception, distinguishing sharply between creatures with a CERS (us, and any other language-users there may be) and those without one. I have been arguing that such a sharp distinction is at best misleading and risks distorting our conception of the cognitive capacities of languageless creatures. Concept possession, even the full-blown kind enjoyed by language users, is not a unitary matter: there is a range of capacities and tendencies that can count towards possession of a given complex of concepts, most of which can be possessed to a greater or lesser degree. For that reason I have been using the word 'concept' in a way that allows languageless deciders to have concepts. However, the notion of non-conceptual content continues to provoke debate; more to the point, the assumptions and frameworks in terms of which it is discussed are relevant to our present interests and need some consideration.

The friends of non-conceptual content start from the claim that perceptual experiences have *representational content*—'content that is evaluable as correct or as incorrect' (Peacocke 2001: 240). That is hard to dispute, given we can say a state whose content is that p is correct just in case p, otherwise incorrect. Now, since it seems that many very humble creatures are capable of representing their environment, I cannot consistently deny that *some* content describable as perceptual is in a natural enough sense non-conceptual. However, it is significant that many of these creatures are not deciders. Dragonflies, bees, and other insects may fall short of being deciders, yet still represent their environment. A crucial consideration is that the information is not *for them* in the way such information is for deciders: it is not for them because it does not guide their behaviour via interpretation, assessment, and decision-making. It affects their behaviour in other ways. So although I can agree that there is such a thing as non-conceptual content, since it can be said to be the content of information that affects the behaviour of many non-deciders, I still have reservations about the notion of non-conceptual content when applied to deciders. This is because I see difficulties in the idea that information which is for the system, as some information must be for deciders, could somehow *fail* to be conceptualized. I will return to this topic in the next chapter. Meanwhile let us consider the reasoning which underlies use of the notion. There are two related but distinct routes along which the friends of non-conceptual content explain their position.

One route starts from the high line about concepts. Peacocke for example takes *conceptual* content to be 'content of a kind that can be the content of judgment and belief' (2001: 243). Given that assumption it seems that if perceptual experiences have contents, then either languageless creatures don't have perceptual experiences, or else the contents of their experiences are non-conceptual. Since the first alternative is hard to take, that is a reason for concluding that at least some perceptual contents are non-conceptual. The suggestion then is that (a) perceptual contents are non-conceptual because *they can be enjoyed regardless of whether the perceiver has concepts suitable for specifying them, or indeed any concepts.*

The other route emphasizes the richness of perceptual experience. When we consider the detailed contents of experiences, it is hard to see how they can be completely captured by means of concepts. How do you get your concepts round the exact shapes of clouds, for example, or the exact character of the lion's roar? So we arrive at the idea that perceptual contents are too rich to be completely conceptualizable: (b) perceptual contents are non-conceptual *because they could not possibly be captured by any concepts.* (See for example Carruthers 2000: 68.)

Conceivably some contents that were non-conceptual according to (a) might not also be so according to (b). It is consistent with (a) that all perceptual contents capable of being enjoyed by conceptless creatures *could* be brought under suitable concepts; but that is obviously inconsistent with (b). It also seems possible that, conversely, (b) could hold while (a) did not. Perhaps (b) holds even though the unconceptualizable contents it envisages could not be enjoyed except by creatures with *some* concepts. However, although the frameworks in terms of which we might wish to pursue the debate about non-conceptual content are obviously relevant to my purposes in this work, pursuing the debate itself, I am glad to say, is not. My aim in this and the preceding two chapters has been to explain and clarify what it is for something to be a decider, and in particular what is involved in the acquisition and use of perceptual information. If we can find informative necessary and sufficient conditions for that, it is all I need. I see no reason also to engage in the project of finding convenient means of *specifying* whatever the information may be: specifying its content. For my purposes that project is dispensable. There is even less reason to engage in the further project of devising means of specifying the contents of perceptual experiences that dovetail into some particular conception of how to do semantics.

It is just as well that there is no need here to seek ways of specifying the information acquired by languageless creatures, since it encounters two obvious difficulties. One is the truism that in general our human, language-dependent conceptual scheme is unlikely to mesh in with the multifarious conceptual organizations of languageless creatures: their information will not necessarily be specifiable in our terms. The other is that by definition languageless creatures could not offer or consider specifications of the contents of their own thoughts, so that our efforts in that direction would lack a constraint which makes it less problematic for our own case. Contrast the case of intelligent language-using aliens. The aliens' conceptual scheme might be largely incongruent with ours; but at least they would be in a position to consider—indeed they would actually be producing—specifications of the contents of their thoughts and judgements.

You might suggest that if the contents of a creature's thoughts or judgements cannot be specified, then it becomes doubtful whether it has any. I see no good reason to accept that suggestion. We can generally tell, even with quite humble creatures such as cats or chickens, *that* they have received information relating to a certain area of their activities. We don't share their concepts, but we can know they have just acquired life-preserving information; for example we can know that the cat has just made a (proto-)judgement roughly on the lines of 'Mouse there'.

8.11   THE CONTENTS OF DECIDERS' INFORMATIONAL STATES

Deciders acquire information, so some of their states have content. I have just argued that there is no need to be concerned to specify just what is the information they acquire; but it may appear problematic that they acquire information at all. What is it, on my account, for their perceptual and other informational states to have content? Am I committed to one or another of the current theories? Do I maintain that these contents are to be explained in terms of causal covariation, or conceptual roles, or teleofunctionally, or what? Two guiding principles need to be kept in mind. One is that it is the system as a whole which has the information that interests us. The other is that there is no reason to presuppose that some single relation constitutes aboutness. I will say something about each principle separately, although they are connected.

It is the whole system that has the relevant information

As a number of examples in Chapter 7 illustrated, what concerns us is not any old bits of information which get into a system somehow, but the system's *own* information: information which is for it, which it can use. Plenty of other sorts of information may make a difference to the system's behaviour. For example, in vertebrates the vestibular (sub)system receives and processes information which helps to keep the animal in equilibrium; but normally that information (about pressure on regions of the feet, for example) is not for the animal as a whole. On the other hand, perceptual information about potential prey may serve as a basis for the animal's choices of course of action: such information is for the animal as a whole.

There is no single relation of aboutness

Here I go along with an approach suggested by Wittgenstein. He urged that there is no single relation which constitutes a word's having reference (1953, sects. 10, 13–15). It is consistent with that approach to hold that there is no single relation which constitutes a creature's information being *about* this or that. The hydra emits poisonous tentacles which paralyse its prey, which it then draws into its mouth and swallows. Assuming this organism is some kind of reflex system rather than a decider, it doesn't have information about anything, so, in particular, has none about its prey. Still, it has built-in patterns of behaviour which enable it to deal appropriately with its prey; and I suggest that that is a useful baseline for thinking about aboutness. The hydra's patterns of behaviour are in a minimal sense directed at its prey; and we might perhaps say its behaviour is 'about' its prey. Similarly much of the behaviour of bees is directed at, and minimally about, nectar or pollen. With deciders, much of whose behaviour results from the system as a whole choosing this or that course of action, such behaviour may be more or less appropriate for it to achieve its current goals. When in the course of its attempts to achieve its goals it deals with this or that feature of its environment more or less appropriately, we can say that its information, as well as the behaviour that information helps to guide, is 'about' those environmental features. If the cat pounces on the mouse it has been stalking, the information which helped to guide its behaviour was about the mouse.

There are surely 'realizing representations', some of which are likely to be particularly relevant to particular contentful perceptions or thoughts. In the cat, for example, there may well be a particular complex of neurones activated just when it is dealing with mice. But as we noticed earlier in connection with conditions for a state to be representational, the further assumption that the realizing representation for a given thought must itself have something like the structure of that thought's linguistic expression seems unjustified. It may be objected that unless the realizing representations have such structure, and unless in addition the elements of the structures are appropriately related to the things and kinds represented, then it is impossible to understand how representation is possible at all. But that objection depends for its appeal on other heavy presuppositions identified earlier.

8.12 CONCLUSION

I have had two aims in this chapter. One was to make clear that the framework invoked by the basic package does not have to be as sophisticated as is presupposed by some currently popular ways of talking about concept possession and beliefs. The other was to show, through examination of the reasoning commonly used to support Evans-inspired assumptions, how the idea of the basic package affords a useful alternative. The 'no decider without language' objection depends on unwarranted assumptions. To put it crudely, it overlooks the possibility of behaving systems intermediate between reflex systems and language users, and imposes excessively strong conditions on the ability to acquire and use information.

The main components of my framework are now in position. But for perceptual consciousness a further condition needs to be identified.

9

Direct Activity

The basic package is necessary for perceptual consciousness, or so I have argued. For reasons to be considered shortly I doubt whether it is also sufficient; but that issue is secondary. The main task of this chapter will be to consider more directly what perceptual consciousness requires. Incoming perceptual information must be *directly active,* a notion that will need careful explanation.

9.1 THE BASIC PACKAGE, CONTROL, AND CONSCIOUSNESS

A decider is by definition able to control its behaviour on the basis of stored and incoming information. It can also interpret information, assess its situation, and make decisions, in however rudimentary a way. Assuming its information is about its environment, could it do those things if it were not perceptually conscious? It is quite natural to assume that the basic package is not only necessary for perceptual consciousness but also sufficient. An influential thought here is that control of behaviour (genuine control, not the simulacrum of it shown by some reflex systems) involves deciding what to do on the basis of stored and incoming information—when deciding what to do includes those moment-to-moment modifications that are normally necessary. We may well wonder how such modifications would be possible without conscious perception of the changing scene of action. But that conclusion is too quick.[1]

Think of situations where someone else is guiding your actions—for example when you are reversing your car. Your friend calls out, 'Three feet to go ... two feet ... two inches ... stop!' That information may enable you to avoid hitting a low wall out of sight from where you are sitting. In this situation you don't need actually to see the wall (whether consciously or unconsciously) since you have another source of information. Now consider another possibility: that for some sensory modality, *all* the perceptual information you receive from that

---

[1] Not, however, on account of zombies! Zombists are right that the basic package is not sufficient for perceptual consciousness, but wrong about the reason. The sole-pictures argument shows that zombies are impossible; so their alleged possibility doesn't prove that the basic package is not sufficient for perceptual consciousness.

source comes in unconsciously, but you are able to use it either when you search your memory, or when it just spontaneously pops into your thoughts. Perception without awareness (subliminal perception) and blindsight seem close to this possibility, so it is not too far-fetched. With those examples in mind we must recognize, it seems, that possibly a decider could control its behaviour on the basis of unconscious perceptual information. If that is right, the basic package has not been shown to be logically sufficient for perceptual consciousness.

That reasoning falls well short of showing that the basic package is not sufficient for the system to be capable of *some* form of conscious perception. At most it shows that the package is not sufficient for conscious perception *of the scene of action*. When your friend is guiding you as you back your car, you consciously hear the spoken directions. Also, the subjects in experiments with subliminal perception are normal human beings, and seem to need to be perceptually conscious in at least some respects if they are to be able to act on the unconscious information they supposedly receive. Blindsight subjects, too, tend to be normal conscious *visual* perceivers except for their 'blind fields'. As for the idea that unconsciously received perceptual information might just 'pop into your thoughts', it is hard to make sense of this unless the popping consists of episodes closely resembling the conscious perception of spoken or written sentences, or perhaps of images. It remains unclear whether a system with no conscious perceptual experience at all could still receive perceptual information in accordance with the basic package. However, there is no need for me to take a stand on this issue.

9.2 WHY THE BASIC PACKAGE SEEMS INSUFFICIENT FOR PERCEPTUAL CONSCIOUSNESS

In blindsight the subject has to be forced to guess what is currently out there but not consciously seen. In subliminal perception the subject might or might not be able to tell what information has arrived subliminally. And all of us, when there is a question of what we saw or heard or tasted at noon yesterday, or an hour or a minute ago, normally have to recollect, to summon up, the relevant information. We have received and retained it; but it is not immediately 'operative', so to speak. It isn't 'forced' upon us, it doesn't directly affect us now; in order to guide our actions it has to be 'called up'. These considerations suggest that there could be an organism all of whose sensory information never affected it directly at the time it was coming in, and could therefore only be used either by being called up, or in some other indirect way.

You might wonder whether such organisms actually exist. It seems unlikely, since the imagined situation appears to conflict with the evolutionary point of sense perception. Plausibly its point is to provide the organism with instantly utilizable information about events in its current environment *regardless* of whether it chooses to summon up this or that particular item. Consider an ordinary rabbit.

It seems to have the basic package and to be capable of sense perception, though its capacities to assess its situation and make decisions need not be very well developed. Assuming that is right, the rabbit perceives things that potentially help or harm it without having to perform any act of summoning up its memories. If there are lettuces in the field ahead of it, it can go and eat them without hesitation. If a fox appears, the rabbit spots it. If the fox is a long way off it may continue eating. If it is close, it stops eating and bounds away. The decision is up to it. But now imagine the situation if, instead of sensory information forcing itself upon the rabbit, the information was not utilizable unless called up, or unless it just popped up (whatever that means), or had some other indirect effect. Such a creature, a 'rabbitoid', would be at a huge disadvantage compared with a real rabbit. That is so regardless of the mechanisms by which information was caused to pop up, especially if this were purely random. Even if there were some kind of sub-personal filtering and triggering of what popped up, the animal would still not be able to exercise its own judgement, as the normal rabbit can when faced with the fox in the distance and the enticing food nearby.

You might suggest that the rabbitoid could continually be interrogating its memory on the lines of 'What's in front of me now?', 'Where's my forepaw now?', and so on. But the more closely we pursue this idea the clearer it becomes that the rabbitoid's situation would be extremely hazardous compared with ordinary rabbits. It could not decide how to avoid dangers or go for gains as promptly and effectively as a real rabbit. Nor could it control its current behaviour without having to bombard its memory with a constant stream of queries. That would be a distraction from its pursuit of its goals. We might wonder whether information in the rabbitoid's memory could somehow enable it to control its behaviour without having to do anything to bring that about.[2] But that would be, if anything, even more damaging to the creature's prospects. That is immediately obvious in the special case where the stored information becomes active at random. If you're trying to escape a fox you need information about its and your *current* positions, not random data about, say, where the nearest lettuces are. The only remotely useful arrangement would be one by which stored information became active when the creature needed it; perhaps via some kind of association of ideas. But that would still lack the enormous benefits real rabbits—and, it seems, all actual deciders— get from information forcing itself upon them when they don't realize they may need it, and haven't been thinking about what they might need. (The rabbitoid is being stalked by a fox: nothing prompts it to wonder whether it might be about to be attacked.)

Imagine we managed to construct an artificial system with the basic package. It looks as if the constructor would have the option of leaving out a feature that we and actual rabbits have: by which incoming perceptual information is not just

---

[2] See Ned Block's 'superblindsighter' (1995: 233), to be discussed in the next chapter (9.13), and the discussions of blindsight and automatism at 10.8 and 10.9.

acquired and stored, but forces itself upon us as it comes in, without our having to call it up or wait for it to somehow turn up. On the face of it (although it is too easy to go wildly wrong in such speculation) the design task would be different if the system only required the basic package and not that extra feature. Surely additional work would be required if incoming information had to be instantly utilizable. Conscious perceptual experience at any rate requires the incoming perceptual information to be instantly utilizable—even if instant utilizability is not logically sufficient for conscious perception.

So I am inclined to think that the basic package is not sufficient for being a subject of conscious perceptual experience. The speculative evolutionary considerations glanced at in connection with the rabbit suggest that species with the basic package but without the additional feature are unlikely to have survived. True, in the case of naturally evolved organisms the basic package may still be nomologically sufficient for consciousness. But that is beside the point, since even if true, it does not explain what it is for something to be conscious.

9.3 THE EVANS-TYE MODEL

It will be useful to contrast the account of perceptual consciousness I shall be setting out with the one offered by Evans and modified by Michael Tye. Evans's idea was that being a subject of conscious perceptual experiences requires: (a) the capacity to receive sensory information; (b) the capacity to think and reason, which depends on a 'concept-exercising and reasoning system'. The former capacity results in 'internal states which have a content by virtue of their phylogenetically more ancient connections with the motor system'; their content is 'non-conceptual'. Since many languageless creatures receive sensory information, they too have these states. However, Evans's view is that their inability to conceptualize prevents them from being perceptually conscious: what makes the difference between them and us is that in our case these states 'also serve as input to the concept-exercising and reasoning system'.

Judgements are then *based upon* ... these internal states; when this is the case we can speak of the information being 'accessible' to the subject, and indeed, of the existence of conscious experience. (1982: 227)

This idea is uncomfortably reminiscent of the Cartesian Theatre model of perception, according to which having perceptual experiences is a matter of the thinking subject confronting a special kind of mental object. As Ryle (1949) pointed out, the Cartesian model cannot do its explanatory job. If perceiving external objects requires something like the internal perception of internal mental objects, how can such internal perception itself be explained without positing further levels of internal perception of additional internal mental objects, hence a vicious infinite regress? If no further levels of internal objects are needed, why the first level? If on the other hand the relation between thinking subject and mental objects is not like perception, what is it? The Cartesian Theatre model provides no satisfactory way to deal with that dilemma. Conscious perception cannot, it seems, be explained in terms of a thinking subject facing internal objects, a sort of ethereal TV show. Can Evans's account avoid that objection?

The kernel of his model consists of, on one side, an array of non-conceptually contentful internal states, and on the other the concept-exercising and reasoning system (CERS), making judgements 'based upon' those internal states. A close analogy would seem to be someone reporting on a picture they are looking at. The trouble is that if that analogy were appropriate the model would not work. The person reporting on the picture not only sees it, but sees it in its full rich detail, including aspects they may not choose to put into words. And they *have* to see its rich detail, otherwise they are not in a position to choose which aspects to report on: if they couldn't see the details there might as well not be any. In this analogy the details of the picture correspond to the non-conceptually contentful internal states in Evans's model. To press the analogy, how can the CERS be conceived of as 'seeing' or otherwise apprehending those non-conceptually contentful internal states that are put into it? Conceiving of the situation on those lines would require the CERS to have something like its own sense organs: not just a system for conceptualizing sensory inputs, but a full-blown perceiver. According to the analogy, only if the CERS were such a perceiver would it be able to make selections from among the unconceptualized inputs. I don't say consideration of this analogy absolutely demolishes Evans's model. The point is that the analogy is natural, yet according to it the model fails to do what it sets out to do because it reinstates the original problem. The CERS was supposed to do something like perceiving the non-conceptually contentful internal states that are its input; but the analogy with reporting on a picture exposes the fact that the model offers no way for *un*conceptualized details to have any impact on the CERS. Such details might as well be absent.

If the model is not to be conceived on the lines of that analogy, what makes the unconceptualized states 'inputs' to the CERS? *Without* something like perception it is mysterious that they are inputs to it at all, rather than having no more relevance to perception than, say, states of the digestive system. It is perfectly intelligible that there should be non-conceptually contentful internal states which get inside the organism *somehow* while remaining outside the CERS: that situation seems to be illustrated by the perceptual systems of certain insects. The difficulty is to understand how the CERS could be in a position to *pick out* states which are then to be conceptualized. Worse, it is a mystery how the CERS could get to grips with those unconceptualized 'inputs' at all; the model seems to make no provision for it to stand in any relevant relation to them. So Evans's own version of the CERS model faces a dilemma. If the CERS has to be conceived of as itself a perceiver, the model fails not only because it is vulnerable to the standard regress objection to the Cartesian Theatre, but because it leaves the existence of 'unreported' details impossible to explain. If on the other hand the CERS is not a perceiver, it is insulated from its so-called 'inputs' to such an extent that it has nothing it can conceptualize, and fails for that reason.

It is common to describe perceptual inputs as 'available' to, or 'poised' for, further processing (Block 1995; Carruthers 1996; Tye 1995: 2000; Botterill and Carruthers 1999). Is that a way out of the dilemma? Can Evans's model explain conscious experience as a matter of non-conceptualized inputs being *available* to the CERS? But 'available' is a weasel word, not even a suitable metaphor.[3] It fails in two respects. First, it doesn't discriminate between conscious and unconscious processes. Each of us has vast amounts of information that is 'available' for thinking about (about what we were doing yesterday, for example; about historical and geographical facts, about people we know) but hardly any of it is currently conscious. Much of that information could also be described as 'poised'—it is so easily accessible to us—yet that doesn't make it conscious.

The second consideration is that the metaphor of a state's being 'available' or 'poised' fails to discriminate between the actual and the dispositional. Conscious perceptual experiences are actual events. When you are listening to a saxophone solo or seeing a buzzard flying overhead, something is *actually* going on inside you. It cannot just be a matter of what is merely capable of being accessed, or poised to do something. Any adequate philosophical account of perceptual consciousness must do justice to the actuality of conscious experience.

Michael Tye's account of perceptual consciousness shares the broad pattern of Evans's model. He too has 'non-conceptual' representations facing a close relative of the CERS. Non-conceptual map-like representations are produced by the sensory systems, and the 'conceptual system' (or 'cognitive' or 'belief/desire system') processes them. He says:

> The claim that the contents relevant to phenomenal character must be *poised* is to be understood as requiring that these contents attach to the (fundamentally) maplike output representations of the relevant sensory modules and stand ready and in position to make a direct impact on the belief/desire system. ... they supply the inputs for certain cognitive processes whose job it is to produce beliefs (or desires) directly from the appropriate non-conceptual representations, *if* attention is properly focused and the appropriate concepts are possessed. (1995: 138; cf. Tye 2000: 62)

This account is not threatened by the counter-example of unconscious but 'available' *beliefs* because Tye's perceptual representations are contrasted with beliefs in four respects: they are sensory representations while beliefs are not; they are outside the 'cognitive system' while beliefs are inside it; they are non-conceptual while beliefs are conceptual; they are 'appropriately poised' while beliefs are not (loc. cit.).

However, his 'PANIC' model (for Poised Abstract Non-conceptual Intentional Contents) still seems vulnerable to the other objection. The metaphor of contents

---

[3] Recall Evans's use of 'accessible' in the quotation above. I used 'present' in the same weaselly way in Kirk 1992.

'standing ready and in position to make a direct impact on the belief/desire system' implies they do not always actually make such an impact. So how can that system take any account of them at all? They threaten to be unconscious. This was essentially the same difficulty as undermined Evans's model. Rather than pursuing the discussion of how the Evans-Tye model might be defended against such attacks I will carry on with the development of my own account, contrasting it where appropriate with the Evans-Tye model.

9.4   CONCEPTS AND THE ACQUISITION OF INFORMATION

One strand of thinking in connection with non-conceptual content goes as follows: 'It would be absurd to suppose that each possible pattern of sensory information that a system is capable of receiving is captured by its own special concept. We can't have a concept for each shade of colour, each creaking sound, and so on.' Such reflections might persuade us that we need to distinguish between a system's merely acquiring or registering some chunk of perceptual information, and its bringing the information under a concept. Perhaps we ought to consider the suggestion that *registering* and *conceptualizing* are two distinct functions. Impressed by that idea we might go on to infer that it must be possible for a system to acquire or register perceptual information without conceptualizing it, as the Evans-Tye account envisages. This might make room for 'poisedness'. Let us examine that suggestion, remembering that we are working within a de-sophisticated framework where all deciders conceptualize, however primitively.

Can registering and conceptualizing be two distinct functions? We may seem to have examples. Any reflex system, hard-wired so that sensory inputs directly caused fixed sequences of behaviour, could be said to acquire or register perceptual information without conceptualizing it. The registration of a given stimulus would then consist merely in its triggering whatever reflex behaviour the system was hard-wired to produce. The artificial giant, which is not a reflex system, also acquires information without (itself) conceptualizing it. Unfortunately 'registration' in such cases is irrelevant to understanding perceptual consciousness. Neither reflex systems nor the giant are deciders; a fortiori they are not candidates for perceptual consciousness. The key consideration is that the information supposed to be embodied in the form of 'unconceptualized inputs' must be *for the system*. There is no problem over information just getting into a system if it is not for the system, or if the system itself does not have to conceptualize it. This is true even when the information in question has effects on behaviour, so long as those effects are not produced via the system's own interpretation, assessment, and decision-making (example: information which gets into the vestibular system and affects balancing movements). The problem is to understand how information which *is* for the system, and therefore usable by it, could be registered without being conceptualized.

In order for a decider to use perceptual information in controlling its behaviour, it must among other things be able to take account of changes in its environment over time. Suppose it is a cat, dependent on mice for a living. Here it comes, chasing a mouse. As the mouse scampers away successively different patterns of light fall on the cat's retinas. To have any chance of following and catching its prey, the cat's cognitive processes must group these different light-patterns together as all connected with the prey; and if the mouse happens to squeak, those sound-patterns too had better be linked up with the same prey. Such groupings and linkings-up seem to be precursors of conceptualization. (The engineering problems they involve are of course extremely familiar to neuropsychologists.) However, they are not special to deciders. There is no reason why reflex systems, provided they have sufficiently complex front ends, should not engage in those activities. Up to this point, then, the cat might as well be a reflex system rather than a decider, in which case the information is not for it. But I am assuming that the cat *is* a decider, and that the information it gets through its senses *is* for it, which means it interprets the information, assesses its situation, makes decisions, and controls its behaviour on the basis of those activities. Given those assumptions, how can whatever perceptual information is *for the cat* escape conceptualization? What could registration be if it did not involve the conceptualization of incoming information? Those considerations, though not decisive, nudge us towards the conclusion that no decider could acquire or register perceptual information without bringing it under concepts, if only in rudimentary ways: no registration without conceptualization.

You might think we could sidestep that conclusion by noting that the perceptual information in question could be tucked away in the system's memory as it was acquired. But that would only defer the problem. The information would still have to be usable by the system. The question recurs: how could that happen without some degree of conceptualization? Unless the use of a given remembered item is linked to conceptualizing it, there seems no possibility of retrieval. You might suggest it could consist in something like images popping up spontaneously. But how would those spontaneously produced memory-images themselves be manageable without some degree of conceptualization, when subjectively similar perceptual experiences are not? We still seem driven to conclude that there can be no registration without conceptualization. However, that would be too quick and too simple. To see why, we need to consider a further question. Is the acquisition or registration of information just a limiting case of conceptualization, or something different in kind?

9.5 REGISTRATION AND CONCEPTUALIZATION

We can use 'registration' for a decider's reception or acquisition of perceptual information about details of the passing scene even when that information is not necessarily brought under what we *ordinarily* think of as concepts. Just now I am in that sense registering subtle variations in the colour of the old brickwork opposite my window, and of the outlines of the bricks themselves, even though I can't even think how to bring those features under my ordinary concepts. The details seem too rich—unless, perhaps, I managed to set up a special system for dividing the visual field into pixels, and learned to use a scheme for assigning colours to each position in a huge grid. In the ordinary sense (closely associated with the idea that having a concept is knowing a word) we don't have concepts for each discriminable shade of colour, or each pattern of surf breaking on the beach, or each possible voice timbre, each smell, and so on. There certainly seems to be a contrast between the way all those fine perceptible details come in, and the activity of conceptualization. That makes it tempting to think of registration as providing the 'matter' for conceptualization (which seems to be how Kant distinguished concepts and 'intuitions'). But the temptation must be resisted. The picture of raw perception supplying the materials on which concepts are exercised is too close to the Cartesian Theatre. Two factors make the picture more attractive than it ought to be.

One is that we actually do exercise our ordinary concepts on materials supplied by perception. Nor is that activity confined to puzzle situations, as when we don't know whether the shadowy shape ahead of us is a rabbit or a clump of grass. We are constantly conceptualizing and reconceptualizing things we can see and hear perfectly well. However, as I will try to make clear, it is a mistake to assume that seeing, hearing, smelling, and so on are totally concept-free: do not involve even the rudimentary concept-like capacities of languageless deciders.

The other misleading factor is that we tend to assume that concept possession is restricted to those full-blown concepts we can use in explicit reasoning. Such concepts tend to be thought of as more genuinely concept-like. But that is not the only relevant sort of concept possession when we are considering deciders. Seeing, hearing, smelling, and so on are themselves exercises of essentially the same capacities as those involved in exercising the concepts we use in explicit reasoning, even though our ordinary vocabulary doesn't encourage that way of thinking. It's true we don't have concepts in the ordinary sense for each particular shade of colour, each possible pattern of breaking surf, each voice timbre. But we do have and exercise relevant concept-like capacities, which are capable of pinning down precise details. Dennett's example of the matching torn edges of a cardboard Jell-O box (such as was used for identification by spies) is a nice analogy with the sort of thing our nervous systems are capable of (Dennett 1991: 376–82). Each spy's torn edge exactly matches the other's; similarly, each perceptual experience, or more generally, each pattern of perceptual information that we receive, can be stored in memory and used as a basis for further thinking. Agreed, we do not have a concept in the ordinary sense for each experience that we can remember, refer to, and think about. But our capacity to store information in that way is very much *like* our use of ordinary concepts.

If that is correct, our vocabulary risks misleading us about the way concepts are involved in perception. Because we connect concept possession with understanding words, we tend to assume that if there couldn't be a word for each shade of colour, there couldn't be a concept for each shade of colour either. That may indeed be correct according to our *ordinary* use of 'concept'; and the thought encourages the notion of concept-free 'registration'. In reality, the capacities exercised in what I am calling registration don't appear to be significantly different from those exercised in conceptualization of the ordinary sort, at least if the linguistic aspects of it are left on one side.[4]

Of course we are ignorant of much that goes on in human and animal brains under the crude descriptions 'acquiring information', 'registration', and 'conceptualization'. Somehow or other the changes caused by the impact of the outside world on a decider's sense receptors influence its processes of interpretation, assessment, and decision-making and thereby enable it to guide its behaviour. How that actually happens in terrestrial creatures, and how it might conceivably happen in other types of systems, are still largely unsolved problems for the sciences concerned—though very actively pursued. Nor does there appear to be any reason to expect a single general solution. It seems quite likely that there are innumerable different ways in which not only organic terrestrial nervous systems, but possible artefacts and extraterrestrial systems, might satisfy the crude descriptions in my sketch of the basic package. But not only am I ignorant of what those ways may be; I suggest it would be beside the point even to attempt to investigate them here. My focus is the what-is-it problem; and for that purpose, I suggest, it is enough to be reasonably clear about the outlines. No doubt these outlines will eventually be characterized in terms of a really scientific psychology. While no such characterization is at hand, I am trying to do it in terms of everyday psychology: terms I have been trying to clarify in the last two chapters.

9.6 TWO POINTS ABOUT INFORMATION AND REGISTRATION

Here two points about information and registration need emphasis. One is that the conception of the basic package built up in the last chapters makes it convenient and on the whole appropriate to think of the acquisition of 'perceptual information' as a matter of *effects typically caused by a decider's sense receptors being exposed to its environment, and typically enabling it to guide its behaviour more adaptively than it would otherwise have been able to.* (Since that covers only perceptual information, it should for completeness be extended to cover other sorts, but we need not attempt that.) This way of thinking about the acquisition or 'registration' of information has to be understood in conjunction with the consideration that deciders interpret incoming information, assess their situation, make decisions,

---

[4] McDowell (1994) opposes Evans's position by claiming that perception necessarily involves conceptualization, though not via the reasoning I find persuasive. (Readers of McDowell will easily see how my position differs.)

and guide their behaviour on that basis. The effects in question either actually have effects in their turn on the system's interpretation, assessment, and decision-making, or are potentially capable of having such effects because they are, as we say, stored in memory: more on this presently.

The second point is that what I am calling the 'acquisition or registration' of perceptual information is not generally a matter of registering facts. When the cat registers the movements of the mouse, it is not a matter of registering *that just now both pairs of legs are outstretched, now they are together again,* .... We may struggle to put into words just what information is registered in any particular case, even when the perceiver has language (which is partly why the notion of non-conceptual content seems to be needed) and in general I think it would be inappropriate to attempt to do so. This is not information of a kind that needs to be expressible by means of 'that'-clauses.

9.7 DIRECTLY ACTIVE PERCEPTUAL INFORMATION: INSTANTANEITY AND PRIORITY

Now for the core of this book. Certain events constitute a decider's acquisition of perceptual information. Such events are registered in the system's memory, if only for a brief period. But in addition they may affect the system in other ways, notably these four:

(a) By directly affecting the system's central processes of interpretation, assessment, and decision-making in ways to be explained shortly—by being *directly active*. This is typically the case with ordinary conscious perceptual information. (You hear a tiger growling outside the door and decide—perhaps rashly—to hop out of the window.)

(b) By various effects on patterns of behaviour and behavioural tendencies, capacities, and abilities. Subliminal perception is one case. (You have been 'primed' to favour a particular reading of an ambiguous word: a disambiguating word or picture has been flashed up subliminally.) Another case is blindsight, where information and appropriate behavioural capacities and abilities are acquired without, apparently, any related experiences.

(c) By causing mental images or other thoughts to 'pop up'. This quite often happens in connection with things we have perceived in the normal conscious way (a). (A memory image of the grapes you spotted earlier in the kitchen floats into your mind and you go downstairs to renew acquaintance with them.)

(d) Without conscious impact. In this case the information is incorporated into the system's general stock of background information. The system may or may not be able to 'call up' the information. When it can call it up the information may be said to be 'poised', at least in Block's sense: the information is 'ready and waiting' (1995: 245 n.7).

Our focus is case (a): directly active perceptual information. I have to try to get reasonably clear about it—for which purpose I can't just say that it's what happens in ordinary conscious perception. Here it is particularly important to keep in mind that the descriptions involved in the basic package are to be construed neutrally, that is, regardless of whether it's known that the system to which they apply actually is perceptually conscious.

Briefly, but not yet very helpfully, my definition of direct activity is this: the events constituting a system's acquisition of perceptual information are *directly active* on the system's processes of interpretation, assessment, and decision-making (its 'central processes') if their effects on them have characteristics which I am calling 'instantaneity' and 'priority'. These are not distinct properties, I think, but the same property viewed in two ways.

By saying that incoming perceptual information has 'instantaneity' I mean it pretty well instantaneously endows the system with certain kinds of capacities, as follows. In the human case they include the capacity to describe the appearance of what we can see, the sound of what we are hearing, and so on. However, verbal capacities are not the only ones that matter, or even the most important. More important are such capacities as being able to recognize what has been perceived when it is presented again in similar circumstances, or when a photo or tape-recording is presented. The most directly relevant and easily identified capacities are the commonplace ones involved in being able spontaneously to produce appropriate non-verbal behaviour. You show you are acquiring visual information with instantaneity if, when you want to open the book in front of you, you reach for where it actually is rather than somewhere else; that you are acquiring auditory information with instantaneity if you look up when your name is called; that you are acquiring olfactory information with instantaneity if after sniffing the contents of two cups you choose the one containing your favourite drink. The sense in which these capacities are acquired instantaneously is that exercising them doesn't require any special acts of recall, any guessing, or any popping up. This characteristic of directly active processes is obviously not shared by case (c) (random popping up of thoughts and images). What about (b) and (d)?

Case (b) includes subliminal perception (or 'perception without awareness') and blindsight. In both types of phenomena the subject acquires instantly at least *some* relevant capacities and abilities. To get an idea of the sorts of abilities that are in question, look round and then shut your eyes. You will probably still be able and ready, for at least a few seconds, to behave in appropriate ways with respect to the furniture and other surroundings. You will be able to avoid bumping into chairs and tables, and to reach for and grasp things like books or plates.

As a way of making vivid the possibility of something like permanent blind-sight without normal vision, Nicholas Humphrey invites you 'to imagine what it would be like if you were to keep your eyes permanently closed, and were to find that you still had knowledge of the position and shapes of objects (with this knowledge being continually updated)'. He suggests that then you might perhaps be in much the same situation as a blindsight patient (1992: 71). Perhaps. However, one feature of blindsight is that the subject is not able to make all the discriminations with respect to their blind fields that they can make with respect to the normally sighted parts of their visual fields. The information they acquire, and the abilities and capacities that go with it, are less detailed than what normal vision supplies—which is one important difference between blindsight and normal vision. An equally important difference is that blindsight subjects are apparently unable to access the information in question without being forced to guess. They have actively to *do* something that people with normal vision (including themselves with respect to the unaffected areas of their visual fields) don't have to do. So even though blindsighted people instantly acquire some of the relevant abilities and capacities, they don't acquire all of them.[5] (The following possibility helps to bring out the point. Someone might have vision impaired in such ways that, so far as their powers of visual discrimination were concerned, they resembled a person with blindsight: the information they received via their eyes would be as coarse and lacking in detail as that which blindsighters receive from the blind fields. But they would still have capacities and abilities that the blindsighter lacks. Notably they would not have to be forced to guess what they were seeing; and their incoming visual information would have instantaneity.)

What about case (d), where the information passes immediately but unconsciously into the individual's general stock of information? The point of the question emerges on recalling the rabbitoid. Why shouldn't information which endows the rabbitoid with the relevant kinds of capacities get into it unconsciously, so that it 'just knows' there's a fox behind it, for example?[6] The information need not just be 'available' to the animal for control of its behaviour, it could even be 'poised' in Block's sense of 'ready and waiting' (and perhaps Tye's sense of 'ready and in position'). Even in that case, however, the rabbitoid's acquisition of perceptual information would lack instantaneity. Certainly the animal would acquire *some* of the relevant capacities, but it wouldn't acquire those which would enable it to decide how to behave without taking any further action. To deal explicitly with this point, let us turn from this rather negative aspect of direct activity (no recall, no guessing, no popping up) to its other aspect, which I am calling 'priority'.

Consider again the evolutionary situation. It is plausible that perceptual consciousness has the function of ensuring not just that information about its environment gets into the organism somehow or other and can be used somehow or other, but that it gets into it so that it can be used to maximum advantage. Of course it's a good thing if perceptual information can be used at all. Even if it gets into the organism only subliminally (case (c)), or otherwise unconsciously (case (d)), it may still help it to guide its behaviour: to achieve goals it already has. But if the

---

[5] 10.8, 10.9 below discuss other kinds of blindsight as well as related topics.

[6] Thanks to Bill Fish for impressing on me the need to give this case special attention.

information not only helps it achieve its existing goals, but helps to ensure that its goals continue to be appropriate in its developing situation, that is enormously better. If the events constituting the system's acquisition of the information perform that potentially life-preserving function, they have *priority* in my sense. More specifically, those events have priority if they act on the organism's central processes of interpretation, assessment, and decision-making *regardless of the information's relevance to whatever goals the organism may currently have.* We can say that information coming in with priority in this sense 'forces itself' on the system's central processes, since it affects them in a way it cannot control (except indirectly, for example by looking the other way or shutting its eyes) regardless of its relevance to its current goals, and regardless of whether it actually gets used. Because the information acts on the system's central processes regardless of its relevance to current goals it enables the system to alter or modify those goals, and may prompt it to do so (but see the end of this section). If I am driving to London along the A1 and see a road block and diversion signs, I may slow down and turn off. Originally my goal was simply to keep going along the A1 till I reached London; but seeing the diversion signs prompted me to alter that goal, thereby (I hope) ensuring that, by avoiding a crash, I achieved my aim of getting to London.

By explicitly specifying that directly active incoming perceptual information has priority as well as instantaneity—by stressing the positive aspects of direct activity as well as its negative ones—we make clear how case (a) is prevented from collapsing into case (d). We rule out the special kind of rabbitoid whose unconscious perception of the fox is as swift as if it had seen or heard the fox consciously. The rabbitoid's perception of the fox may be, as far as it goes, instantaneous in the usual sense; but it doesn't have instantaneity in my special sense because it doesn't come with *all* the relevant sorts of capacities. The information the rabbitoid acquires doesn't force itself on it in the sense explained, and so doesn't give the animal the opportunity to revise its current goals, even if it is highly relevant to its survival. The information just feeds into its total stock, and has effects on its decision-making only as other background beliefs do: that is, only to the extent that it is relevant to current goals. Not that the system must be able to make a *judgement* to the effect that a given piece of information is relevant. The point is that something like relevance to current goals is often a factor in causing stored information to have effects on assessment and decision-making.

Case (d), illustrated by the rabbitoid, might suggest that a decider's acquisition of perceptual information could have the first characteristic of direct activity (instantaneity) without the second (priority). But that is ruled out by the definitions. Instantaneity is so defined that it involves acquisition of *all* the right kinds of capacities, including those which manifest priority. Nor could there be priority in the absence of instantaneity, because a system's acquisition of the right kinds of capacities is a matter of its *being able to decide* to behave in a certain way on the basis of the information in question, not a matter of behaviour being automatically triggered, as with reflex systems. Since the priority in question is priority of incoming perceptual information, there is no possibility of such information having that kind of priority without also instantaneously endowing the system with the right capacities. That is why instantaneity and priority in my special senses can be thought of as respectively the negative and the positive aspects of direct activity, rather than distinct properties.

Note that priority does not imply that the subject's current goals actually *are* modified whenever that would be appropriate. All sorts of factors may interfere, for example inattention, ignorance, rashness. The point is that the effects which the events constituting acquisition of incoming perceptual information have on the system's central processes *enable* it to modify its current goals if it chooses to do so, without having to call anything from memory or guess or wait for something to pop up. But those remarks may still leave you puzzled.

9.8 A HOLISTIC APPROACH TO DIRECT ACTIVITY

Just *how* do the events constituting a system's acquisition of perceptual information 'act on' its central processes? In particular, what kinds of activity constitute priority? If you want an answer specifying actual mechanisms I have nothing to offer—but nor, so far as I know, has anyone else, although neuroscientific investigations are being pursued at a furious pace. Ignorance of mechanisms is not the main problem from a philosophical point of view. We need to understand the general structure of the processes involved.

Here we face what looks uncomfortably like a dilemma, as the discussions around the sole-pictures argument in Chapter 4 showed. The Cartesian Theatre model cannot be correct. If we attempted to explain consciousness in terms of anything like a homunculus in front of an ethereal TV screen, we would still have to explain how it perceived events on the screen; and so on. That is certainly a dead end. Even the much more sophisticated Evans-Tye account comes dangerously close to that model. But if there is nothing like an internal TV screen we seem to face an equally unappealing alternative: the processes involved just fire off uselessly into the void. Can we escape that choice?[7]

The aim is to understand how a system can be a subject of perceptual consciousness. On the one hand we have to beware of picturing a little micro-subject surveying or monitoring the processes involved; on the other we also have to beware of assuming that a sub-process could constitute conscious experience all on its own. Instead, we need some way of conceiving of perceptual consciousness according to which it contributes to the working of the system as a whole. These considerations suggest we need a holistic approach. Some of the considerations offered in connection with the sole-pictures argument also point in this direction. We need to conceive of what we can (still) call 'acquiring' and 'taking account of'

---

[7] If you think Dennett's 'multiple drafts' idea gets us out of this fix, see 11.6 below.

'directly active' information as integrated whole processes rather than as relational. Give up thinking of non-conceptual representations as distinct from but 'poised' or 'available to', and processed by, an Evans-type concept-exercising and reasoning system. Instead, conceive of certain large-scale complex processes as wholes, whose coordinated activity *constitutes* the system's taking-account-of-directly-active-perceptual-information.

On the face of it, such a holistic approach would release us from the threatened dilemma. But can we really understand the proposal? To mention one problem: how could we detect the processes involved?

9.9 CAN WE REALLY UNDERSTAND DIRECT ACTIVITY HOLISTICALLY AND NOT IN TERMS OF 'POISEDNESS'?

For reasons already considered we are forced to use vague language. The risk is that it is so vague that dubious assumptions slip past unnoticed. Is there a hidden slide from intelligible functionality to mystery? An 'and-here-a-miracle-occurs' move? I believe we can rule that out fairly straightforwardly.

First, a remark about instantaneity. The capacities which a decider instantaneously acquires in acquiring perceptual information don't come in ready-made behavioural packets, each consisting of a given particular piece of information causing a particular piece of behaviour. Reflex systems, and also more complicated systems such as Block's machines, have such packets; but what a decider does depends on what it *chooses* to do. So the events/processes constituting a decider's acquisition of perceptual information cause it to be *able* to behave in certain ways if it decides to do so: they *enable* it to guide its behaviour. It can avoid bumping into the tree; it can run in the right direction to catch the mouse; and so on. It is in that sense that a decider instantaneously acquires the capacities in question.

The functions that have to be performed by various interacting processes in order for a decider to be able to act in those ways on information-based decisions (in order for there to be the relevant sort of instantaneity) are evidently pretty complicated. But although a detailed account of how they were actually performed would have to wait for solutions to some serious neuro-engineering problems, I know of no reason why it should involve philosophical problems over and above those discussed in earlier chapters: problems about, for example, concept possession and the acceptability or otherwise of behaviouristic accounts of the mind.

Now, directly active incoming perceptual information somehow results in the system being put in a position to *consider and take into account* incoming information without having to guess, probe its memory, or wait for something to pop up; and being *prompted to modify its current goals*. Does that take magic? Or may we assume that those high-level functions are clear and respectable enough for our purposes, and can be implemented in ways we have a reasonable chance of eventually understanding? I suggest the answer depends on whether my explanations of instant-aneity and priority make it possible to discover whether these descriptions apply to a given system. I think they do.

First, I suggest that experienced observers would sooner or later be able to tell in most cases (though we know there will be indeterminate cases too) whether or not a given system had the right kinds of behavioural capacities and dispositions. Obviously the observers must interact with the system, and their sensory resources must be appropriate to its own. (Human testers without special equipment wouldn't be able to make much progress with systems communicating exclusively by radar, for example.) They might start by establishing that its dispositions were those of a decider. This would require them to discover its needs, wants, and sens-ory systems, to the extent that its behaviour revealed them—as in general, surely, it would. Next they had better examine its internal workings to check that they are consistent with its really being a decider—in line with the moderate realism of folk psychology—and not a pseudo-decider like many of the systems considered in Chapter 7. Finally, they can consider whether the system has the additional special capacities and dispositions involved in direct activity. They should have no difficulty discovering whether exposure to the things around it instantly equips it with the capacities involved in instantaneity. (The bird is instantly able to peck at the right spot on the lawn for catching the worm; the chimp carries the nut to a suitable stone for cracking it.) As to priority, it shows up in the way a creature clearly set on pursuing one objective can be diverted as soon as it spots a potential predator or alternative prey. No single observation will be enough to ensure that our observers are faced with a genuine case of priority rather than of some more or less automatic reflex. But they can deepen their investigations by engaging in a variety of behavioural interactions with the system, and also by studying its internal workings. I take it that in general (again allowing for indeterminate cases) they will be able to tell whether its internal processing is in accordance with its classification as a decider with direct activity: a *decider-plus*.

Unfortunately there is no magic formula determining whether that processing conforms to the moderate realism of everyday psychology. The best we can do, I suspect, is to bring to bear considerations like those offered in Chapter 7. Folk psychology seems to me to imply little that is clear or positive by way of real-ism; my thought is that it nevertheless does imply something. Most importantly, I take it to imply that a system is not intelligent unless on occasion it cobbles together its own ways of responding to what it takes to be its situation; and that it doesn't make its own decisions on the basis of distinct sensory modalities unless this involves distinct processes constituting its interpreting specifically visual information, or auditory information, or olfactory information (which is why the machine-table robot failed to qualify as a decider). If a system's behavioural capa-cities are consistent with its being a decider-plus, and if its internal processing meets the few constraints suggested by the examples in Chapters 7 and 8, then it is a decider-plus.

So I think the functions involved in instantaneity and priority, complex though they are, are clear and respectable enough for our purposes and raise no special philosophical difficulties. Somehow or other the production of internal processes and of behaviour reflecting those functions can be engineered—because it has been, at least in our own case. In spite of our ignorance of the details, therefore, I don't think they involve philosophical difficulties beyond those of correct description.

This conception contrasts sharply with the Evans-Tye model, notably in respect of (a) poisedness; (b) conceptualization.

(a) The metaphor of poisedness has no role in the proposed model. Direct activity is to be conceived of as an integrated process, not intelligibly divisible into a 'poised' non-conceptual representational/experiential component and a conceptualizing component. An experience of smelling eucalyptus, for example, is not split into two distinct items: scenting eucalyptus on the one hand, and being aware of it, noticing it, attending to it, and the like, on the other. Instead there is an integrated process of experiencing-the-smell-of-eucalyptus. Certainly, in human brains we can distinguish sense-receptor-caused activity in the projection areas of the cortex from activity in other regions, such as the frontal lobes involved in planning. Such physical and functional divisions are indeed consistent with the Evans-Tye model. States of the projection areas might correspond to that model's non-conceptualized representations/contents; processing in the frontal lobes and other regions might correspond to activity of the CERS. But what then would correspond to the former being 'poised' or 'standing ready and in position to make an impact' on the latter? What would be the difference between their being so poised and not making an impact, and their being not just poised, but actually making an impact?

According to the Evans-Tye model, that difference would be the difference between the experience being phenomenally conscious but not conceptualized or otherwise thought about, and its being both conscious and conceptualized. But here the model gets into trouble. Keep supposing for argument's sake that states of the projection areas underlie non-conceptual representations/contents, and frontal-lobe processing underlies activity of the CERS. If the former makes no impact on the latter, how can it even be noticed or attended to—how can it even be conscious at all? That is the problem noticed earlier, and the Evans-Tye model seems stuck with it. But if, to get over that difficulty, the model is modified so that it is only when there is an actual impact on the cognitive processing that representations are poised, the cost is to give up the original idea that they are not conceptualized. That brings us to the second main difference between the model proposed here and the Evans-Tye model.

(b) The physical substrate of direct activity in humans must be some pattern of neural activity. As just explained, this activity should be in principle capable of being identified via a combination of behavioural and internal investigations. No doubt the physical substrate will have distinguishable components that are in principle locatable. Some may be roughly identifiable as the arrival of a given piece of perceptual information within the system, others as the further processing of that information in various ways. But that does not imply that there are components separately identifiable as 'a nonconceptual representation', 'conceptualization of the representation', or 'poisedness'. That is a second major contrast with the Evans-Tye model.

So much for my account of the direct activity of perceptual information. I have argued that direct activity is necessary for conscious perception. But it is vital to know whether it is also sufficient, in the sense that if a system has it, then some of the events occurring in it constitute its having conscious perceptual experiences. We saw in the last chapter that zombies (if they had been possible) would have had the basic package; we can note now for later reference that they would also have acquired directly active perceptual information, since this is just a matter of the exercise of capacities and functions all of which are specified neutrally. In the next chapter I will defend the claim that direct activity is sufficient for conscious perception; but some further points must be noted first.

9.10 SIGNIFICANCE OF DIRECT ACTIVITY

Direct activity is hugely important if I am right. It makes all the difference between a mere decider such as the rabbitoid and something with phenomenally conscious perceptual experiences. Yet any of a whole range of different additional features might have been added to the basic package instead of this one. What makes this particular feature so special? Without further explanation, picking on direct activity may seem arbitrary. In fact it is not, for reasons already suggested.

Direct activity makes a strong and distinctive contribution to survival. Without it, an organism would be at best in the same position as the rabbitoid. It would acquire perceptual information all right, but the information wouldn't automatically enable it to modify or abandon its current goals if doing so would help it to gain a benefit or avoid a threat. That is a sufficiently critical advantage to explain the importance of direct activity. Not that the evolutionary history of conscious perceivers necessarily included a transitional phase when rabbitoids roamed the earth: far from it. As we noticed, if such creatures ever occurred at all they would probably have become extinct very rapidly, forming, at best, a twigless branch of the evolutionary tree. I suggest instead that deciders with direct activity evolved directly from creatures that were not themselves deciders, yet were close enough to them to be able to look after themselves better than rabbitoids would have done. (Remember that there are likely to be many organisms that neither determinately have the basic package nor determinately lack it.)

You may wonder why I single out the effects of incoming perceptual information on, in particular, the system's processes of interpretation, assessment, and decision-making. What makes its effects on *those* processes so important? The answer has to do with the fact that we are concerned with perception. The events in question constitute the system acquiring a certain sort of information: learning, in fact. But the point of perception is to guide decision-making, hence behaviour, which means that the way the information gets into the system has to be so integrated with its overall functioning that it is enabled to guide its behaviour on the basis of such information. The system can't be said to use information unless it has some control over its behaviour; and it can't be said to have control over its behaviour if sensory inputs simply cause behavioural outputs in a reflex manner. Guiding its behaviour has to involve something like decision-making. But when decision-making concerns environmental features about which the system is currently receiving perceptual information, it inevitably depends on the system's interpretation of that incoming information, and also on its assessment of its current situation. I don't see how incoming perceptual information's direct effects on the system's workings can fail to affect not only its processes of decision-making, but those of interpretation and assessment as well.

Creatures are not making decisions all the time they are consciously perceiving, of course—or not decisions as ordinarily so classified. However, decision-making processes of a kind are going on all the time, as part of the system's interpretation and assessment. Interpretation, assessment, and decision-making seem to be inextricably linked.[8]

9.11 DEGREES OF CONSCIOUSNESS AND THE RICHNESS OF PERCEPTUAL INFORMATION

I have emphasized that relatively humble organisms—perhaps even creatures less complex than mammals and birds—may be perceptually conscious. I can't say much about this, not being a zoologist; my best hope is to offer suggestions for basing better-informed judgements in particular cases. One general consideration that needs to be kept in mind is this. The sensory equipment of very humble animals, and for that matter of relatively simple artefacts, may differ from our own not just in respect of the aspects of the environment to which they are sensitive, but in respect of the richness of the information they are capable of collecting: its 'bandwidth'. Some creatures have visual or other sensory systems with greater bandwidth than that of human vision (I believe eagles are an example); but just now I am concerned with those where the bandwidths are considerably less. In that respect, therefore, it seems to make sense to talk of *degrees* of consciousness. Creatures incapable of making more than a small number of discriminations in

---

[8] The remarks in this section seem to me at least consistent with the view encouraged by Milner and Goodale (1995) and others that 'The functional role of conscious visual perception ... is to support reason, recall, and reflection. It is only indirectly to guide (better, to select) actions in the here-and-now' (Clark 2001: 511).

any sensory modality may still have 'some small dull Perception, whereby they are distinguished from perfect Insensibility'; but it seems reasonable to view them as having a lower degree of consciousness than we do.

There is another reason for a similar conclusion. As we have noticed, there is scope for it to be indeterminate whether a given system has the basic package. If a system which only indeterminately has the basic package also has the special feature of direct activity, then a reasonable conclusion seems to be that it is also indeterminate whether it is perceptually conscious. Although that view is quite widespread (Dennett 1991; Tye 2000), some readers are likely to find it unsatisfactory or even outrageous: surely perceptual consciousness is all-or-nothing, either present or absent?[9] They will concede that some creatures may have less rich perceptual consciousness than ours. They will also concede that we have different levels of consciousness, often noticeable when we are between sleep and waking. But they may still insist that even when consciousness is faint or very limited, it is still there. If that is right, there is no room for indeterminacy. I suggest, however, that there is nothing but prejudice in favour of this assumption. We even have some evidence to the contrary. It comes from one of Laurence Weiskrantz's blindsight subjects:

DB was questioned repeatedly about his vision in his left half-field. Most commonly he said that he saw nothing at all. If pressed, he might say in some tests, but by no means all, that he perhaps had a 'feeling' that a stimulus was approaching or receding, or was 'smooth' (the O) or 'jagged' (the X). But always he stressed that he saw nothing in the sense of 'seeing', that typically he was guessing, and was at a loss for words to describe any conscious perception. (1986: 31)

'Perhaps had a feeling' suggests it is indeterminate whether or not there is perceptual consciousness there. The fact that DB stuck to such descriptions even when pressed suggests that the intuition that perceptual consciousness must be all-or-nothing is not a serious objection to my position.[10]

9.12 PHENOMENAL CONSCIOUSNESS IN GENERAL

Although I am focusing on perceptual-phenomenal consciousness, I must say something about the what-is-it problem for phenomenal consciousness in general. I maintain that being a decider with direct activity—being a decider-plus—is

---

[9] Many would agree with McGinn that 'The emergence of consciousness must . . . be compared to a sudden switching on of a light' (1982: 14). Chalmers holds that, on the contrary, 'there is probably a continuum of conscious experience' (1996: 105), but insists it is determinately present or absent. I am suggesting both views are mistaken.

[10] I am not assuming that because DB had difficulty deciding whether he was consciously seeing, the reality in question was indeterminate. We often have ambiguous evidence about determinate matters. But if the boundary between deciders-plus and other systems is indeterminate, perhaps DB is evidence for real indeterminacy. DB was not commenting on a matter where observation might have misled him: he was not observing at all. See 10.8.

both necessary and sufficient for perceptual-phenomenal consciousness, but not that it is either necessary or sufficient for all the varieties of phenomenal consciousness noted at 5.1. I suggest, however, that what goes for perceptual-phenomenal consciousness may be modified and extended so as to apply to other cases of phenomenal consciousness.

In *Raw Feeling* I briefly explained how that might be done (1994: 169–74). The broad idea is that we can achieve a grasp of non-perceptual types of phenomenal consciousness on the basis of a grasp of perceptual types. Perhaps the processes involved in the non-perceptual types are relevantly similar to those involved in the perceptual types. For example, if there were brains in vats (detached brains, stimulated exactly as they would have been if they had been functioning in a living person) the processes inside them would be relevantly similar to those involved in direct activity. I believe we could justifiably say there was phenomenal consciousness in such cases in spite of the fact that the vat-brain is not *perceptual*-phenomenally conscious, at least if it is agreed that perception involves interacting with external things. But even in normal people, certain processes not directly involved in perception may still have effects on the system's central processes closely similar to the direct activity of the events constituting acquisition of perceptual information. We can reasonably speculate that these would probably constitute hallucinations, hence episodes of phenomenal consciousness.

I am not suggesting that other cases of phenomenal consciousness are to be *defined* in terms of perceptual consciousness. The point is simply that it seems possible to understand how there can be such cases on the basis of our understanding of the nature of perceptual-phenomenal consciousness. The topic demands more extended treatment than would be appropriate here.

9.13 WHY IS IT LIKE THIS?

Suppose I am right about the explanation of why there is *something* it is like for you when you perceive things, and something it is like for me when I perceive things: that it is explained by our both being deciders-plus. You may complain that I've stopped half-way: something important still needs to be explained. Why, given that a certain system is perceptual-phenomenally conscious in the first place, do its individual experiences have precisely the subjective characters they do have, rather than others? Why is it like *this* for me to see a ripe tomato, for example—especially if what it's like for you is different?[11]

In Chapter 5 we noted that Nagel has supplied powerful reasons why it is impossible to solve the general 'what-it's-like' problem: how to get from viewpoint-neutral

---

[11] This is one way to present the explanatory gap. Levine says, 'For a physicalist theory to be successful, it is not only necessary that it provide a physical description for mental states and properties, but also that it provide an *explanation* of these states and properties ... why it is like what it is like to see red or feel pain' (1993: 128).

facts about any arbitrary creature to what its perceptual experiences are like. His argument for that particular conclusion works because (I think) the concepts in terms of which we describe the character of our perceptual experiences cannot be fully grasped except by those who have had experiences of the kinds in question, or at least are capable of imaginatively constructing them. In general a knowledge of viewpoint-neutral facts cannot convey such concepts. When it comes to the special problem of understanding why our own experiences are as they are, however, given that the relevant viewpoint-neutral facts are as *they* are, the situation is different. We already possess the necessary concepts. The problem is to understand what connects these neutral facts with just these experiences, rather than with others, which on the face of it seem as well qualified to occupy the functional roles provided by the neutral facts. So why *is* it like this?

Recall the idea of 'transposed qualia' (the inverted spectrum being a special case). If it is a genuine possibility, the problem of why it's like *this* is perhaps not particularly pressing: it then starts to look like a brute primitive fact. However, I have argued that cases of transposed qualia in the relevant sense (without physical differences) are impossible; and I will not tackle the why-is-it-like-this problem in this book. One reason is that it is not really to the point. My present project is the what-is-it problem: to make it clearly intelligible how something can be a subject of phenomenal consciousness at all. The why-is-it-like-this problem is a further topic, and doing justice to it would divert attention from what is central. Besides, I have dealt with the topic at some length elsewhere (1994, especially 186–216). But one important consideration is worth stressing now: we need to distinguish significantly different readings of the question 'Why is it like *this?*' Some readings incorporate misconceptions and don't raise serious problems; and in one important sense of the question—the sense invoked in Jackson's example of Mary the scientist—it is a mistake to assume that an explanation could possibly be provided.

Let me emphasize that although I believe that in certain special conditions there could be something analogous to the inverted spectrum, I do not think it would be *explicable* in terms of merely physical differences. And although by definition there would be no behaviourally detectable differences in such cases, there would on my account be internal functional differences. Provided the right internal and external functions were performed, it wouldn't matter what materials the system was composed of.

9.14 CONCLUSION

I hope that in the light of the discussions in this chapter, the concept of directly active perceptual information has turned out to be no more problematic than the concepts involved in specifying a decider. My contention is that when the second lot of capacities is added to the first—when some of the events constituting a decider's acquisition of perceptual information are directly active—then it is perceptual-phenomenally conscious. Those two conditions are individually necessary and jointly sufficient for the system to be a conscious perceiver. If section 9.9 is sound, direct activity doesn't make the what-is-it problem harder.

But it doesn't automatically solve the problem. Some readers will object that there could be a decider-plus which was not perceptually conscious.

10

Gap? What Gap?

The sole-pictures argument shows that zombies are impossible, but does nothing to explain why anything should be phenomenally conscious in the first place. As a framework for such an explanation I have introduced two notions: the basic package and direct activity. Any system with the basic package is a decider; any decider with directly active perceptual information has the 'basic package-plus' and is a decider-plus. I have argued that the basic package-plus is at least necessary for perceptual-phenomenal consciousness. What has to be shown now is that it is also sufficient—not just nomologically, but in such a way that contradiction or other incoherence would be involved in a decider-plus not being phenomenally conscious.

Throughout it remains crucial that the concepts in the framework be taken neutrally: their applicability must not depend on a presupposition to the effect that the system described is phenomenally conscious. The task now is to explain how those neutral descriptions ensure that certain consciousness-involving descriptions must also apply, in spite of the fact that we don't seem able to define the latter in terms of the former. I will offer my explanation in the first sections of the chapter, then deal at some length with all the serious objections I know of.

10.1 EXTENDING THE SOLE-PICTURES ARGUMENT

The conditions which have to be satisfied for a system to be a decider-plus are broadly functional. Though explained in terms of everyday psychology they require only that the system possess certain neutrally specified capacities, and that there be certain neutrally specified relationships, causal and other, among processes inside and outside it. Zombies are an example, though a special one; they would have been just like us in all functional respects. If zombies had been possible they would have been deciders-plus; but the sole-pictures argument showed that zombies are not possible.

What about other kinds of deciders-plus? Could there be any without phenomenal consciousness? I claim the basic package-plus is sufficient—c-sufficient—for phenomenal consciousness, and will defend that claim in three stages. First, in this section I will extend the sole-pictures argument so as to rule out the possibility of a decider-plus which is not phenomenally conscious, on the provisional assumption that being a decider-plus satisfies all the purely functional conditions necessary for perceptual-phenomenal consciousness. In the second stage I will defend that assumption (10.2–10.5). In the third stage I will discuss objections (10.6–10.15).

First, then, to explain how the sole-pictures argument can be extended so as to rule out the possibility of a decider-plus without phenomenal consciousness, given the following provisional assumption:

(A) The basic package-plus includes all the purely functional conditions necessary for perceptual-phenomenal consciousness.

If, given (A), a decider-plus could still be without phenomenal consciousness, there must be some condition C such that:

For any arbitrary decider-plus without phenomenal consciousness, satisfaction of C would result in its becoming phenomenally conscious.

Given (A), satisfaction of C cannot involve any functional differences, at least none relevant to whether or not the decider-plus in question is phenomenally conscious. It cannot affect the system's behavioural dispositions or capacities, for example, or how it processes information. But now recall what was said in Chapter 4 about 'epistemic intimacy'. This was shorthand for the ways in which phenomenally conscious subjects engage cognitively with their phenomenal experiences; attending to and comparing experiences are two examples. Now, the cognitive processing involved in such activities has to be really *about* the experiences in question, and the latter must be genuinely attended to or compared (although, for reasons given in the last chapter, we have to conceive of such attending and comparing holistically). In the light of the sole-pictures discussion we shall see that satisfaction of condition C cannot result in any such genuine aboutness, attending, or comparison.

Since by (A) all necessary functional conditions are assumed to be satisfied, satisfaction of C must depend on certain special entities or properties which, when appropriately associated with the basic package-plus, make the system phenomenally conscious. The key consideration is that these special items cannot relevantly affect cognitive processing. If they did, that processing would not satisfy the purely functional conditions, contrary to assumption (A): the system's cognitive workings would be in some relevant respects different. If the special items have no effects on the system's cognitive processes, however, how can they provide for epistemic intimacy? We are back with essentially the same situation as we considered in connection with sole-pictures.

There are differences. My zombie twin is my exact physical duplicate, while now we are dealing with any arbitrary decider-plus, whose qualifying functions and capacities are specified at a high level of generality which does not demand particle-for-particle resemblance. My zombie twin is a purely physical system; there is no such restriction on the arbitrary decider-plus. E-qualia are defined as non-physical; the special items whose association with the basic-package-plus are supposed to underlie perceptual-phenomenal consciousness might be physical, so far as condition C is concerned. Finally, e-qualia are causally inert, while there is nothing to prevent these special items from having *some* effects, even on the system's cognitive processing, so long as they make no difference to the functions and capacities belonging to the basic package-plus. For all that, essentially the same argument can be used here. There are two crucial facts: (a) the special items have no relevant effects on the system's basic package-plus functions and capacities; (b) there are no other factors which could ensure that its cognitive processing was about or otherwise epistemically intimate with the special items. (a) was established in the last paragraph; now for (b).

Possibly the special additional items which are supposed to make the system phenomenally conscious—assuming there is such a condition as C—are *isomorphic* with those cognitive processes which enable its acquisition of perceptual information to qualify as having instantaneity and priority. Possibly those special items are also *caused*, as appropriately as possible, by those cognitive processes. But the sole-pictures argument shows that isomorphism and causedness do not help; they cannot ensure that the system is epistemically intimate with the special items. Further, as in the special case of my zombie twin, so in the general case of an arbitrary decider-plus, there is no other relation to do that job. Therefore, given our provisional assumption (A), there cannot be such a condition as C. In full: if the basic package-plus satisfies all the purely functional conditions necessary for perceptual-phenomenal consciousness, then it satisfies all the conditions necessary for perceptual-phenomenal consciousness.[1]

In the next few sections I will defend and try to enhance the intuitive appeal of assumption (A): that the basic package-plus does indeed satisfy the purely functional conditions for perceptual-phenomenal consciousness. I believe these sections will also have a tendency to show, independently of the extended sole-pictures argument, that the basic package-plus is also sufficient for consciousness. We can start from an example.

10.2   ZOË

Assume that cats are deciders-plus, and suppose our cat Zoë is sitting at the foot of a tree and spots a mouse, at the same time hearing a dog further away. She is receiving two lots of perceptual information: visual information about the mouse, a potential source of fun and food; auditory information about the dog, a potential source of danger. Neither of these lots of information causes her to do anything. The sight of the mouse doesn't automatically trigger mouse-chasing behaviour; the

---

[1] So this book offers a refutation of Block's contention that 'We have no conception of a ground of rational belief to the effect that a realization of our superficial functional organization that is physically fundamentally different along the lines I have specified for Commander Data is or is not conscious' (2002: 405; see 7.8(e) above).

sound of the dog doesn't trigger dog-fleeing behaviour. Some kind of interpretation, assessment, and decision-making goes on before Zoë acts—though my
lengthy acquaintance with this animal suggests that those processes are not very
sophisticated.

There are several different dimensions of information here, not just the broad
grouping of visual information on the one hand and auditory information on the
other. There is also information about the relative spatial locations of the mouse
and the tree, the sizes and shapes of mouse and tree, the loudness, timbre, and
temporal distribution of the dog's barks, and so on. At any given instant many of
these different sorts of information are coming in simultaneously.

Since we are assuming the incoming perceptual information is directly active, it
affects Zoë's processes of interpretation, assessment, and decision-making in the
ways explained in the last chapter: with instantaneity and priority, continuously
and uncontrollably. The visual information relating to the mouse affects those
processes differently from the auditory information relating to the dog. Indeed,
that the events in question constitute her acquisition of *information* at all depends
on their affecting those processes in different ways. The mouse-information
ensures that Zoë knows which way she can go to get close to the mouse; the dog-
information ensures she knows which way she can go to get away from the dog.
Those are just two examples of what the integrated processes of information-
acquisition with instantaneity and priority enable the cat to do; there are countless
others.

The question now is not whether all that is enough to ensure there is something
it is like for this animal, although I think it is. The question is whether she has all
the *purely functional* properties necessary for being phenomenally conscious. I aim
to persuade you that she does.

10.3 BEING ABLE TO TELL THE DIFFERENCE

Zoë sees the mouse and hears the dog. Being a decider ensures there is one clear sense
in which she can tell the difference between those two different events. If behaviourism had worked, we could perhaps have said that this was just a matter of being
able to behave differently in relation to seeing a mouse from how she would behave
in relation to hearing a dog. But in Chapter 7 we concluded (at least I did) that
behaviourism doesn't work: the nature of the internal processing matters. Still, if we
consider Zoë purely as a decider, momentarily leaving direct activity out of account,
the fact that she can behave differently with respect to the two animals when she sees
the one and hears the other ensures that there is one respect in which she can tell the
difference between those two events. It is not the decisive respect, however.

Receiving perceptual information isn't only a matter of acquiring certain capacities; it also involves internal events. We are assuming Zoë is a decider-plus, and
able to decide how to behave on the basis of directly active incoming perceptual

information. It follows that telling the difference between the mouse (which she sees) and the dog (which she hears) involves also telling the difference between different *internal* processes ultimately caused by the mouse and the dog respectively. These are the processes which constitute her acquiring directly active visual information about the mouse, and directly active auditory information about the dog. I am not saying Zoë is *thinking* of those internal processes or that she conceptualizes them as such; surely she does neither of those things. But neither am I saying that the difference merely causes her to behave differently: far from it, since the assumption is that the processes in question are involved in direct activity, where incoming perceptual information does not necessarily cause any behaviour. The point is that *in* telling the difference between the sight of the mouse and the sound of the dog Zoë is also telling the difference—in a way which does not necessarily involve the causation of any particular behaviour—between what are in fact internal processes, when the existence of such different processes is part of the moderate realism of everyday psychology.

It might be objected that in order to tell the difference between those internal processes Zoë must have special concepts for them. Carruthers for example has argued that:

… any system capable of conscious perception must be able to discriminate the events within it that carry perceptual information *as* events carrying such information, … (1996: 154)

That strong claim requires Zoë to have a concept of *information*: something I rather doubt she has. Carruthers attempts to support his claim via the assumption that if an organism's experiences are *like* anything, then it 'must be capable of representing, and of distinguishing between, its experiences as such' (1996: 155). I see no good reason to accept that assumption. I claim Zoë can in effect represent and distinguish between the internal events which are *in fact* different internal processes, and constitute her acquisition of different sorts of perceptual information, simply by representing and distinguishing between their external causes (the mouse and the dog's barking). I believe that when she does that she has conscious experiences; but I don't see why she should need special concepts for them as such. Concepts such as that of *experience*, I suggest, can be acquired only by creatures cognitively more sophisticated than cats or even babies. Zoë gets along perfectly well with her own crude concepts (*edible stuff, quasi-mouse, quasi-dog*, or whatever). When she brings those concepts into play in the course of seeing the mouse and hearing the dog they perform dual roles. They don't just enable her to deal appropriately with the animals out there in her environment; they also enable her to distinguish, in a way which does not necessarily involve any particular behaviour, between the internal events constituting her acquisition of two sorts of directly active information: mouse-caused visual information and dog-caused auditory information. *In effect* she distinguishes between those two sorts of internal events; but we don't have to suppose she can also distinguish between them 'as such': as internal events or experiences.

If it had been at all appropriate to think of the situation on the model of the Cartesian Theatre we should now have been able to imagine something like Zoë's 'self', or her 'inner eye', lodged inside her and monitoring visual, auditory, and other perceptual information as it comes in, much as we look at the TV and listen to its soundtrack. But that model is unworkable. Whatever may be the details of what's happening in Zoë's case, they cannot fit that picture. Instead we have to think of what happens holistically. There are integral processes which include the effects of incoming perceptual information on the cat's processes of interpretation, assessment, and decision-making in such ways that they *constitute* her becoming able to, for example, 'take account of' and 'attend to' the differences between the internal processes caused by seeing the mouse, and those caused by the dog's barking.

If a metaphor helps, perhaps we need that of a dimension, or a domain of activity, in which such difference-telling takes place. Not that there is some special physical space where it occurs. The point is that it is helpful to think of a dimension or domain of activity concerned with making connections between the acquisition of directly active perceptual information on the one hand, and the production of behaviour on the other, when that domain of activity is neither the simple acquisition of information (which could in principle just go straight into memory, as with the rabbitoid) nor just the causation of behaviour.

When the information about the mouse and the dog are coming in with instantaneity and priority, the events constituting their acquisition can be thought of as having an immediate *impact*—but not any sort of impact. It is by hypothesis an impact on the animal's interpretation, assessment, and decision-making. Clearly the impact of the events constituting the mouse-caused visual information is different from that of those constituting the dog-caused auditory information. We could say they strike the cat differently.[2] Such differences are what enable her to base her decisions on the information as it comes in. If that is right, then it seems to me that she has all the purely functional properties required for there to be *something it is like for her*.

In that case our provisional assumption (A) ceases to be an assumption and becomes a premiss; and by the argument of 10.1 we can conclude that Zoë is phenomenally conscious. In terms of the metaphor just introduced, we can say that the domain of the direct action on Zoë's central processes of the events which constitute her acquisition of perceptual information has a further description: it is *also* the domain of perceptual-phenomenal consciousness.

In what follows I will go over the same ground from different angles with the aim of reinforcing the claim that Zoë has the purely functional properties necessary for perceptual consciousness.

---

[2] Since we have to conceive of such events holistically, we cannot separate acquisition of the information from interpretation, assessment, and decision-making (9.8, 9.9). Certainly the events more directly caused by the impact of the dog and the cat on Zoë's sense receptors can be thought of separately from processing further downstream. But my remarks about 'impact' and 'striking' should be construed on the lines of 'being-struck-by-the-mouse's-running'.

10.4 ZOË'S ABILITIES

Suppose for argument's sake that although Zoë is a decider-plus she lacks phenomenal consciousness: there is nothing it is like for her. If there is nothing it is
like for her when she spots the mouse and hears the dog barking, then what it's like
for her as the mouse stays within view is exactly the same as what it's like for her as
the dog stays within hearing: that is, *like nothing at all.* In that case, though, how is
she able to do the things she actually can do? How is she able both to respond
instantly and appropriately to changes in the mouse's movements, for example,
and—because the incoming information enables her to revise her current goals—
to leg it up the tree if the dog comes closer, without (like the rabbitoid) having to
call up stored information, or guess, or just wait passively till it chances to pop up?
How could all that happen if there were nothing it was like for her?

You might object that these rhetorical questions get us nowhere. Nothing
prevents the information from coming in unconsciously. What is there about
deciders-plus which rules that out? But that suggestion is inconsistent with at least
our *ordinary* notion of the unconscious reception of perceptual information.
Certainly we take in some perceptual information unconsciously. But that is
intelligible only because we can contrast it with the case where we acquire the
information consciously. If we pick up some piece of perceptual information
unconsciously it does *not* immediately enable us to decide to modify our current
goals, or immediately to act accordingly.[3] It lacks instantaneity and priority. And
if we happen to possess language, acquiring information unconsciously doesn't
immediately enable us to say what the information is. But in the case of a decider-
plus, directly active incoming perceptual information does enable it to modify its
goals, and does immediately equip it with the other capacities involved in instantaneity and priority. Since the objection requires incoming information to be
acquired unconsciously in spite of the subject's acquiring those and related capacities, the objection is in effect no more than a denial of my thesis: it doesn't
amount to an independent objection.

But we can do better than just record that the objection begs the question. My
contention is that the instantaneity and priority of the incoming perceptual information endow Zoë with *all* the purely functional properties necessary for perceptual-
phenomenal consciousness; and the objection does not seem to damage that
contention. When we reflect on this example it is hard to see how Zoë could fail to
be conscious. How could the events constituting her acquisition of that information
be factors in her deciding to modify her goals, unless she were conscious? It seems
that the only intelligible way for her to acquire *all* of those capacities is for there to be
something it is like for her: one thing it's like for her to see the mouse, something else

---

[3] At 10.8, 10.9, and 10.13 below I take account of experimental evidence for the view that many
of our movements are guided by unconscious perception.

it's like for her to hear the dog barking, and so on for all the different packets of perceptual information she acquires. At the very least, I do not see how any further functional conditions would need to be met.

Higher-order theorists are likely to object that, on the contrary, it's quite easy to conceive of something being a decider-plus without perceptual-phenomenal consciousness. They might say perceptual information could be acquired 'transparently': without the content's including 'a dimension of *seeming* or *appearance*' (Carruthers 2000: 184). They might add that this additional feature can be provided only if the subject is capable of higher-order thought. The trouble is that this extra feature seems necessary only if you conflate two distinct conceptions of perceptual-phenomenal consciousness. On one conception (the one I am appealing to) it is sufficient for perceptual-phenomenal consciousness that there be *something it is like* to perceive this or that thing. The other conception requires in addition something on the following lines: that the subject be *aware of having the experience*, or be *capable of being aware of having the experience*. Certainly we human beings can and do have higher-order thoughts about our experiences; but that is not the point. The point is that appealing to the second conception of perceptual-phenomenal consciousness, which obviously entails a capacity for higher-order thought, comes too close to begging the question. I will return to that line of objection later.

10.5 PROVISIONAL CONCLUSIONS

Subject to further consideration of possible objections, I conclude that what was provisionally assumed at the beginning of this chapter is true. That is:

(A) The basic package-plus satisfies all the purely functional conditions necessary for perceptual-phenomenal consciousness.

In section 10.1 I extended the sole-pictures argument and its supporting discussions to show that:

(1) If the basic package-plus satisfies all the purely functional conditions for perceptual-phenomenal consciousness, then it is c-sufficient for perceptual-phenomenal consciousness.

It follows that:

(2) The basic package-plus is c-sufficient for perceptual-phenomenal consciousness.

In the last chapter I argued that the basic package-plus is c-necessary for perceptual-phenomenal consciousness, or at least for central or typical cases. I conclude that it is both c-necessary and c-sufficient at least for central or typical cases of perceptual-phenomenal consciousness. One way of presenting this point—one of my two major contentions in this book (the other being that zombies are not conceivable)—is to say that we are not dealing with some merely 'brute' identity. By the extended sole-pictures argument, any system satisfying the necessary functional conditions is *also* perceptual-phenomenally conscious for that reason. No merely natural or nomological or brute necessity has to be invoked.

You may be wondering why I have not discussed attention, for example, or long- and short-term memory, or how visual processing involves the detection of a host of different features, or any of the numerous other aspects of human perception that are under such close scientific investigation today. The reason is that I am throughout concerned to focus on the functions that must be performed in *any* system that could count as perceptual-phenomenally conscious. There seems to be plenty of scope for wide differences, among kinds of decider-plus, in how their defining functions are performed. It is hard to imagine how anything could perform them if it were not capable of some degree of attention, for example; but is that a matter of c-impossibility? It would be interesting to consider whether attention is strictly implied by the basic package-plus; but that is only one of many trails that I cannot follow up here.

10.6   SOME MISCONCEPTIONS

At this point I want to forestall a few possible misunderstandings:

'The concepts you use in your explanations—the ones in the basic package and those involved in explaining what you mean by "directly active"—are too vague to be useful. For that reason alone it's hard to know what to make of your explanations.'

The main concepts are certainly vague. But they are no vaguer than those in rival explanations, for example those favoured by 'pure representationalists' such as Dretske and Tye, or by exponents of the various 'higher-order' theories such as Armstrong, Carruthers, Lycan, and Rosenthal; or by Dennett. For that matter they are no vaguer than the concepts routinely used by neuroscientists when they describe what they take to be the functions of various neural features.[4] (These and other rival accounts of perceptual consciousness are briefly considered in the next chapter.) True, two wrongs don't make a right; but there are explanations for this vagueness. As suggested in Chapter 5, in order to see what the what-is-it problem amounts to we have to use our everyday concepts; nor does it seem possible to find hygienic substitutes.

'The vocabulary you use to specify the basic package and the special feature is pervaded by implications of consciousness. It's not surprising you feel you can claim to have explained perceptual consciousness in those terms; but really you haven't. You've just

---

[4] You might hope that mathematical or cognitive scientific concepts could overcome the difficulty of vagueness; but it ain't necessarily so. Gregory Mulhauser (1998) defines 'representation' and 'function' in terms of algorithmic information theory. When it comes to applying them to his central project of explaining consciousness in terms of a 'self model', he assumes without argument that they usefully coincide with the ordinary notions which share the same names. I would argue that they don't.

helped yourself without acknowledgement to the rich implications of your chosen vocabulary. As Robert Van Gulick has put it, "The challenge is to specify roles that could be filled only by qualitative states (without just begging the question by building explicit qualitative conditions into the definitions of the roles)" (2003: 342).'

The charge is serious, but I believe I have avoided it by requiring the vocabulary for the basic package and direct activity to be construed neutrally. On that basis the relevant psychological functions can be specified *without* begging the question. Is it suggested that that approach is unfeasible? Why? Surely we can say of a creature or a robot that it satisfies all the detectable conditions for being a conscious perceiver, when those conditions don't involve direct or obvious knowledge of whether it is genuinely conscious. You may suspect there is still logical room for it to lack consciousness. But in that case the concepts in question do *not* logically imply it, and the objection fails for that reason. Even if, as I maintain, there is no logical room for the conditions to be satisfied and the system to lack consciousness, we can still apply the concepts without knowing that fact. So even if it is true (and it may be) that the concepts in question are pervaded by implications of consciousness, that doesn't impair the legitimacy of my approach. This conclusion is reinforced by the fact that zombists such as David Chalmers are happy to agree that zombies have all those features of normal people that he calls 'psychological' (in contrast to 'phenomenal' ones).

'You don't go any way towards explaining how individual states of perceptual consciousness are realized.'

My main project is to contribute to solving the what-is-it problem: the general problem of what it is for something to be a subject of perceptual-phenomenal consciousness. My contention is that what it is, is to be a decider-plus. Given that a system is a subject of perceptual-phenomenal consciousness in the first place, the project of explaining why its individual experiences have whatever characters they do have is a different project, not attempted in this work.

'A lot of philosophical effort is currently being devoted to getting clear about qualia, but it's unclear what you think qualia are.'

One reason is that my approach to the what-is-it problem in terms of the basic package plus direct activity has no need to introduce the term. Another is that I suspect it encourages and is encouraged by the jacket fallacy. I have deliberately avoided using the word 'qualia' except when forced to do so by the need to discuss arguments for or against zombies. I am content to take it that qualia are what zombies are supposed to be without. Since I don't have to use the notion, I don't have to take a stand on the metaphysics of qualia—fortunately, since the debate is becoming scholastically complicated. I believe the basic package-plus story helps to render at least some aspects of that debate obsolete.

'No matter how much you refine your specifications of the basic package, direct activity, instantaneity and so forth, there will always be non-standard ways of implementing them which leave the system without perceptual consciousness.'

A common complaint, reinforced by reference to ingenious examples such as Block's machines, the homunculus-head, and Commander Data. However, I think it bundles together two distinct objections: (a) that I have failed to take account of some relevant functions; (b) that no functional account whatever could capture what is essential to perceptual consciousness. If I really have taken account of all relevant functions, and if none of the objections to functionalism damages my account, there cannot be any 'non-standard' implementations which both satisfy my conditions and leave the system unconscious. To take what is certainly a tricky example, the homunculus-head is conscious on my account because its internal workings mirror all those that are involved in performing the functions in a normal human brain.

I accept I may be open to objection (a) and await suggestions about what vital functional features my account leaves out. Recall, though, that the discussions in Chapter 7 illustrated several ways in which the complex of everyday psychological concepts used to specify the basic package cooperate to rule out a range of other implementations which may at first have seemed to qualify, including the Block machine and the machine-table robot. A similar point applies to the notion of direct activity. That a specified system merely appears to be a decider-plus is not enough: its internal workings must be consistent with the moderate realism of everyday psychology.

Block's interesting example of Commander Data can be construed as a challenge to accounts based purely on functions specified in terms of everyday psychology. 'Any account of that kind leaves too much underdetermined', Block could say. 'It will always be possible to implement the favoured functions in non-standard ways. So far as your account is concerned, Commander Data might or might not be phenomenally conscious.' If the arguments in this and the preceding chapter are sound, functions specifiable in terms of everyday psychology *are* enough to determine that the system in question is perceptual-phenomenally conscious; so I think the challenge has been met.

As for objection (b), it is the chief focus of discussions later in this chapter.

10.7 WHAT THIS ACCOUNT DOES

Having noted some things my account doesn't set out to do and (I believe) didn't have to attempt, let me summarize what I think it does.

(a) The overall project can be seen as that of explaining how a mere object can at the same time be a conscious subject. I think my account simplifies the task by looking for the minimal requirements for a subject of perceptual-phenomenal consciousness, aiming to side-step the special problems raised by our own highly sophisticated capacities such as language-guided concepts and self-awareness. The definitions of 'decider' and 'directly active incoming perceptual information' may well apply to quite humble creatures, and could in principle be applied to suitably constructed artefacts.

(b) My account focuses on identifying certain key functions, defined neither causally, mathematically, computer-scientifically, nor teleofunctionally, but every-day-psychologically. I have tried to make clear how this approach is well-conceived for the what-is-it project, acknowledging that some philosophers regard any func-tionalist approach to the problem of consciousness as misconceived.

(c) I have tried to show how any decider-plus is necessarily also a subject of conscious perceptual experience. I have explained why I don't think the job can be done by means of definitions, and why in any case the project has no need of such definitions; and will say more in that vein shortly. The aim has been to make it not just rationally compelling but intuitively appealing that being a decider-plus is necessary and sufficient for perceptual consciousness, thereby helping to break the spell of the zombie idea and throwing light on the nature of consciousness.

I hope some readers will find what I have said persuasive; many will feel they know any number of decisive objections. Discussing what appear to be the most serious ones will help me further to clarify my approach. First, some difficulties arising from empirical work.

10.8 BLINDSIGHT

Many examples of blindsight in the literature pose no problems for my account. They fall unambiguously into category (b) of the four introduced at the start of section 9.7. In such cases, incoming visual information does not qualify as directly active because either the subject has to guess what it is, or this has to be made apparent by indirect procedures (on which see Weiskrantz 1997: 67–70). However, certain blindsight cases can seem like a counter-example. These are where the subject performs an action guided by information coming from the 'blind field' with what appear to be instantaneity and priority. DF, for example, 'was able to modify the posture of her hand to match the orientation of a slot towards which she was reaching, yet she was unable to *perceive* the orientation of the slot' (Milner *et al.* 1991: 424; see also Milner and Goodale 1995). It is even said that some blindsighters can catch objects thrown into their blind fields.[5] If these subjects really do receive visual information that is directly active in my sense, and if they really have no visual experiences in their blind fields, then of course they are a counter-example. But I can resist that conclusion. At least three alternative responses to the evidence, all consistent with my position, seem available.

The first is that DF actually does have a conscious experience, but that it is unlike normal seeing because it derives from only some of the many processes that are integrated in normal vision. Normal vision includes information about edges, contrasts, colours, and shapes, for example. In DF's case, little more than the

---

[5] Milner and Goodale's DF is described as 'very good at catching a ball or even a short wooden stick thrown towards her' (Milner and Goodale 1995: 128)—but not as catching things 'in her blind field'.

orientation of the slot seems to have any impact on her central processes. To the extent that this impact comes with instantaneity and priority, my account requires it to be conscious. However, the incoming information would be so impoverished in comparison with normal vision that it is perhaps not surprising if the subject denies seeing anything. Here it is interesting to consider Weiskrantz' remarks in connection with a series of trials involving his subject GY, who was asked to press keys to indicate both whether he detected the orientation of a moving light, and whether he had any kind of relevant experience. Replying to the question 'What did you see?', GY said 'I didn't see anything'. Weiskrantz reports that on another occasion 'GY, in response to the same question in a closely similar stimulus situation, said it was difficult to know *how* to describe his experience. "You do not actually really sense anything", he said. He then added, "the difficulty is the same that one would have in trying to tell a blind man what it is like to see".' Weiskrantz comments, 'The nearest I have been able to come to a description of his awareness in this situation is that it is a kind of knowing that there is movement, as pure movement, and being aware of its direction, but in the complete absence of any identity of what it is that is moving . . .' (1997: 66. See also the quotation at 9.11). GY's remarks and Weiskrantz' interpretation seem consistent with the hypothesis that GY does have some kind of conscious experience in the trial situation, but that it is so different from normal vision that it seems not appropriately describable as a visual experience: there is *something* it's like, but it's not like normal seeing. Perhaps DF similarly has a perceptual-phenomenal experience of some kind. (Interestingly, Milner and Goodale say 'It appears that under some circumstances GY does not have blindsight for motion; he is actually able to perceive motion' (1995: 83).)

Another way in which (what I know of) the experimental evidence could be interpreted consistently with my account would be to say that the blindsighter's grasping behaviour is automatic: a matter of mere reflexes. This suggestion allows for a sense in which incoming visual information is 'active'—it influences the subject's behaviour—but not directly active in my sense because it does not engage the person's central processes. Admittedly this seems an unlikely explanation for such activities as pressing a key to indicate the direction of a light; but it is perhaps not implausible for DF's grasping and orientation movements, especially if learned reflexes are allowed to count, as they perfectly well could be.

A third alternative explanation would be the one proposed by Milner and Goodale (1995), who say that 'Blindsight is paradoxical only if one regards vision as a unitary process' (86). As is well known, they find empirical support for the view that there are two streams of visual processing in the brain onwards from the visual projection area V1. The 'ventral' stream goes through the temporal lobes to the areas associated with conceptualization, planning, and language; the 'dorsal' stream goes through the parietal lobes to the motor areas. The evidence suggests that this second stream has the function of guiding action, including not only quick 'reactions' such as in hitting or catching a fast ball, but also the positioning and guiding of detailed limb movements at normal speeds, as when one unconsciously avoids tree-roots in one's path. Milner and Goodale suggest that this second stream's contents are not available to conscious thought; while the first is. Is this suggestion consistent with my account?

Yes, because the 'dorsal' stream of visual processing bypasses the subject's processes of conceptualization and planning. That implies it does not impinge on the central processes of interpretation, assessment, and decision-making, and for that reason is not directly active in my sense (which of course does not prevent it from being directly active in other senses). To the extent that Milner and Goodale's suggestion fits the empirical facts, therefore, it is compatible with my position.

However, it may be urged that DF's visual information must surely be interpreted, assessed, and decided on to some extent. If that is right, there seems to be room for a further alternative explanation of the phenomena. Perhaps what we ordinarily think of as the person's behaviour may be controlled (in the sense relevant to deciderhood) by two or more distinct components or subsystems (different in character from the two streams of visual processing invoked in the last suggestion). One of these components is the person's 'central' processes. These processes qualify as central because they constitute what would normally be thought of as the person's interpreting, assessing, deliberating, and choosing. In particular they are involved in the ordinary use of language. But in addition to this central component, the present suggestion is that there is another component, which normally operates independently of the central component. Like the latter, it too engages in a certain amount of interpretation, assessment, and decision-making, although the processes in this subsystem might be cruder than those in the central system. If that were the case, blindsighted object-catching might be accommodated. Because the subsystem was itself a decider-plus in spite of operating to a large extent independently of the main system, it would be perceptual-phenomenally conscious on my account. But because it did not involve the person's *central* processes of interpretation, assessment, and decision-making, and in particular was not in control of the use of language, the person as a whole could not sensibly be described as conscious of the motion of the object within their blind field. There would be some perceptual-phenomenal consciousness of the event in question, but its subject would be the subsystem, not what we call 'the person'. (There are obvious analogies with split-brain cases.)

That speculative suggestion does not seem wildly implausible given the complexity of the human organism. There seems plenty of scope for subsystems to incorporate their own interpretation and decision-making. Conceivably the digestive system is an example, although perhaps it is too self-contained to be a pertinent illustration. On my account it is only those processes of interpretation, assessment, and decision-making which are integrated as suggested in Chapters 6 and 7 that are 'central', and that determine whether the system as a whole, rather than just some subsystem, is perceptual-phenomenally conscious.

Evidently, the question whether any of the above alternative explanations gets at all close to the facts, and if so which, must await further empirical work.

10.9 AUTOMATISM

In sleep-walking, post-epileptic behaviour, and other cases of 'automatism', a person performs quite complicated actions yet seems unaware of what they are doing, or aware of it but not fully in control. This may appear to confront me with a dilemma. Either a person acting under automatism can have control of their behaviour in spite of not being perceptual-phenomenally conscious; or else perceptual-phenomenal consciousness doesn't after all require the ability to decide what to do on the basis of directly active perceptual information. So being a decider-plus is either not sufficient for perceptual consciousness, or not necessary.

The vast complexity of human perceptual and motor systems brings with it a vast range of potential impairments to normal functioning. Precisely how normal functioning is impaired in the various kinds of automatism is of course an empirical question; and the crude characterization above leaves room for different kinds of deficits to be involved even when the symptoms are superficially similar. My response to the challenge of automatism can therefore vary with the details of the case.

To start with sleep-walkers: although they seem to exhibit some degree of central control of their behaviour, I gather they are less than fully aware of what is happening around them. That suggests that not all the processes involved in normal functioning are brought into play. Admittedly there can hardly fail to be some degree of interpretation, some assessment of the situation, and some decision-making; but those central processes seem to operate at reduced levels of efficiency. An explanation emphasizing their relatively low efficiency would allow a somnambulist to have some degree of phenomenal consciousness of events (perhaps intermittently) while not being able to recall the episode later. In such cases, some perceptual information would be directly active on the subject's 'central' processes, hence the person would be perceptual-phenomenally conscious; in which case automatism of that sort is not a counter-example. This explanation might also be appropriate for post-epileptic automatism (discussed in Block 1995: 239–41).

An alternative explanation might be based on the last, highly speculative, hypothesis described in the last section. It would allow sleep-walking to be explained in terms of behaviour controlled not via the subject's central processes of interpretation, assessment, and decision-making, but via a subsystem. The direct activity of perceptual information on that subsystem (or those subsystems) would constitute phenomenal consciousness and enable the subject to decide on the quite complicated sequences of behaviour sometimes observed; but such consciousness would only be that of the subsystem; and the failure of incoming perceptual information to engage with the subject's central processes would account for the clumsiness of the behaviour, its disconnectedness from waking projects, and the subject's failure to remember it once fully awake.

What if the automatistic subject is conscious but not in control, as apparently occurs in post-epileptic states? This seems less of a problem for my account than the in-control-but-not-conscious case. It is one of the cases where, as noted earlier, we can take perceptual consciousness with the basic package-plus as standard, and use it as a basis for accounting for deviant cases. As with paralysis, it seems that the central processes involved in normal perception may be engaged even when the subject has lost normal control of behaviour.

Let me re-emphasize that the suggestions in this and the last section are speculative. If research eventually demonstrates that in some cases a subject's basic package-plus capacities are active when the subject is not phenomenally conscious; or if it is shown that in some cases the subject is phenomenally conscious but lacks the basic package-plus (though I don't see how that could be done), then I am just wrong. So far neither of these cases seems to have been demonstrated, either for automatism or for blindsight.

Reflection on automatism and blindsight can prompt the thought that Descartes may have been right, and that all or most animals—even Zoë—might not be perceptual-phenomenally conscious. But beware of the distorting influence of the zombie idea. Of course we can *imagine* that animals are not conscious; but that doesn't warrant the conclusion that deciders-plus might not be conscious. I don't say it is inconceivable that animals should resemble blindsighters for the whole range of their sensory experiences. What I do say is that it is inconceivable (in my sense: c-impossible so far as we can tell) that a decider-plus should fail to be phenomenally conscious. I believe that many animals are deciders-plus, but my account of perceptual-phenomenal consciousness leaves it open whether any actually are. It's an empirical question.

10.10 GENERAL OBJECTIONS TO FUNCTIONALIST ACCOUNTS

Two common objections to functionalist accounts of consciousness have been disposed of already: the alleged possibilities of 'absent qualia' and 'transposed qualia'. This whole book is a reply to the zombie version of the absent qualia objection; non-zombie versions are dealt with in some of the discussions in Chapter 7. As to transposed qualia, I have argued that the sole-pictures argument against zombies also shows that the relevant case of transposed qualia (the one where there is complete physical duplication) is also impossible. But there are plenty of other objections to consider. Many are to functionalism in general, and not well aimed at the view advocated here—even if it is functionalist at all.

Objection F: 'You must be crazy if you think any description in functional terms can possibly be equivalent to a description of an experience. As Searle says, "If you

are tempted to functionalism, I believe you do not need refutation, you need help"
(1992: 9).'

Reply F: This objection misses my own account by miles. I do not maintain that
any functional description is equivalent to a description of a conscious experience.
I have given this off-target objection first place because too many critics still
assume that all varieties of functionalism are committed to that claim, and I want
to forestall the misconception: it makes their task far too easy.

Levine, for example, in his book *Purple Haze*, assumes that 'Functionalism is
the view that mental states, including qualia, are definable in terms of their causal
roles . . .' (2001: 96; see also his 1993: 134). And Chalmers routinely assumes that
functionalists are committed to functional accounts or analyses of 'what it means
to be phenomenal' (for example his 1996: 15). Once functionalists have been
saddled with this view it is easy to object that 'causal role is not all there is to our
concept of qualitative character' (Levine 1993: 134), or that 'Although conscious
states may play various causal roles, they are not *defined* by their causal roles'
(Chalmers 1996: 105). Nothing I have said commits me to the view that there are
functional definitions of everyday mental concepts, or reductive equivalents for
consciousness-ascribing descriptions. If anyone thinks there are such definitions,
I think they are mistaken for the reasons considered in Chapters 2 and 5. To recap-
itulate: for many types of experience, characterizing them requires possession of
the necessary concepts; but those concepts cannot be acquired by anyone who has
not had the relevant type of experience; they are viewpoint-relative. If that is right,
the more general concepts in terms of which functional roles might be characterized could not be used to construct expressions equivalent to descriptions using
viewpoint-relative concepts. No possible viewpoint-neutral definitions could
characterize the various 'feels'; no functionalist approach could possibly succeed—
if functionalism entailed there were such characterizations. But why should it?
Why should it attempt to solve the 'what-it's-like' problem? I argued in Chapter 5
that no one ought to attempt that because it can't be done. What Chalmers offers
as a reason why a 'functionalist' account could not possibly succeed ignores what
reasonable functionalists are trying to do.

Objection G: 'There's more to that objection than you've managed to do justice
to. The fundamental point is that there's a difference in *nature* between functional
concepts and the concepts in terms of which we think about experience—and that
seems to entail there's a difference in nature between the properties involved:
between the mere performance of functions and the occurrence of conscious experiences. Functional concepts are *relational*, while the concepts we normally use to
characterize conscious states are not. Consciousness is *intrinsic*, and therefore
cannot be just a matter of psychological relations among mental states. A mark of
the difference is that you have no explanation of how the "first-person" concepts
we use to describe our experiences are related to the "third-person" ones you use to
describe the performance of functions.'

Reply G: Certainly these concepts are different in nature. But that is explicable on the basis of the fact that being a decider-plus is what ensures that an object is also a consciously perceiving subject. Once something qualifies as a subject of conscious experiences there's scope for it to acquire its own special concepts, concepts different in kind from those which observers might employ in describing what was going on. These concepts are suitable for thinking about the character of the subject's experiences from the subject's own point of view. Typically they will be viewpoint-relative.

Once we understand how there can be conscious subjects it seems unremarkable that there should be concepts specially apt for characterizing their own experiences. It is a consequence of the way such first-person concepts are acquired that what they apply to should *seem* to be insulated from those facts and relations which nevertheless, if I am right, constitute conscious-subjecthood. Normally a subject is justified in using a viewpoint-relative concept in connection with his or her own experiences purely by the occurrence of that experience itself, independently of observation or other evidence. I don't need to consult the dentist to find out whether I have toothache, and I don't need to understand the functional basis of toothache or other pains in order to be able to acquire the relevant concepts. That makes it natural to assume that the *existence* of phenomenally conscious perceptual experience is independent of the relationships involved in the basic package-plus. Yet if my earlier reasoning is sound, the existence of phenomenally conscious perceptual experiences depends entirely on those relationships. It is therefore beside the point that subjective, viewpoint-relative concepts are different in kind from the viewpoint-neutral concepts used to specify the basic package-plus.[6]

Objection H: 'You're still missing the point. You say all that's involved in perceptual-phenomenal consciousness is states and processes performing certain functions; specifically, the functions involved in direct activity. But the absolutely fundamental point is this: what's essential about phenomenal properties is their *feel*. According to Kripke, "Pain ... is not picked out by one of its accidental properties; rather it is picked out by the property of being pain itself, by its immediate phenomenological quality" (1972: 152). Relatedly, what makes states conscious according to Chalmers is "that they have a certain phenomenal feel, and this feel is not something that can be functionally defined away" (1996: 105). Functional states and processes can't have such feels; at least, even if they are associated with such feels, the feels can't be *essential* to them. You're just whistling in the dark.'

---

[6] Consider a remark of Howard Robinson's when discussing materialism: '... unless there is some reductive analysis of how the mental concepts capture the physical properties, ... it is difficult to see why there should be need for new concepts to capture experience, unless it were that they captured different properties from those caught by the physical vocabulary' (1998: 175). That seems to overlook the points illustrated by landscape features and digital images. There is no problem of 'new concepts' capturing different properties if the descriptions attributing those properties are strictly implied by P.

Reply H: One component of this objection can be dismissed quickly. It's true that feels cannot be 'functionally defined away': such definitions are not to be had; but we have seen that nothing requires me to look for them. The kernel of the objection is this: although feels are 'essential' properties of conscious states, they cannot be essential properties of functional states. I will not challenge the assumption that feels are indeed essential properties of conscious states. I do challenge the assumption that conscious states cannot *be* functional states. If my toothache is a functional state, and its feel is essential to it, then that feel is essential to that functional state, implausible though that may seem. But consider why it seems implausible. It is only because functional facts *strike us*, on the face of it, as remote from phenomenal facts. Facts about behavioural and other capacities, and about causal and other relations among processes, just don't seem capable of constituting facts about sensations or perceptual experiences. But the way things strike us cannot settle the matter. I have argued in some detail that certain facts about behavioural capacities, and about causal relations among the processes which underlie those capacities—vitally including facts about the system's internal arrangements— *do* constitute facts about perceptual consciousness, incredible though that may have seemed at first. If that is right, and if feels are essential properties of conscious states, then feels are essential properties of some functional states, and the objection collapses.

Objection I: 'Like all functionalists, you are confused over relations between what actually performs a given function—the occupant of the functional role—and the function itself. In Levine's words your approach embodies "an unwarranted assimilation of role player to role" (2001: 98). He agrees that his experience of the red of his diskette case performs a certain function, whatever exactly it may be. But, as he points out, the character of the experience seems quite independent of the fact that it performs that function. It can even seem that an experience with the same quality could have performed a different function:

> However complex the description of the functional role played by ... my reddish visual experience of the diskette case, it seems like the right way to characterize the situation is that the reddish experience is *playing* a certain role, not that it *is* a certain role. The point is that you don't show that a property is itself relational merely by finding a relational description that uniquely identifies it. It might still be that the property itself is intrinsic .... (2001: 98)

In a nutshell, although you claim to offer a solution to the what-is-it problem, all you really offer is a solution to the 'what-does-it-*do*' problem: a solution which may be interesting, but doesn't perform as advertised.'

Reply I: That last remark gives me a neat way to nutshellize my reply. I claim that to solve the what-does-it-do problem *is* to solve the what-is-it problem. To explain: I have argued that any system with the basic package-plus is thereby necessarily phenomenally conscious. If that is right, then necessarily anything which does the right sorts of things (provided that takes account of its internal arrangements) *is* the right sort of thing. That, I think, disposes of the main thrust of the present objection. There is no 'unwarranted assimilation of role-player to role' because in the general case there couldn't be a role-player at all unless the role were being played: there could be no perceptual-phenomenal consciousness without the basic package-plus.

So much for the general case. But what about particular cases? Am I saying that each individual phenomenally conscious experience is just the playing of some role? Surely the force of the present objection is much greater for particular cases. And Levine's example is not of consciousness in general but of a specific phenomenal character: the reddishness of his current visual experience. He holds that a 'colour quale' has its own 'substantial and determinate' character, which is intrinsic to it; so he finds it natural to assume that a quale is independent of any role that may be performed. You may therefore protest that my approach leaves the heart of the objection untouched. Can I seriously deny that his experience *has* a specific intrinsic character?

Of course not. I think the account of perceptual-phenomenal consciousness I am offering explains *how it is* that there is such a thing as experiences with specific intrinsic character. The key consideration now is epistemological. In line with Replies G and H, the subject of a conscious experience doesn't have to consider its relations to other things in order to be in a position to judge either that it's happening, or what its character is. That alone warrants the use of the word 'intrinsic', since from the subject's point of view it might as well be intrinsic. As we noted, once perceptually conscious individuals have come into existence they can develop their own viewpoint-relative concepts and deploy them whenever instances occur—*without* having to reflect on those instances' relations to other things, or even knowing about those relations. That is consistent with the episode in question being from another point of view 'extrinsic' or relational, since the occurrence of an experience with that character depends on the episode's relations to other states, inputs and outputs.[7]

You might still wonder what on earth a functional account of a perceptual experience with a specific character would be like. Could there be such an account? I won't discuss this question at any length because my project is the what-is-it problem, and I have discussed this further problem elsewhere (1994: 175–209). But a few remarks may help to avoid misconceptions. The *existence* of conscious perceptual-phenomenal experiences has already been provided for. They exist just in case there are deciders-plus: systems with the basic package, some of whose perceptual information is directly active. By providing for the existence of perceptual-phenomenal experiences in general, provision has thereby been made for them to have their own distinctive characters. For it makes no sense to suggest there could be conscious perceptual experiences *without* distinctive characters.

---

[7] Support for this line comes from a remark of Carruthers, who points out that there may be 'recognitional concepts of experience . . . ', whose concepts are not 'relationally or causally defined', while those concepts nevertheless pick out relational properties (2000: 78).

Certainly we need to consider how we can explain the differences between these characters. An important step in that direction is to recall that the central processes of interpretation, assessment, and decision-making in a decider-plus are differentially sensitive to different patterns of incoming perceptual information—as Zoë's central processes were differentially sensitive to visual information about the mouse and auditory information about the dog. Do we need to take account of the details of the *physical* processes which actually realize the processes thus functionally conceived? Not beyond what is necessary for determining the patterns of discrimination and sensitivity. What matters, I would argue, is the *structure of contrasts* determined by the system's total set of discriminatory capacities and sensitivities. This structure gives perceptual experiences their particular characters (Kirk 1994).

When these points are developed I think it is possible to see how the different specific characters of conscious experiences can be understood to be a matter of functional relationships. But given the complexity of most actual perceptual systems and the range of discriminations they are capable of; given also the range of different possible deciders-plus, calling for almost indefinitely extended disjunctions of possible interconnections among functional set-ups, it is hard to see how there could be graspable functional accounts of the specific characters of different types of experience.

The following objection is closely related to the last, but makes a distinct point relating to causation.

Objection J: 'According to functionalism, to be in a mental state is to be in a state which performs a certain role in mediating between inputs, outputs, and other mental states. It doesn't matter what performs that role so long as it gets performed somehow. For example a functionalist account of being in pain might be that it is a state typically caused by damage to the body and typically causing winces, groans, or screams, depending on the severity of the damage (much too crude, but it illustrates the point); and whether this role is performed by C-fibre firing, or by activity in silicon chips, or in some other way, makes no difference to whether the subject is in pain. On this approach, a mental state is the property of *having some other property* (perhaps a neurophysiological one) which performs the role in question. In that sense, functionalism treats mental states as "second-order" properties. Now, *second-order properties are not causally efficacious.* "It is the state that fills the functional role, not the state of having a state that fills the role, which does the causing of behaviour" (Jackson and Pettit 1988: 387). The first-order state of C-fibre firing (or whatever) does the work; the second-order state of *having* a state that does the work does no work. So your functionalism entails a kind of epiphenomenalism. Or at any rate, either pains and other mental states are not functional states, in which case your functionalism is mistaken for that reason; or else they are not causally efficacious, in which case your own claims are exposed to the extended version of the sole-pictures argument, and you are mistaken for *that* reason.'

Reply J: The literature on this topic is getting complicated, and it would involve a long detour to engage in it (see Block 1990; 1997; Fodor 1990; Jackson and Pettit 1988; Kim 1993; 1998; Pereboom 2002). Fortunately I need not engage in it to any depth: I will briefly indicate why I think my position is not exposed to the objection.

I certainly hold that the qualities of our experiences, such as those of smelling eucalyptus or being in pain, are causally efficacious, so I don't think I am exposed to the sole-pictures argument. But even if some kinds of functionalism get into difficulties over second-order properties, I don't think mine does. On my account, having a perceptual-phenomenal experience with a certain quality is a functional property in this sense: it is what it is on account of its relations (causal and other) with other states or processes inside a decider-plus. Now, plausibly a neurological state is *not* in general what it is on account of its relations with other states or processes: it is a state of certain neurones, glial cells, neurotransmitters, or other elements of the brain, not depending for its existence on its relations with things outside itself. For that reason I could not consistently hold that the neural state or process was *identical* with the having of an experience; nor do I. What I can consistently hold is that, when it is occurring inside the right sort of system, it *constitutes* the having of an experience. It would be misleading to say that if having that experience has effects (for example certain thoughts) then what causes those effects is the neural state or process. What causes them is having-that-experience; and having-that-experience is not the same thing as the processes which constitute it in the system as a whole. Now, it may be objected that since nothing is going on but low-level neural processes, they are the only things that could possibly be doing any causing. But recall the example of relief rain, where large masses of air are forced upwards by the shape of the mountainside. In one sense nothing is going on but multitudinous interactions between, on the one hand, particles of the various gases which compose the air, and on the other, particles of the various minerals which compose the surface of the mountain. But in another sense something else is going on too, because those same micro-events, taken together, constitute the macro-event of the mountainside causing large masses of air to rise. When we say the mountainside causes the air to rise, we are *redescribing* (aspects of) those same micro-events. The fact that we can do so explains why the events involved in the numerous micro-causations can constitute a single event of macro-causation. By the same reasoning, the events involved in numerous micro-causations among nerve cells, neurotransmitters, and so on, can constitute an experience's causing certain thoughts. So I think I can consistently maintain both that experiences and their qualities are causally efficacious, and that items at lower levels of description and explanation are also causally efficacious—because the lower-level causal transactions constitute the higher-level ones.

This does not imply that the higher-level descriptions must figure in any laws there may be which cover interactions at lower levels. Together with more than one level of description, we have more than one level of explanation. If the higher-level processes are covered by a science, it will be a 'special science' other than neuro-biology. Its concepts will have been arrived at for different purposes from those of the lower-level science, and its sentences will not in general have equivalents at the lower level. In that sense the higher-level science will be autonomous. But since its descriptions all apply *in fact* to events and processes covered by the lower-level science, everything it provides for will be provided for, in its own special and perhaps restricted way, by the lower-level science. It is worth adding that if the processes involved are all physical, then all the truths statable in terms of the higher-level science—including those about causal relations—will be strictly implied by a sufficiently wide-ranging subset of P, the totality of physically statable truths, though obviously much more remains to be said.

10.11   THE 'EXPLANATORY GAP'

To say there is a gap between the physical facts and the facts of consciousness is just a way of describing an aspect of the mind-body problem. Even eliminativists have to concede that some explanation is called for, even if there are no 'facts' of consciousness. Levine offers a more sophisticated treatment. The aim of his book *Purple Haze*, he tells us,

> was to establish that, when it comes to conscious experience, we face a kind of Kantian antinomy. On the one hand, we have excellent reason for thinking that conscious experi-ence must be reducible, in the requisite sense, to a physical phenomenon, and, on the other hand, we don't see how it could be. (2001: 175)

He says 'The explanatory gap is primarily an epistemological problem, not neces-sarily a metaphysical one' (10). But just what is that problem? He mentions several features which collectively account for what he thinks is special about the problem of naturalizing consciousness. Two key ideas are those of 'gappy identities' and 'thick conceivability'.

He maintains there is a 'sharp epistemic contrast' between 'gappy' identities and standard cases such as that of water and H_2O (81). Suppose for argument's sake that 'the reddish qualititative character of a certain visual sensation' is R, and 'its neurophysiological character' is B, and that it is suggested that R = B (where 'R' and 'B' are singular terms referring to properties). Materialists will find the hypothesis that R = B useful; anti-materialists will demand an explanation. (My own suggestion for solving the what-is-it problem does not entail psycho-physical identities. The only identity I am committed to is between being a subject of perceptual-phenomenal experience and being a decider-plus.) Levine claims that although in that particular case the demand for an explanation of the identity is intelligible, in many cases, such as that of the identity of water with H_2O, it would be unintelligible. So 'R = B' is a gappy identity, while 'Water = H_2O' is not. He thinks attempts to play down this contrast all fail, and takes his reasoning 'to reveal the existence of a genuine explanatory gap, a genuine distinction between gappy and non-gappy identities' (90).

I don't find a relevant contrast here. True, the psycho-physical case is special in all sorts of ways, and any identities required to explain it are likely to raise queries. But the intelligibility of a demand for an explanation of identity is a matter of degree; there is a wide spectrum of empirically based identity claims. Some scarcely call for explanation at all (for example, 'An eclipse of the sun consists of the moon getting between the sun and the earth'). Others are less immediately intelligible; I think that includes even 'Water is H2O' (which does after all leave room for queries, and requires some chemistry together with 'bridging principles' such as 'Water is liquid between zero and 100 degrees Celsius') as well as trickier examples like 'Rainbows are an effect of the distribution of refracted light in raindrops between the observer and the sun' (where the relevant bridging principles need a considerable amount of explanation). No doubt psycho-physical cases are at the difficult end of this spectrum; but arguably the contrast Levine alleges depends on the extent to which the relevant bridging principles are accessible. To be sure, in the case of consciousness and the physical we don't have any generally accepted bridging principles anyway, still less any easily grasped explanations which make them generally accessible. But I discern no relevant epistemic contrast here—although obviously there is still a difference between the more and the less intelligible cases.

Levine discusses the 'conceivability argument' against materialism that we considered in Chapter 3. His initial definition of 'conceivability' is that 'a situation S is conceptually possible (conceivable) relative to representation R just in case S, when thought of under R, is judged possible' (40). As we saw, such liberal definitions make the conceivability argument unworkable, so Levine introduces 'thick conceivability'. A situation is thickly conceivable relative to a representation R 'just in case it's conceptually possible relative to R, and any derivation we can construct from R to a conceptually impossible representation R* will include gappy identities in its premises' (87). (A derivation may include bridging principles.) He reconstructs the conceivability argument on that basis, and finds that version more impressive (though he still does not endorse it). Notably, from the point of view of our concern with the what-is-it problem, he claims that zombies are conceivable in his thick sense. Since that sense is clearly not the one used in my sole-pictures argument, I don't think the conceivability of zombies in that sense is to the point, even though he remarks that 'The conceivability of zombies is ... the principal manifestation of the explanatory gap' (79). All that really matters, from his point of view, seems to be that in spite of there being apparently irresistible reasons to think that materialism is true, and that zombies really are impossible, we have no good explanation of this. I don't see how the apparatus of gappiness and thick conceivability improves our grasp of that predicament. Certainly I don't see that it is an obstacle to my projects in this book.

Suppose we had in front of us a really satisfactory explanation of why zombies are impossible, such as I have been trying to construct. Some people would still be unconvinced, and might insist there were 'gappy identities' in the explanation: identity claims that in their opinion could intelligibly be queried. For them, zombies would still be thickly conceivable. I suggest that would be their problem, not mine. It can't be necessary for functionalists or physicalists to make everyone else accept the truth when it's put to them.

10.12 AWARENESS OF EXPERIENCES

Levine thinks the explanatory gap 'widens' when we come to what he calls the 'problem of duality'. This consists in the fact that on the one hand our awareness of conscious experiences seems to imply that *two* states (the experience itself and our awareness of it) are related, while on the other hand 'experience doesn't seem to admit of this sort of bifurcation' (2001: 168). There are certainly some real problems in this area. One of them manifests itself in the appeal of two equally mistaken models of consciousness: the Cartesian Theatre and the e-qualia conception. We considered this problem in the last chapter, where I suggested we need an account of perceptual-phenomenal experience according to which such things as 'taking account of' and 'attending to' experiences are integral processes, to be conceived of holistically. The coordinated activity of certain relatively large-scale internal processes *constitutes* the system's taking-account-of-directly-active-perceptual-information.

Levine suggests 'It is the quale, the phenomenal experience, that at once has the qualitative character that is "for me", present to my mind, and is also the awareness of itself' (173). I find the idea of a quale that is 'the awareness of itself' obscure, and don't see how it contributes to solving a genuine problem. I suspect we have here an example of how familiarity with sophisticated human forms of consciousness can dazzle us. Being aware *of* states of consciousness implies a more sophisticated mentality than just being perceptually conscious and having a point of view. However, Levine reformulates his suggestion: 'A way to put the problem of duality is just this: how could anything like a point of view exist?' (177). That formulation is certainly less puzzling.

Levine seems to have lumped together two distinct conceptions. My approach offers a way of simplifying a complex of problems. Plausibly, what evolved first were creatures with limited perceptual consciousness and a limited kind of point of view. If such creatures were aware *of* their conscious states at all, it is only in the sense in which a baby may be aware of a flashing light or a pain: such organisms are just *in* those conscious states; they don't know *that* they are in them. It seems reasonable to say a mouse can be phenomenally aware of a cat; but not also to say it's aware *that* it's aware of the cat. That would implausibly require it to have some concept of awareness. Such creatures don't have what Levine calls 'phenomenally constituted thoughts'; yet if they are phenomenally conscious, they still have qualia in the usual sense. If that is right, the problem of perceptual-phenomenal consciousness can be separated from the special difficulties Levine focuses on. In the case of such creatures, duality as he presents it in his puzzling formulations doesn't exist; there is only the problem of how they can have a point of view and be perceptual-phenomenally conscious.

On my approach, relatively simple creatures have phenomenally conscious experiences by means of which they are aware of things in their environment—and it is the creatures themselves, not their individual states, which are aware. Advanced creatures like ourselves have an additional capacity: they can be aware of their experiences and other mental states as such. This sophisticated awareness doesn't seem specially problematic compared with similarly sophisticated aware-ness of other types of mental states—for example, awareness of what one wants. If this approach works, Levine's quale which 'is also the awareness of itself' is a chimera. No mental state is aware of anything: it's the whole organism which is aware of whatever it may be.

10.13 CARRUTHERS'S CRITIQUE

Peter Carruthers has developed a sophisticated 'higher-order thought' theory of phenomenal consciousness (1996: 2000). In expounding and defending it he criti-cizes its rivals, including earlier versions of my own account. Discussing his criti-cisms will further reinforce and clarify my position, which he classifies together with the 'first-order representational (FOR)' theories of Fred Dretske (1995) and Michael Tye (1995). His critique of FOR theories has two stages. The first consists of building up a case for the existence of 'non-conscious' mental states, particularly those he calls 'non-conscious experiences'. The second is a challenge to FOR theor-ists to explain the difference between them and conscious experiences.

In support of the claim that there are non-conscious experiences Carruthers appeals not only to examples such as blindsight, but also to the experimental evidence about two streams of visual processing in the brain that we have already noted. How can any FOR theory accommodate this evidence? In particular, how can my own account accommodate it? Carruthers assumes my view is that 'for a perceptual state with a given content to be phenomenally conscious, and to acquire a "feel", it must be present to the *right sorts* of decision-making processes—namely, to those which constitute the organism's highest-level execut-ive'; and he doesn't see how this 'could transform an experience which isn't phe-nomenally conscious into one which is' (170). But that attack is off-target. Carruthers has a sound objection to the view that perceptual-phenomenal consciousness is just a matter of information being 'present' or 'made available' to certain cognitive systems. As he points out, essentially the same objection can be made to Tye's position. 'It remains mysterious', Carruthers says, 'how *poisedness*—of either the conceptual or action-guiding variety—could be sufficient to confer *feel* on otherwise similar, but non-poised, states which lack it' (178). He is right.

But the view to which that is a sound objection is not mine. As I have tried to show, there is a crucial difference between information being merely poised or available, and its being directly active.

The difference is illustrated by the difference between the rabbit and the rabbitoid. For the rabbitoid, incoming perceptual information is immediately stored in memory, and is 'available' and 'poised' in the sense that the animal can use it if it calls it up. But the information isn't directly active: it isn't forced on the rabbitoid. In my terms, the rabbitoid's incoming perceptual information lacks priority: it doesn't immediately give the animal the opportunity to revise its goals. For that reason I have argued that the rabbitoid is not perceptual-phenomenally conscious. In contrast, the normal rabbit's incoming perceptual information does seem to be directly active: it does seem to have priority; and if that is right, it is why the rabbit is phenomenally conscious. So I claim my account is untouched by Carruthers's objections.

You might for a moment suspect that essentially the same objection could be extended from mere poisedness to direct activity. Why should direct activity confer 'feel' upon incoming information? But I have anticipated that objection. The extended sole-pictures argument shows that there couldn't be a decider-plus without consciousness; the rest of this chapter is aimed to enhance the intuitive appeal of my approach. However, one or two further comments on Carruthers's points will be useful.

First, that there should be an 'on-line action-guiding perceptual system, which is charged with detailed fine-grained control of movement, which responds very swiftly, and whose contents are not conscious' (Carruthers 2000: 166) raises no difficulties for the proposal that it is direct activity which makes for consciousness, as I pointed out when discussing blindsight. On the other hand, some of the conclusions Carruthers draws from the existence of these two systems seem overstated. He asserts that 'most of the time when you act, the perceptions which guide your actions on-line are not conscious ones; and the perceptions which are conscious, and which feed into your thoughts about what you are doing, are not the ones which guide your movements' (166). The evidence he mentions doesn't imply that our movements are not to *any* extent guided by conscious perceptions; only that their detailed execution is not so guided. That is consistent both with actions in general being guided by conscious perception, and with a high proportion of normal-speed movements being largely so guided.

Carruthers asks why 'conceptualisation should give rise to phenomenality in any case. How can the mere availability of a perceptual content to concepts and thought transform it into one which is appropriately *subjective*, having *feel*, or "what-is-it-likeness"?' (173 f.). As he points out, this question amounts to a challenge to explain why phenomenal consciousness should have emerged only at a rather late stage of evolution rather than at earlier stages. My reply is embodied in earlier chapters. I am concentrating on perceptual-phenomenal consciousness. In Chapter 6, I argued that only deciders are perceivers in the fullest sense. I have argued since that the special feature which is additionally necessary for perceptual-phenomenal consciousness depends for its realization on the system's having the basic package. None of that implies that 'conceptualization gives rise to phenomenality'. My approach is obviously consistent with phenomenal consciousness having evolved quite early.

The following remarks summarize Carruthers's challenge to FOR theories:

> The resources available to a FOR theorist in tackling the problem of phenomenal consciousness ... consist just of first-order analog intentional contents together with first-order functional roles. ... the recurring problem for a FOR theorist is to explain, in purely first-order terms, what it is about some, but not other, analog intentional contents which confers on them the properties distinctive of phenomenal consciousness. (178 f.)[8]

Three points summarize my response to that challenge. First, my position is not adequately characterized as a FOR theory in Carruthers's sense because it doesn't rely on availability or poisedness but emphasizes direct activity in the sense explained. Second, direct activity exists only in deciders, which are capable of a kind of belief and thought (subject to the qualifications developed in Chapter 7). Third, what confers the property of 'feel' on my account is direct activity; and that is not just a matter of contents and functional roles, but of how the relevant functions are performed.

A word about formulations of theories of consciousness in terms of 'states' (or 'experiences') which acquire 'properties'. I can't say such formulations are false, since the language of properties is elastic. Being 'directly active' is, after all, a property of the events constituting the acquisition of perceptual information, and so, loosely, also a property of perceptual information. But I suggest that those ways of putting things tend to encourage a misconception. The picture conveyed is of a something (a 'state', 'experience', or 'content') which may exist with or without certain properties: those of phenomenal consciousness. Carruthers represents me as claiming that this 'something' acquires those properties on being 'made available' to the controlling processes. I have just explained why that is a misrepresentation. But the picture is also misleading because it tempts us to the jacket fallacy: it makes it too easy to think we have to look for a property which a state, experience, or content might or might not have, analogously to the way that, for example, a door might or might not be painted red, or a person might or might not be wearing a jacket. That gets us uncomfortably close to the Cartesian Theatre model. I suggest it is better to think of states of phenomenal consciousness as states of a whole system. When the system is in some particular conscious state (for example that of being phenomenally conscious of the blue sky) there are processes which constitute the whole system's being so conscious; but there need be nothing—nothing which remains the same, like the door—which could have constituted the system's being conscious but for the fact that it lacked a certain property.

---

[8] Nothing I have to say turns on Carruthers's use of the analog/digital distinction.

10.14 'WORLDLY-SUBJECTIVITY', 'MENTAL-STATE SUBJECTIVITY', AND HIGHER-ORDER THOUGHT

Carruthers might retort that I have been overlooking a crucial distinction: between getting information about the 'worldly-subjective' property of the sky's blueness, and getting information about the 'experientially subjective' property of the experience of that blueness. He would then restate his objection by saying that I cannot account for that distinction. To elaborate.

In one sense, bats have a different point of view from us simply because their sensory systems are radically different from ours. Carruthers says that because there are such differences in the way the world is perceived, 'the world takes on a subjective aspect by being presented to subjects with differing conceptual and discriminatory powers' (2000,128). He agrees that FOR theories have no difficulty over that sort of subjectivity. What the experience of bats *would be like*, however, if bats were phenomenally conscious (as they aren't if he is right) involves a quite different kind of subjectivity—and again that is surely correct. He describes these two sorts of subjectivity as 'worldly-subjectivity and mental-state-subjectivity' (129). So far so good.

However, he goes on to assert that first-order theorists have to deny the reality of this distinction. According to him, only higher-order theories can provide for it. As I understand it, I find the reality of the distinction undeniable, but see no reason to take up higher-order theory. In outline he conceives of the situation as follows:

(1) Perceiving the world involves representing objects and properties in it, in whatever 'worldly-subjective' modes of perception the subject may have.

(2) Such perception can occur 'transparently', that is, without there being anything it is like for the perceiver: without phenomenal consciousness (2000: 123, 183 f.).

(3) However, in our own case at least, much perception is not transparent but phenomenally conscious: the subject's mental states *themselves* 'take on a subjective aspect' (128).

(4) That requires higher-order representations: 'states which meta-represent the subject's own mental states' (128).

(1) is unproblematic, but the other claims are tricky to assess. (2) is acceptable *only* provided it is restricted to a narrow range of cases: to blindsight, to 'perception without awareness' (subliminal perception) or to creatures like the rabbitoid. But clearly Carruthers intends it to apply also to the perception of all creatures who lack the sophisticated capacities for higher-order thought that he describes. In that sense I think my arguments undermine (2). Claim (3) is capable of being construed innocently. It may be taken to be contrasted with (2) when that too is construed innocently, and to mean simply that much of our own perception does not

resemble blindsight or perception without awareness. But Carruthers clearly means (3) in a sense in which it entails (4). How can he justify (4)?

Apparently aiming at such justification, he asserts that first-order theorists must deny there is 'any real distinction' between 'the analog properties which our experiences represent as figuring in the world', and 'phenomenal properties of the organism's experience of the world'; and goes on to say that such theorists are 'committed to claiming that phenomenal properties of experience just *are* the analog properties of the world represented in experience; ... that the what-is-it-likeness of experience is just a matter of *the world being like something* for the subject when represented in experience in some distinctive analog way (vision, echolocation, or whatever)' (129). So far as I can see, he makes these claims because the versions of first-order theory uppermost in his mind are those of Dretske and Tye. He has a point against those versions. But mine is significantly different. It is not the mere fact that the world is represented in some distinctive way which constitutes there being something it is like to experience it; it is the fact that the events constituting the acquisition of perceptual information are directly active: have simultaneity and priority. When—but only when—they are directly active, the organism's experience of the world can be said to have its own 'phenomenal properties'.[9] Since these properties obviously cannot be identified with properties of things in the world, I don't fall into the error Carruthers detects.

10.15 MORE OBJECTIONS

Objection K: 'There's still a way in which you're begging the question. In effect you're confusing what Block calls *access* consciousness with *phenomenal* con-sciousness. Recall what he says: "Phenomenal consciousness is experience; the phenomenally conscious aspect of a state is what it is like to be in that state. The mark of access-consciousness, by contrast, is availability for use in reasoning and rationally guiding speech and action" (1995: 227). He argues that there can be access-consciousness without phenomenal consciousness, using the example of the "superblindsighter". Ordinary blindsight subjects lack *both* access-consciousness and phenomenal consciousness in their blind fields, so they don't illustrate his point. However, he suggests that "a blindsight patient could be trained to prompt himself at will, guessing what is in the blind field without being told to guess. ... Visual information from his blind field simply pops into his thoughts." Block

---

[9] Not that such properties can be conceived of on the jacket model: as if the experience were a something which might or might not have them. The point is that if there is something it is like for the subject to experience things in the world—as when incoming perceptual information is directly active—then we may correctly *describe* the situation in those terms. That is consistent with the view that direct activity is a matter of integrated processes which do not permit an ontological distinction between an experience and the subject's having it.

concludes that "The superblindsight case is a very limited partial zombie" (1995: 233) because such a person is access-conscious but not phenomenally conscious of what is in their blind field.'

Reply K: I will concede something to the objector, although it's a poisoned chalice. If the suggestion is that phenomenal consciousness in Block's sense has no functional implications whatever, so that its presence or absence leaves behaviour and behavioural capacities completely unaffected, then I concede that phenomenal consciousness *in that sense* is radically different from the consciousness of a decider with directly active perceptual information. But in that case phenomenal consciousness would be completely epiphenomenal. The suggestion that there is such a thing would just be a version of the e-qualia story, or at least exposed to the extension of the sole-pictures argument. In any case, if the present objection relies on the assumption that phenomenal consciousness *is* epiphenomenal, then it itself begs the question. It does nothing to undermine my argument that being a decider-plus is c-sufficient for there to be something it is like.

That apart, I don't think I'm begging the question at all. The superblindsighter's blind-field visual information conspicuously lacks direct activity. Having to 'prompt yourself at will' is as different as could be from acquiring perceptual information with instantaneity and priority. Since nevertheless Block submits the superblindsighter as a case of 'access-consciousness', the objection is off-target. So evidently I'm not confusing access-consciousness in that sense with phenomenal consciousness.

In a footnote Block discusses among other things a 'super-duper-blindsighter whose blindsight is every bit as good, functionally speaking, as his sight', but says that he chose the superblindsighter to make his point 'in part to avoid conflict with the functionalist' (246 n.16). He also notes that he could put his point in terms of three 'types of access: (1) truly high-quality access, (2) medium access, and (3) poor access'. Actual blindsight patients have (3), superblindsighters have (2), and super-duper-blindsighters, 'as well as most of us', have (1). I think the extension of the sole-pictures argument, especially when taken together with the other reasoning in the earlier part of this chapter, shows that these examples do not provide materials to refute the contention that being a decider-plus is logically sufficient for being perceptual-phenomenally conscious. If *all* the functions of direct activity really are performed in the super-duper-blindsighter, then that individual really has perceptual-phenomenal visual consciousness, not blindsight at all.

Block's notion of 'access' will bear a closer look. He says:

A state is access-conscious (A-conscious) if, in virtue of one's having the state, a representation of its content is (1) inferentially promiscuous . . ., that is, poised for use as a premiss in reasoning, (2) poised for rational control of action, and (3) poised for rational control of speech. (1995: 231)

He adds that these conditions are jointly sufficient, but not all necessary: specifically, (3) is not necessary because he wants to allow some languageless creatures to have A-conscious states. (In response to comments, he states he 'didn't intend to imply that principles of logic or good reasoning are necessary for A(-consciousness) or that animals cannot have A. I meant to appeal to the use of a representation in reasoning, even if the reasoning is poor' (278).)

The notion of 'use of a representation' makes me uneasy for reasons indicated at 8.5 above. But my chief worry is this. Block seems to assume that the only relation functionalists can appeal to in this context is one of *quality of access*, together with the idea of content being 'poised' in the sense of 'ready and waiting' (245 n 8). As I hope is clear, the relation of direct activity is not a matter of quality of access. Even the rabbitoid's perceptual information can be of the same high quality as that of the standard rabbit. What matters is that although the rabbitoid's information may perhaps be poised in the sense of 'ready and waiting', it is not directly active. Even high-level access-consciousness does not entail direct activity, it seems. For that reason it doesn't entail phenomenal consciousness by my account.

Objection L: 'You have conceded that creatures other than deciders can be said to perceive. Why shouldn't they have perceptual consciousness of a kind? Even if prawns are not deciders, why shouldn't they feel pain? Indeed, why shouldn't much simpler creatures such as the amoeba still have "some small dull Perception"? Pleasure and pain, especially, are very basic to survival, and must have come early in the evolutionary story; so even a creature with no other kind of consciousness might still have pleasure or pain.'

Reply L: I argued earlier that the basic package is necessary for perception in the full sense, so that creatures such as Galen Strawson's Weather Watchers, who supposedly perceive their environment in spite of lacking control of any behaviour, are impossible: they would perceive no more than litmus paper or photographic film do. However, I have conceded that some kinds of reflex systems, which by definition lack the basic package, can still be said to perceive, so the objection may appear to have some force.

There seem to be just two ways in which the objection may be pressed. One would be to suggest that there is a special non-functional 'conscious component' to the creature's perception: something which makes the difference between just having the right behavioural and processing capacities, and being perceptually conscious. Let's call this special component x. How could x make any contribution to the creature's life? By hypothesis the creature has no directly active perceptual information. Also by hypothesis, it doesn't even acquire information in the sense explained and discussed in Chapters 6 and 7. Does x have any relevant effects on its internal processes? No, since by hypothesis x has no functional impact. What, then, could make the difference between x's having something to do with this creature's life, and its having no connection with the creature at all? The only possible reply seems to be that x is *caused* by processes inside the creature; it might also be isomorphic with certain significant aspects of those internal processes. But by the extended sole-pictures argument, x's being caused by such processes, or isomorphic with them, does nothing to ensure that the creature is conscious. So the x-theory cannot account for perceptual consciousness.

The other way to pursue the objection would be to concede that consciousness plays a functional role, but urge that it could be less complex than the one I have picked on. What might that possibly be? One suggestion would be *reactivity*. But if mere reactivity, or even only a very high level of reactivity, constituted perceptual consciousness, then we'd have to count things like litmus paper and cameras as perceptually conscious, which they aren't. A more promising suggestion would be that a 'representation' becomes conscious when it passes a certain threshold of activation. But then, why should high activation levels result in consciousness in the first place? The only possible answer would have to be in terms of functions; and I would need to be told what is wrong with the arguments I have offered for picking on the functions involved in the basic package-plus. To repeat, I concede that I may have picked on the wrong functional roles. But I have given my reasons, and can only wait to see what further objections there are to the ones I have chosen.

The idea that pleasure and pain are basic has understandable appeal. Although Aristotle knew nothing of evolution he was aware of the dependence of perceptual capacities on others, remarking that 'whatever has sense-perception also has pleasure and pain and both the pleasant and the unpleasant; and whatever has these also has desire. For this is a reaching out for the pleasant ...' (*De Anima*, 414^{b}6). However, there seem to be good reasons why creatures whose behaviour is explicable on the basis that they are reflex systems, even if not pure reflex systems, cannot be regarded as serious candidates for being subjects of sensation (*pace* Nicholas Humphrey (1992), who ascribes sensations even to the amoeba). There seems to be nothing happening in such systems that could actually *constitute* their having sensations. To start with, not being deciders, they have no interpretation, assessment, or decision-making. So whatever processes constituted their having sensations would have to be located somewhere in their various reflex subsystems. The trouble then is that these may well be independent of each other, in which case there can be no reason why a single reflex should not have its own proprietary sensation—regardless of whether or not it was connected to the rest of the system. But that would entail that the system as a whole didn't have any of these sensations, contrary to the suggestion.[10] When you reflect further there seems no way for this suggestion to be slotted into the evolutionary story. Even if individual reflexes had sensations (an idea I find unintelligible) there is no way that those sensations could contribute to the creature's survival because they couldn't be sensations *of* the total creature. If you still think there could be such sensations anyway, what prevents the subsystem in a piano which consists of a single key plus linkages to hammer and strings from having its own sensation? Again: there is nothing that

[10] This does not imply that a conscious system could not have subsystems that were also conscious. On the contrary, I think the homunculus-head would be an instance. The claim I am attacking is that a reflex system as a whole might be conscious. If its only consciousness were that of its separate reflexes, there would be nothing to constitute its own consciousness.

could constitute its having a sensation. The idea seems impossible to entertain except on the basis of something like the Cartesian Theatre, or the associated idea that consciousness is a sort of psychic paint, which can be applied to or withheld from any sort of mental state whatever—an assumption I take to have been demolished by the extended sole-pictures argument.

Objection M: 'In many cases the cause of an action cannot be conscious perception. For example, when my hand accidentally comes into contact with a hot surface and I pull it back, the movement occurs *before* I feel the heat. Nor is this phenomenon confined to mere reflexes: the same happens when playing fast ballgames. How do you reconcile that sort of thing with your account of perceptual-phenomenal consciousness?'

Reply M: Recall the discussion of automatism. I am not saying *all* behaviour occurs as a result of decisions based on conscious perception. Reflexes such as automatic withdrawal of the hand from heat don't even appear problematic for my account. Nor, I suggest, are the almost instantaneous reactions of skilled tennis-players. In effect they have trained themselves so effectively that many of their actions are close to reflexes; to the extent that that is true, again they don't make difficulties for my account. Perhaps I should re-emphasize that I am not recommending a traditional variety of functionalism, according to which what makes a state conscious is its *causal* role. The situation is more complicated. There is perceptual-phenomenal consciousness when the events constituting a decider's acquisition of perceptual information have instantaneity and priority. Plenty of perceptual information may also come in unconsciously, as is apparently the case with the heat-reflex and acquired tennis-return reflexes.

10.16 WHY THERE WILL ALWAYS SEEM TO BE A GAP

We noticed in the last chapter that zombies would be deciders-plus. So if the arguments in this book are sound, they would be phenomenally conscious and not zombies after all. Indeed, if I am right, zombies are actually inconceivable in the only sense that matters. Why then is the zombie idea so tempting? Anti-physicalists tend to make much of this question, but really there is no mystery here. The what-is-it problem arises from the fact that human beings are both objects and subjects: objects whose behaviour and internal workings are open to observation and describable in terms of viewpoint-neutral concepts; subjects whose thoughts and feelings, though not open to observation, are still describable—in terms of viewpoint-relative concepts. There is a gulf between these two kinds of concepts, which makes it too easy to imagine that the 'objective' kind might apply even if the 'subjective' kind did not. Associated with that gulf, of course, is the gulf between being a mere observer of such an organism, and being that organism itself. These gulfs form a daunting obstacle to attempts on the what-is-it problem.

The point is illustrated by the reasoning by which it is sometime argued that because functional roles can be revealed by third-person observation, the presence of phenomenal consciousness cannot. We noted early on that Chalmers reasons in this way (3.7). The mistake, I suggest, is to assume that observation alone could reveal whether the playing of such roles was or was not c-sufficient for perceptual-phenomenal consciousness, ignoring the fact that philosophical explanations are also necessary. The slip seems to be essentially the same as Leibniz's nearly three centuries earlier, when he remarked:

We have to admit that perception, and what depends on it, cannot be explained mechanically, that is, by means of shapes and movements. If we imagine a machine whose construction ensures that it has thoughts, feelings, and perceptions, we can conceive it to be so enlarged, while keeping the same proportions, that we could enter it like a mill. On that supposition, when visiting it we shall find inside only components pushing one another, and never anything that could explain a perception. (*Monadology*, §17)

True, their targets are different. Leibniz is attacking mechanism, so writes of seeing components pushing one another; Chalmers is attacking functionalism, so writes of functional roles being revealed by observation. But the same basic error occurs. Both philosophers assume that the failure of observation to reveal the existence of a logical connection (strictly, in my terms, a c-necessary connection) from observable physical processes to conscious experience proves there is no such connection at all. Leibniz, like today's anti-physicalists, finds it easy to imagine the machinery churning away in the absence of conscious experience; both assume their thought experiments settle the matter. (Could Leibniz really have supposed that gazing at the machinery would help? Surely he started off from the assumption that perception and thought couldn't possibly be mechanical processes.) Both philosophers neglect the possibility that a sound approach to the nature of perception might make clear that what on the surface appear to be unrelated types of processes should be related as I claim they are: that there should be no more to the occurrence of conscious experiences than there is to performance of the relevant functions by physical processes.

Because of those two gulfs—between observer and subject, and between viewpoint-neutral and viewpoint-relative concepts—the zombie idea seems likely to continue to be a seductive source of confusion.

11

Survival of the Fittest

Why prefer my account to any of its numerous rivals? I will briefly consider the main alternative approaches, though without much detailed criticism; there is plenty of that in the journals. Two hors-dœuvres precede the main discussions: one on neuroscientific and scientific-psychological accounts, the other on the irrelevance of the traditional metaphysical doctrines.

11.1 SCIENTIFIC-PSYCHOLOGICAL AND NEUROSCIENTIFIC ACCOUNTS

Undertaken from a scientific standpoint, theorizing about consciousness has two characteristics which mark it off from the projects of this book. One is that for obvious reasons it typically focuses on consciousness in human beings. The other is that it typically aims primarily to throw light on the mechanisms. These differences prevent straightforward comparisons between scientific approaches and my own. I am concerned with consciousness in general, whether in terrestrial creatures or in other possible systems, and have nothing to say about mechanisms.

When scientists do speculate on the functions which matter from the point of view of understanding consciousness, their assumptions tend to link them with one or other of the main philosophical approaches to be considered later. For example Alan Baddeley tentatively suggests that the subject is conscious of whatever information is processed in 'the central executive component of working memory' (1997: 333), which brings him close to Evans. Edmund Rolls favours the idea of 'higher-order linguistically-based thought processing' (1999: 252). And Weiskrantz' (1997) suggestion that consciousness requires a 'commentary' is also close to the higher-order thought idea, and has affinities with Dennett's notion of 'probing'.[1] The 'global workspace' notion developed by Bernard Baars (1997) is one way of attempting to get a grasp of the relevant functions, but it is not much more than a metaphor, and seems to leave much scope for conflicting interpretations, as do the other suggestions.

---

[1] Among other things Weiskrantz says, 'Phenomenal awareness itself, in our view, results from the delivery or potential delivery of a report' (1997: 76). Dennett's notion of 'probing' and the 'higher-order thought' approach will be discussed later: 11.6, 11.11.

The functions I have been discussing in the crude terms of everyday psychology could surely be more adequately characterized on the basis of a more scientific psychology. For that reason as well as others, my approach is heavily subject to revision in the light of scientific work. However, I think the two main contributions of this book—demolition of the zombie idea; and the account of perceptual-phenomenal consciousness in terms of the basic package-plus direct activity—offer reasonably solid grounds for supposing that, contrary to what some philosophers have argued, if neuroscientists can explain the processes underlying conscious experience, and in particular how those processes perform the functions involved in the basic package-plus, then they will in fact have explained 'experience itself' (Chalmers 1996: 118).

I will comment on two features of some of the more philosophically orientated suggestions from neuroscientists and neuropsychologists. One is a distinction between two kinds of consciousness: simple and complex, or 'primary' and 'higher-order' (Edelman and Tononi 2000); or 'core' and 'extended' (Damasio 1999). The simpler kind of consciousness is supposed to be included in the complex kind, and to be present in relatively humble organisms. According to Edelman and Tononi, primary consciousness is 'the ability to generate a mental scene in which a large amount of diverse information is integrated for the purpose of directing present or immediate behaviour' (103). This kind of consciousness depends on four main factors: perceptual categorization; concepts; memory; and 'value constraints' (roughly, facts about the organism that were selected during evolution and exert pressure on how the brain develops and on the formation of neural circuits). That those four main factors come into the story is pretty obviously entailed by the basic package; they also, plausibly, entail it. On the other hand, it is not clear whether Edelman and Tononi's primary consciousness involves what I would call direct activity as well as the basic package. They might accept that it does involve it; further clarification of what would constitute a 'mental scene' might make that clear.

The other feature is an emphasis on the importance of a conception of the 'self'. Damasio says the simplest kind of consciousness, 'core consciousness', 'provides the organism with a sense of self about one moment—now—and about one place—here'. It is 'not dependent on conventional memory, working memory, reasoning, or language' (16). He also says of consciousness in general that it 'consists of constructing knowledge about two facts: that the organism is involved in relating to some object, and that the object in the relation causes a change in the organism' (20). Now, regardless of how the details of this account may be elaborated, it clearly demands considerably more sophistication from conscious subjects than mine does. I see no reason why what is counted as the lowest level of 'consciousness' (in effect, the basic package-plus and nothing more) should require the subject to have the conceptual or other means to know that something outside it *causes a change in it.* On my account it is enough if the outside world does in fact have relevant effects on the organism. In addition, I see no reason why all conscious subjects should have a 'sense of self' at all, unless that is just a way of saying they must discriminate between themselves and things outside them. In this connection it is notable that there has long been a tendency on the part of theorists to feel that some kind of reciprocal or reflexive processes involving the concept of a self are necessary in order to account for the peculiarities of consciousness.[2] That assumption goes beyond what I know of any good reasons to accept.

11.2 DUALISM AND PHYSICALISM

Dualism and physicalism are traditionally treated as approaches to solving the mind-body problem. In fact they contribute nothing. However, there are significant differences between the ways they make their null contributions.

Dualism amounts to asserting that the what-is-it problem has no solution. It takes consciousness to be a brute fact which cannot be understood, even though its manifestations can be richly described. According to dualism there just is this special non-physical stuff, or there just are these special non-physical properties, and they take care of all the puzzling features of thought, consciousness, and other mental phenomena. Dualism tells us nothing about why non-physical stuff, or non-physical properties, should be capable of providing for any aspect of mentality at all. No reason is ever given why, alongside the non-physical stuff that is allegedly involved in consciousness and thought, there shouldn't be unconscious, unthinking non-physical stuff as well. So dualism is only the ghost of a solution to the mind-body problem. (Idealism has the same problems, together with its own special ones.)

Physicalism too, regarded purely as a metaphysical thesis, has nothing to say about the mind. But in contrast to dualism its purely metaphysical component leaves scope for illuminating accounts of mentality. Strictly, my account is neutral between dualism and physicalism. Practically it favours physicalism, since if successful it explains how a purely physical system can be a subject of phenomenal consciousness.

There is a notorious lack of evidence in favour of dualism, and masses of evidence for the view that the physical domain is closed under causation: that every physical event that is caused at all is caused physically. If that is true it demolishes all kinds of interactionist dualism, since it leaves no room for a non-physical mind to affect the physical world. It thereby forces dualists to adopt epiphenomenalism, parallelism, panpsychism, or the like, which in turn forces them to concede that a parallel zombie world is logically possible—something I have argued is inconceivable in the relevant sense; in which case those positions are untenable too.

---

[2] For example: 'The particular subjective experience of consciousness depends on self-awareness, which arises from both the recursive ability to embed mental models within mental models and the mind's possession of a high-level model of the capabilities of its own operating system' (Johnson-Laird 1983: 477. See also Mulhauser 1998; LaBerge 1997).

11.3   WITTGENSTEIN AND SARTRE

Some philosophers propose that we need a different kind of philosophy. Perhaps we should adopt a Wittengsteinian approach:

But can't I imagine that the people around me are automata, lack consciousness, even though they behave in the same way as usual?—If I imagine it now—alone in my room— I see people with fixed looks (as in a trance) going about their business—the idea is perhaps a little uncanny. But just try to keep hold of this idea in the midst of your ordinary inter- course with others, in the street, say! Say to yourself, for example: 'The children over there are mere automata; all their liveliness is mere automatism.' And you will either find these words becoming quite meaningless; or you will produce in yourself some kind of uncanny feeling, or something of the sort.

Seeing a living human being as an automaton is analogous to seeing one figure as a limiting case or variant of another: the cross-pieces of a window as a swastika, for example. (Wittgenstein 1953, sect. 420)

On the face of it Wittgenstein's remarks are consistent with the account of percept- ual consciousness offered here. They appear to be concerned only with our powers of imagination; and he is surely right about the difficulty of imagining the situa- tion he describes. However, his overall approach is not consistent with my account. This is not the place for extended Wittgensteinian exegesis, but I do want to explain why I think my account does something that needs to be done, while he appears to regard such accounts as superfluous or even misguided.

One of his guiding thoughts is that 'only of a living human being and what resembles (behaves like) a living human being can one say: it ... is conscious or unconscious' (1953, sect. 281: I discussed this passage briefly earlier: 7.9). I take it the point is that the system of concepts that concerns us here applies prim- arily to living human beings—on account of the patterns of behaviour typical of living human beings, not on account of what happens inside their skulls. Wittgenstein recognizes that our behaviour depends on what goes on inside our skulls; but he seems to think the details are irrelevant: only the behavioural outcome matters. If that *is* his idea, then in Chapters 6 and 7 I have offered reasons for thinking that, on the contrary, the nature of the internal processing matters too.

Peter Hacker offers a nicely clear-cut construal of Wittgenstein according to which 'That human beings and higher animals are conscious creatures is not an empirical truth, but a grammatical one. ... The assertion that human beings are conscious ... only has a use as a grammatical proposition. It might be employed as part of an explanation of what the expression "human being" or "conscious" means.' On that interpretation Wittgenstein's point is that it's because such assertions are merely 'grammatical' that it is not 'intelligible' that 'human beings, behaving just as they normally do', should really be not conscious at all (1990: 525). I don't think that is an adequate response to the zombie idea.

For one thing, since by definition zombies are not human beings, it misses the point to say it's unintelligible that *human beings* should lack consciousness. A Wittgensteinian might retort that since (also by definition) zombies have exactly the same behavioural capacities and dispositions as normal human beings, it's also unintelligible that there should be such creatures. Although this 'grammatical' point could not be claimed to be directly connected with the meaning of the expression 'human being', it might still be held to be connected with that expression indirectly (via the claim that only something sufficiently like a human being can intelligibly be said to be conscious or unconscious). That would be a weak response, though, since the zombie idea is thought to be an objection to such views. Even if Wittgenstein wasn't a behaviourist in any straightforward sense, the line of thought we are considering is too behaviouristic to damage the zombie idea; it comes too close to begging the question. I agree that the idea of zombies is in a sense not 'intelligible', but that view needs solider support than Wittgenstein offers.

Much the same goes for the views of Sartre in *Being and Nothingness*. He has a lot to say about consciousness in a broad sense, much of which is relevant to our concerns. His key thoughts are not too remote from Wittgenstein's. According to Sartre, when we are looking at other people and in other ways interacting with them, we typically see them *as* conscious beings. In his jargon, we see each person as a 'for-itself' (*pour-soi*). But we can also see them as things: each as an 'in-itself' (*en-soi*). The attitude we have to another person—to a living body in its aspect as 'for-itself'—is quite different from, and not reducible to, the attitude we have to a body as an 'in-itself'. It's not that there is a Cartesian mind, a special kind of 'psychic object' somehow yoked to the body. There is nothing over and above the body, although it has these two 'aspects': as for-itself and as in-itself; 'there are no "psychic phenomena" there to be united with the body' (1958: 305). What needs emphasizing is that Sartre just takes it for granted that there *are* these special entities, these 'for-itselfs'. As with Wittgenstein, either Sartre is just a behaviourist—a position we have seen good reasons to reject (and which he himself also rejects)— or he assumes there are no problems over explaining what it is for something to be a for-itself. Either way, he leaves the what-is-it problem untouched.

I am not saying Sartre set out to solve the what-is-it problem and failed. It seems he was more concerned to throw light on the nature of consciousness by spelling out what he took to be the main significant features of human existence, taking for granted that there are such entities as the for-itself. Heidegger similarly takes for granted that there is such a thing as 'Being-in-the-world'. (For discussion see McCulloch 1994.)

11.4 BEHAVIOURISM

Philosophical behaviourism is a partially persuasive attempt to explain the nature of mind, with its own distinctive solution to the what-is-it problem. Under 'philosophical behaviourism' I include all views according to which mental life is just a matter of engaging behaviourally with the world, including other people— and nothing else. Here is a slightly tighter characterization:

Philosophical behaviourism is the claim that for a system to have mental states of any kind is just a matter of its behaving or being disposed to behave, or capable of behaving, in certain ways.

This characterization does not require behaviourists to provide necessary and sufficient conditions, expressible in terms of behaviour and dispositions, for each individual mental state or state type. It is enough that nothing other than behaviour and dispositions or capacities is necessary for having mental states. This variety of behaviourism thereby escapes some of the most obvious objections to other varieties. Just which 'certain ways' of behaving matter is open to negotiation.

Philosophical behaviourism is fiercely opposed not only to Cartesian dualism but to any account of mind according to which what we sometimes call our 'inner' lives are inner in any way but metaphorically. According to it, having a mind in general, and having conscious experiences in particular, involve no special class of entities or properties, but only activity in the world—of beings with certain capacities. This rules out zombies very directly. Since by definition they would share all our behavioural dispositions and capacities, they would share all our mental states, including those involving consciousness, hence *wouldn't* be zombies.

While this approach has much that is valuable, it fails if only because the nature of the inner processing matters. If there is a problem anything like the one I set out to solve at the start of this book, behaviourism doesn't address it. A fortiori the same goes for eliminativism.

11.5 OTHER FUNCTIONALISMS

No doubt my position is a variety of functionalism—though only in a very broad sense of that elastic term. I want to emphasize one or two ways in which it differs from other varieties and is not exposed to the objections which may undermine them. The broadly functionalist idea I find acceptable is simply that mental states depend for their existence on the performance of functions, when these (and hence the mental states themselves) are determined by certain kinds of relations among a system's inputs, outputs, and internal states. By that criterion all the main accounts of consciousness to be discussed later in this chapter are varieties of functionalism. They differ only in which functions they pick out as the relevant ones. It is worth noting how functionalism contrasts with the psycho-physical identity theory. On its own, the identity theory is objectionable because it fails to say anything about *what matters* about those particular brain processes which it says are identical with mental states, about what makes them mental states at all. Functionalism offers to supply that deficiency—and in doing so, renders the identity theory redundant. (If functionalism is true, and the physical universe is as physicalists suppose, there is no need to establish any psycho-physical identities. It is enough to show that the relevant functions are in fact performed by purely physical items.)

Just which functional relations among inputs, outputs, and internal states matter for perceptual-phenomenal consciousness is what I have been trying to make clear enough in the course of explaining the basic package and direct activity. Causal relations are vitally important, but *how* things are caused is also important, as shown by some of the examples in Chapter 7. It is not enough for the causal relations in a decider to satisfy broad overall constraints: they have to be such that all the system's processes of interpretation, assessment, and decision-making are appropriately integrated.

Some varieties of functionalism are objectionable because they ignore the nature of the internal processing (Putnam's early 'machine functionalism' is an example). Others are objectionable because they require semantic reductions of statements about mental states in physical or functional terms, or would 'define psychological states in terms of causal relations among sensory inputs, internal states and behavioral output' (Baker 1985: 1.). Others misleadingly identify mental states with either functional roles or physical properties. And some assume that functionalism is committed to the view that pains, for example, are dispositions (Pereboom 2002). If functionalism is taken to imply any of those views, the basic package-plus view of perceptual-phenomenal consciousness is not functionalist.

Chalmers regards what he calls 'reductive functionalism' as 'the most serious materialist option' (1996: 164). By 'reductive functionalism' he understands a view according to which consciousness is 'conceptually entailed by' (or 'logically supervenient on') the physical 'in virtue of functional or dispositional properties'. I certainly maintain that consciousness is so entailed, and therefore count as a 'reductive functionalist' according to that characterization. However, he goes on to assert:

reductive functionalism does not differ much from eliminativism. Both of these views hold that there is discrimination, categorization, accessibility, reportability, and the like; and *both deny that there is anything else that even needs to be explained.* The main difference is that the reductive line holds that some of these explananda deserve the name 'experience', whereas the eliminative line holds that none of them do. Apart from this terminological issue, the substance of the views is largely the same. ... Neither is a view that takes consciousness seriously. (1996: 165, my emphasis)

Perhaps that last remark should just be construed as teasing. In case anyone takes it seriously, and in order to make things as clear as possible, here are three ways in which that passage seriously misrepresents at any rate some kinds of functionalism, and certainly fails to cover the basic-package-plus approach. First, in common with many functionalists, I am trying to deal head-on with the what-is-it problem. I accept that there *is* conscious experience: I am trying to explain precisely that fact. Since eliminativists deny there is such a fact, that difference cannot be described as merely 'terminological'. Second, that aim entails that we 'take consciousness seriously'. Third, and most important, I hold that what has to be explained is, precisely, the existence of conscious experience. It may be true that for some functionalists, their philosophical explanations lead them to conclude that in order to explain consciousness all they have to do is explain things like 'discrimination, categorization, accessibility, reportability, and the like'. If so, it misrepresents their position to imply that they start off by denying that there is anything else to be explained. They think they have earned the right to say precisely that—but only *after* they have explained that consciousness involves no more than those things. Whatever some functionalists may assume, I emphatically do not 'deny that there is anything else that even needs to be explained'. On the contrary, I accept that there *is* something else that needs to be explained: that is the what-is-it problem.

11.6 DENNETT ON 'MULTIPLE DRAFTS' AND 'JOYCEAN MACHINES'

For someone whose notable contributions to the philosophy of mind include a book called *Consciousness Explained,* Dennett's own account of consciousness is elusive. Like Ryle, he is understandably cautious about committing himself to any particular -ism, such as behaviourism or verificationism. ('Damn all -isms', Ryle used to say.) But the uncertainty does not concern which ready-made label to apply to his position: it concerns what that position actually is.

Broadly, his approach is to reject two familiar sources of worry (the alleged possibilities of absent and inverted qualia) as nothing but symptoms of the baneful influence of the Cartesian Theatre. Of course I agree that zombies are impossible. However, as explained in Chapter 7, I think the absent qualia possibility in a broader sense is genuine. I also think something like transposed qualia is a possibility once internal physical/functional differences are allowed, but has no adverse implications for a naturalistic approach. Dennett's approach seems excessively behaviouristic, as when he remarks, 'What qualia *are,* Otto, are just those complexes of dispositions. When you say "*This* is my quale," what you are singling out, or referring to, *whether you realize it or not,* is your idiosyncratic complex of dispositions' (1991: 389).

His account has two phases: an outline of recent scientific findings and theories on the evolution and nature of human consciousness; and a set of fresh metaphors designed to remove philosophical confusion. Let us consider his two main metaphors: those of 'multiple drafts' and 'Joycean machines'. The question is whether they throw enough light to disperse philosophical perplexities and confusions over consciousness. If they do, there is indeed no need for a special philosophical 'theory' of consciousness on top of the scientific facts.

First, then, multiple drafts. This is a metaphor for the widely accepted model of mental activity as involving a vast number of parallel processes. Perception in particular involves sensory inputs being elaborated, modified, and 'interpreted' simultaneously, by specialized subsystems, along many parallel tracks in various parts of the brain. There is no 'headquarters' or 'inner sanctum within the brain, arrival at which is the necessary or sufficient condition for conscious experience' (106). Among the events thus distributed over the brain are many 'events of content-fixation'. Although these occur at precise times and places, their occurrence is not sufficient for consciousness; indeed, 'it is a confusion, ... to ask *when (one of them) becomes conscious*' (113). Over time, 'these distributed content-discriminations yield ... something rather like a narrative stream or sequence'. 'At any point there are multiple "drafts" of narrative fragments at various stages of editing in various places in the brain' (113).

That metaphor, together with the scientific story, is intended to loosen the grip of the Cartesian Theatre model—a tendency which doesn't vanish, Dennett points out, when we give up Cartesian dualism. I don't think the metaphor does the trick. The most salient reason is the least serious: the metaphor offered as a replacement for Cartesian ways of thinking is itself Cartesian. Drafts are composed and read by someone. If metaphorically there are draft narratives inside the brain, the metaphor implies there is someone in there writing and reading them: just the picture it was supposed to displace. True, Dennett's idea is that the 'narratives' are assembled by processes which do *not* involve internal authors; but his metaphor tends to suck us back into the Cartesian quicksands rather than help us out of them. More serious is the question whether the metaphor helps to explain the difference between conscious and unconscious processes. Indisputably not all brain processes are conscious. But what makes some of them so? Dennett replies in terms of a further metaphor, 'probing'. 'Probing this stream (of Multiple Drafts) at different places and times produces different effects, produces different narratives from the subject' (113; cf. 135 f.). But what is probing? One interpretation would be that it is whatever the subject has to do in order to be able to produce a verbal statement of the content of experience. The few indications Dennett gives suggest that the subject is either asked a question or at any rate produces a statement (113, 135, 143, 169 f. Weiskrantz (1997) seems to recommend such an approach: see n.1 above). But if you are inclined to think that some languageless creatures are conscious (as he seems willing to concede) you will resist the suggestion that language-dependent probing is necessary. If probing is necessary at all, it had better not require language. But then what can it be? Some sort of intentional act, apparently; but that has awkward implications. For example, if our conscious states depend on probing, it seems we could avoid unpleasant experiences such as headaches by simply not probing in the first place—which is absurd. If probing is not an intentional act, though, we are given no clues as to what it might be.[3]

---

[3] There is useful critical discussion of Dennett's thoughts on probing in Carruthers 1996. See also Kirk 1993, on which this section draws.

The point of Dennett's second main metaphor, 'Joycean machines', emerges with his synthesis of evolutionary accounts of human consciousness. The primate brain 'consists of a conglomeration of specialist circuits designed to perform particular tasks in the economy of primate ancestors' (188). To the resulting problem of 'higher-level control', the idea of a 'pandemonium' architecture promises a solution. But this architecture yields a nervous system without the capacity to plan ahead. Somehow human minds go beyond this primate basis, with the ability both to reflect on what is going on and to consider what might come next. Dennett suggests that human consciousness consists of culturally evolved software of a 'serial' kind, installed in the hard-wired 'parallel' architecture we largely share with our languageless primate cousins. We are born with brains equipped with a vast range of specialist subsystems but a lot of plasticity. We then acquire 'an already invented and largely "debugged" *system* of habits' (193), most notably those involved in possession of language. The flow of spoken and unspoken monologues is analogous to the flow of instructions and data through a standard sequential computer. (The metaphor's name alludes to the internal monologues in Joyce's *Ulysses*.)

Exploiting this metaphor of Joycean virtual machines, Dennett says,

> I hereby declare that YES, my theory is a theory of consciousness. Anyone or anything that has such a virtual machine as its control system is conscious in the fullest sense, and is conscious *because* it has such a virtual machine. (281)

That certainly looks like a commitment to the view that a Joycean virtual machine is both necessary and sufficient for consciousness. But consider the suggestion that serial software is imposed on hard-wired parallel architecture. As he says, for any machine whose hard-wired architecture is parallel, there is in principle a hard-wired serial machine that can do anything it can do (1991: 217 f.). So the claim that the underlying architecture in our case is parallel and not serial seems to have no specific relevance to the philosophical question of what it is for something to be conscious. Similarly for the 'virtual machine' idea. Any virtual machine can in principle be hard-wired, so from our point of view it cannot matter whether the Joycean machine is virtual or hard-wired. If the idea is to do useful work on the philosophical problems of consciousness, therefore, we can leave the question of serial versus parallel architecture on one side. But what now remains of the claim that a thing is conscious 'because' it is controlled by the right kind of virtual machine? Dennett's language is at best misleading. How serious is the claim that it's a *machine*? Saying it is a 'system of habits' (193) makes no commitment to its being a machine in any interesting sense. Without that commitment, what is offered as a 'theory of consciousness' boils down to no more than the claim that consciousness consists of behaving like a language-user.

Nor can Dennett consistently go beyond that position. To impose constraints on the nature of the internal processing would conflict with his views on the ascription of content, according to which those ascriptions are independent of any consideration of the nature of processes inside the organism. So it seems he could not consistently deny that the generalized Block machine, for example, instantiated a Joycean machine, in which case he must accept that it would be conscious—in the teeth of arguments to the contrary noted in Chapter 7.[4] The metaphor of the Joycean machine, like that of multiple drafts, may be useful for directing empirical work in the right directions; neither metaphor seems very helpful for throwing light on the philosophical issues.

11.7 PURE REPRESENTATIONALISM

Today many philosophers hold that the character of a conscious experience is its *representational content* (Dretske 1995; Tye 1995). I will call this broad approach 'pure representationalism'; it is also referred to as 'intentionalism'.[5] (Dretske and Tye differ slightly in their accounts of what it is for a state to be representational. Dretske does it on the basis of 'information-providing function', which is supposedly fixed by evolutionary factors. Tye does it on the basis of causal covariance: roughly, a given state represents whatever it is caused to covary with under optimal conditions, which are those where the state performs its evolutionary function. We can ignore those differences.)

You don't have to be a pure representationalist to agree that many conscious or phenomenal states *are* representational. If I see a rabbit lolloping by, my experience represents a rabbit. What distinguishes pure representationalism is the thesis that a state's being conscious or phenomenal involves nothing *more* than its being representational: in Tye's words, 'phenomenal character can be *identified* with representational content of a certain sort' (1995, p. xv, my emphasis). The identity claim is crucial.

If phenomenal character just is representational content, the task of explaining phenomenal consciousness is simplified. At least it is simplified if we assume externalism: the view that, broadly, for a state to have representational content is a matter of its being appropriately related to things in the world. Dretske and Tye are externalists, and like all externalists, they reject the idea that something can be *intrinsically* representational. Given externalism, then, we seem to have a reasonable grasp of how there can be representational content; in contrast we seem to have scarcely any grasp of how there can be phenomenal character (before reading this book).

On the other hand pure representationalism is counter-intuitive. That conscious perceptual states are representational is unproblematic; that their

---

[4] Dennett insists that any program capable of a reasonably sophisticated conversation 'would have to be an extraordinarily supple, sophisticated, and multi-layered system, brimming with "world knowledge" and meta-knowledge and meta-meta-knowledge …' (1991: 438)—which seems to rule out a Block machine (though at the price of giving up behaviourism). But it hardly refutes the suggestion that the system's innards could be so different from our own that it did not instantiate a Joycean machine.

[5] For a broader type of intentionalism see Siewert 1998.

phenomenology is *nothing but* their representational content seems paradoxical. There are two main problems. One is that merely to say phenomenal character is representational content leaves us wondering what makes it conscious. Tye recognizes this; his response is his PANIC story.

The other problem is this. It is pretty well universally agreed that states subjectively indistinguishable from genuine perceptual consciousness can be caused in non-standard ways. For example, a state phenomenally just like the one involved in my seeing a meteor last night might have been caused by stimulating certain cells of my visual cortex. Now, if in the particular case of some individual, some of their perception-like states were *usually* caused non-standardly (taking normal human beings as the reference class), then, on externalist assumptions, the representational *contents* of those states for that individual would be different from what they were for the rest of the population. Either those states would fail to represent at all, or perhaps (it might be claimed) they would represent the states of that individual's brain. Either way, if pure representationalism is correct, those states would necessarily be *perceptual-phenomenally* different too. But it is hard to deny that subjectively indistinguishable states—hence phenomenally exactly similar states—may be caused in different non-standard ways. That is a big problem for pure representationalism.

Swampman—an exact duplicate of Donald Davidson produced by the freak action of lightning on a log in a bog (Davidson 1986)—makes an interesting test case. Externalists agree that because Swampman lacks appropriate connections with things in the world he lacks genuine beliefs, desires, and other intentional states, including memories. That is in spite of the fact that, being from the skin inwards an exact duplicate of Davidson himself, he is indistinguishable from Davidson (once he has cleaned himself up) and behaves just as if he shared Davidson's beliefs, desires, memories, and the rest. In time, no doubt, he will acquire appropriate connections with his environment; but we are talking about the first moments of his existence. All externalists will agree with those remarks; but they will not agree over whether Swampman has phenomenal consciousness from the start.

What does the basic-package-plus-direct-activity account of perceptual consciousness imply about Swampman, still assuming that representational contents depend on external relations? Being exactly like Davidson in all respects not dependent on relations with things in the world, Swampman qualifies as a decider-plus. But now recall that being a decider-plus does not depend on the possession of full-blown concepts (Chapter 8). That is just as well, since even a moderate externalism could hardly allow that Swampman has any concepts other than, perhaps, purely logical and mathematical ones, even though he certainly has all the internal arrangements necessary for a very highly sophisticated and world-involving conceptual system indeed. Concepts are intimately linked with beliefs: what concepts you have depends at least partly on what beliefs you have. Because Swampman lacks the necessary links with things in the world, too much is still indeterminate for him to count as having the same beliefs or concepts as Davidson himself—if he has any at all. For that reason, although Swampman acquires information and, indeed, perceives things in the same sense as that in which all deciders-plus perceive things, he doesn't perceive things in the full-blown way Davidson himself does. So although on my account Swampman is perceptual-phenomenally conscious, and (for example) sees the water all round him, he doesn't perceive *that* there's a lot of water around him because he doesn't yet have a water-concept appropriately linked with his actual environment. For all he knows, he might be on Twin Earth.

Dretske's representationalism contradicts that conclusion. On his view Swampman perceives nothing and has no experiences or qualia: a Swampman-like replacement for you 'would get the same information you get (through its "eyes", "ears", and "nose"), but these systems . . . would not have the biological function of providing information . . . . [For that reason] There would . . . be no experiences *of*, no beliefs *about*, no desires *for*, these objects. There would be no qualia' (1995: 126). I am inclined to take those consequences as a *reductio ad absurdum* of Dretske's position. Why shouldn't there be something it is like for Swampman? Dretske's defence of ordinary externalism is powerful, but he carefully refrains from claiming his arguments establish pure representationalism itself. I think this book provides good reasons against at least his version of pure representationalism.

Tye notes that if we construe representation on the causal covariation model,

. . . no obvious difficulty arises for the claim that some of Swampman's inner states represent things. States in his head certainly track various external environmental states, just as mine do. . . . So it is natural to suppose that . . . optimal conditions obtain and hence that there is sensory representation of those external states. (1995: 154 f.)

On that basis Swampman represents things after all. But it still remains counter-intuitive to insist that what his experiences are like depends on his relations with things in the world. Pure representationalism connects representational content and subjective quality too tightly. I suggest that, given that the basic package-plus account does all that is needed, there is no good reason to cling to pure representationalism.

As we have seen, my account is consistent with holding that a system can be phenomenally conscious without satisfying the necessary conditions for being *perceptual-phenomenally* conscious. Swampman is one illustration; brains-in-vats would be another. So it is consistent with my account that the phenomenal quality of a system's experiences should be wholly determined by its internal processes, regardless of whether they are contentful at all.

Pure representationalism and zombies

There is a special sense in which pure representationalists are committed to the possibility of zombies. Because externalists hold that 'phenomenal character ain't in the head' (Tye 1995: 194), they have to count Swampman as a zombie of a kind, at least to start with. In Dretske's words, 'There can be counterfeit thinkers (i.e. zombies) for the same reason there can be counterfeit $100 bills: the counterfeits are objects that do not stand in the right relations to other things. They do not, for example, have the right history' (1995: 185 n. 13). But that is not the sense of 'zombie' which is at issue in this book. We are concerned with zombies in the sense of creatures indistinguishable from us not only internally, but in respect of their external relations. Pure representationalists could not allow the possibility of a zombie world in that sense: physically just like the actual world (as physicalists take it to be), but phenomenally different (cf. Tye 1995: 195). In such a world, as they are at pains to try to explain, there would be all the relations of representation that hold in the actual world, and therefore all the same instances of phenomenal consciousness.

11.8 HIGHER-ORDER PERCEPTION

Locke asserted that 'Consciousness is the perception of what passes in a Man's own Mind' (*Essay* II.i.19). Without further explanation, this suggestion conjures up the deceptive picture of a homunculus facing a procession of 'mental phenomena': the Cartesian Theatre. It puts the original problem one step back. The problem is that we are faced with the world, and want to explain how we can have conscious perceptual experience of it. We are told that instead of perceiving the world directly, we (or if not we, then some component of ourselves) perceive a representation of the world. If it was a problem how being faced with the world gives rise to conscious experience of it, essentially the same problem returns. How can being faced with an image or other kind of representation give rise to conscious experience of it or of the world?

But perhaps that objection is unimaginative. Data are scanned or monitored by computers, so at least part of the underlying idea cannot be objected to. If Locke's original conception of internal perception is too crude, why not revise it in terms of computer scanning or monitoring? In *A Materialist Theory of the Mind* David Armstrong argues that consciousness, or rather what he calls 'introspection', is a kind of 'inner sense' (Kant's phrase). In introspection the organism perceives its own mental states and, he suggested,

If we make the materialist identification of mental states with material states of the brain, we can say that introspection is a self-scanning process in the brain. The scanning operation may itself be scanned, and so on, ... (1968: 324)

Armstrong doesn't say much to explain the nature of this scanning, apart from the point that introspection in this sense is 'the getting of information or misinformation about the current state of our mind' (326). But that point is vital. One reason is that it entails that what acquires the scanned information is the system as a whole, not just some subsystem. It would not have been enough for the outputs of the scanning to be put into some subsystem, rather than (somehow) into the system as a whole; even very humble reflex systems can incorporate that sort of scanning. Once that has been made clear, though, it becomes hard to think of what is going on as a kind of 'inner sensing' or any kind of perception. The system doesn't somehow confront its own 'mental states', as the perceptual model implies. Instead, it just acquires information about them. But since we know the acquisition of information can occur unconsciously, this account of 'introspection' seems at best an incomplete solution to the what-is-it problem. (Güzeldere 1997 offers further criticism.) In any case it seems too narrowly confined to the problem of mechanisms, not focusing sharply enough on the question of what functions are necessary for perceptual-phenomenal consciousness.

11.9 HIGHER-ORDER THOUGHT

That leads us to an alternative higher-order account of perceptual consciousness, according to which it involves not higher-order perception, but higher-order thought (HOT). The most straightforward account of this type is David Rosenthal's original version:

Conscious states are simply mental states we are conscious of being in. And, in general, our being conscious of something is just a matter of our having a thought of some sort about it. Accordingly, it is natural to identify a mental state's being conscious with one's having a roughly contemporaneous thought that one is in that mental state. (1986: 335)

This explanation of the difference between conscious and unconscious perception has the great merit of being clear. The former is perception we have suitable thoughts about; the latter is perception we have no suitable thoughts about. But that clarity comes at a cost. Is it plausible that every case of conscious perceptual experience is one we have some *actual* thought about? Although many conscious perceptual experiences do involve thoughts about them, the thoughts seem to follow the experiences rather than being what made them conscious in the first place. If I experience a sudden twinge of toothache it tends to make me think about it. But the notion that what made it conscious was having a thought about it is strange. That particular version of the higher-order thought account of perceptual consciousness seems at odds with the facts.

Rosenthal knows that. He goes on to suggest that the conscious-making thoughts need not themselves be ones we are conscious of having. Indeed, he thinks higher-order thoughts are 'typically' not conscious (1997: 744, 745). But that concession undermines the initial appeal of his approach. If we are not conscious of having the thoughts in question, why suppose we are having them at all? The mere fact that positing them helps the theory is not much of a recommendation. What extra benefit is there from having those thoughts: couldn't we have got on perfectly well without them?

To overcome such difficulties other types of higher-order theories have been suggested (for example Carruthers 1996; 2000; Lycan 1996; 1997). I will focus on the latest version of Peter Carruthers's account, some important aspects of which we have already considered. It is a 'dispositionalist' account: a mental state's being phenomenally conscious is a matter of its being 'available' to be thought about by the subject rather than (as on Rosenthal's approach) actually being thought about.

A central feature of Carruthers's account is that perceptual contents are passed to two (or more) short-term memory stores, C (conscious) and N (non-conscious), from where they contribute to the control of action. The contents of C (which are intentional and 'analog') feed into the processes of 'conceptual thinking', which include higher-order thoughts involving 'mind-reading'. The contents of N feed into other processes, notably 'action schemas' and motor control. There is also a 'standing-state belief' box, whose contents are interaccessible with those of conceptual thinking. Carruthers holds that 'the conscious status of an experience consists in its *availability* to HOT' (227). But since standing beliefs are also available to higher-order thought yet not phenomenally conscious, more has to be said. What ensures that some perceptual contents are not just available to be thought about, but phenomenally conscious? The crucial difference is said to be the presence of a 'mind-reading' or 'theory of mind faculty'. This subsystem understands among other things the distinction between 'is' and 'seems', alternatively understands experience 'as a subjective, representational, state of the perceiver'. It enables the subject to have thoughts of the form 'This has a distinctive *seeming* distinct from the *seeming* of that', or 'This *experience* is distinct from that' (241). Carruthers argues that the presence of the mind-reading system has effects on the contents of the short-term memory store C. He thinks this is a consequence of the sort of semantics he favours, which is 'consumer semantics' (either functional- or inferential-role semantics, or teleosemantics, contrasted with informational or causal co-variance semantics: see his 2000: 102, n.6; and 241–57). The distinctive feature of his account is that he thinks that whereas the contents of C would otherwise have been merely 'first-order representations of the environment (and body)', the availability of these contents to the mind-reading system confers on them an additional content:

Each experience of the world-body becomes at the same time a representation that just such an experience is taking place; each experience with the content *red$_a$*, say, is at the same time an event with the content *seems red$_a$* or *experience of red$_a$*. (242)

I find this hard to follow; but let us suppose he is right about this sort of 'dual content'. The question is whether he is also right in his further, crucial, claim that this dual representational content is what constitutes the 'feel' of a phenomenally conscious experience (2000: 243 f.).

Is Carruthers's account necessary for perceptual-phenomenal feel? I believe my earlier arguments show it is not. The mind-reading subsystem requires the subject to have such concepts as *seeming* or *subjective state*. That implies quite a high degree of conceptual sophistication; I have argued that such sophistication is unnecessary for being a subject of perceptual-phenomenal consciousness.

Is his account sufficient for perceptual-phenomenal feel? Again, I don't think so. So far as I can see it does not provide for what I have argued is necessary: direct activity. Even if incoming perceptual information is endowed with the sort of dual content Carruthers claims it acquires from being available to the mind-reading subsystem, the information is still only *available* to that and the thinking subsystem. This seems to leave a Carruthersian organism in the same situation as the rabbitoid: perceptual information comes into it and is available for control of behaviour, but it doesn't have the right actual effects. Mere availability, I have argued, is not enough.

Relatedly, Carruthers's account requires the *content* of a representational state to be enough by itself to ensure that it is phenomenally conscious. Yet he takes a lot of trouble to establish that many contents are not conscious. Even though conscious experiences may have the right sort of dual content, why shouldn't unconscious states have that sort of content too? What guarantees that this special sort of content is conscious?[6] It is mysterious that a state's content alone should make so much difference.

I tentatively diagnose that higher-order thought accounts conflate two distinct conceptions of what it is for an experience to be phenomenally conscious. One is standardly expressed by saying that:

(a) For an experience to be phenomenally conscious is for there to be *something it is like* to have the experience.

The other is that:

(b) For an experience to be phenomenally conscious is for the subject either *to be aware of* what the experience is like, or at least to be capable of being so aware.

A remark of Rosenthal's encourages this diagnosis: 'When a mental state is conscious, it is not simply that we are conscious of that state; we are conscious of being in that state' (1997: 741). That claim needs to be defended by argument: unsupported, it just begs the question (for further discussion, see Dretske 1993). The arguments for higher-order accounts would work if we could legitimately assume that an account of phenomenal consciousness according to conception (b) would also be an account of it under conception (a). But the two conceptions are plainly different. The effect of assuming they are not significantly different is to make the supporting reasoning seem more compelling than

---

[6] Alex Byrne (2001) raises the same objection in his review of Carruthers 2000. It is true that Carruthers discusses the suggestion that his account entails that a Freudian unconscious (something he rejects) would contain phenomenally conscious experiences (2000: 266 f.). But that is not the objection just raised in the text.

it is. Those who insist that we need an account of what it is for there to be something it is like to perceive the world do not have to accept that being aware of *what* an experience is like is the same as there being *something* it is like to have it. They insist that conception (b) is more sophisticated than conception (a). Conception (b) requires the subject to have something like appropriate concepts of experience; (a) does not.

How could two such different conceptions have become conflated? One reason may be a train of thought inspired by considering the first-person case. There is something it is like for me to see the blue sky. How do I know that? Only by having a higher-order thought about the experience. Moreover, it can seem that the only way we can tell with reasonable certainty whether there is something it is like for other people is what they say—and they cannot say anything relevant unless they have higher-order thoughts about their experiences. That reasoning is obviously defective, since it disregards the non-verbal behavioural and other evidence we have for phenomenal consciousness. I am not alleging that this reasoning is consciously engaged in by higher-order theorists, only that some of their remarks are puzzling unless something on those lines is covertly influential. (Weiskrantz' remarks about 'commentary' come close to it: 1997: 75 f.) Although Rosenthal cannot be charged with explicitly endorsing it, he is impressed by the thought that if we are conscious of something, then we know about it. If that means only that when we are phenomenally conscious of a tree, for example, then we know something about the *tree*, it is very plausible. If it means that when we are so conscious, we also know something about the *experience* of the tree, it just begs the question (see also the discussion of Zoë at 10.3).

A consequence of refusing to concede that (a) and (b) are two distinct conceptions, and that what goes for phenomenal consciousness according to one of them doesn't necessarily go for it according to the other, is that higher-order thought theories have to accept that phenomenal consciousness requires more cognitive sophistication than most animals or even babies can plausibly be supposed to have. The basic-package-plus-direct-activity account, in contrast, allows relatively unsophisticated creatures to be phenomenally conscious. (Levine 2001 and Siewert 1998 provide further criticisms of higher-order accounts.)

11.10 CORE POINTS

Any attempt to solve the what-is-it problem has to steer through a jungle of misleading theories and assumptions. My brief discussions of the principal ones may have distracted some readers from the true path, so I will end by recalling this book's core points.

The idea of zombies is interesting for two reasons: because if a zombie world is possible, then physicalism is false (Chapter 2); and because it embodies a conception

of phenomenal consciousness which, though seductive, is fundamentally misconceived. The book undertakes two main projects: to expose the incoherence of the
zombie idea, and to explain what it is for something to be perceptual-phenomenally
conscious.

None of the arguments purporting to establish the possibility of zombies is
compelling (Chapter 3). Further, the zombie idea entails the e-qualia story, which
the sole-pictures argument shows to be incoherent. Zombies are therefore impossible (Chapter 4). That completes the book's first main project and undercuts
some of the most influential objections to broadly functionalist approaches to
phenomenal consciousness.

It does not explain what consciousness is: it does not solve the what-is-it problem.
A solution to the what-is-it problem would help us with the is-it-like-anything
problem. The what-is-it-like problem, however, is distinct from those other two,
and is for Nagelian reasons impossible to solve. Solving the what-is-it problem
demands less than some would claim (Chapter 5).

My strategy has been to use certain concepts of everyday psychology that we
understand reasonably well as a basis for understanding the ones that perplex us,
and in particular for understanding what matters in perceptual-phenomenal consciousness. I have assumed that everyday psychology is moderately realistic.

The first stage in pursuing this strategy has been to articulate a complex of
capacities—the basic package—which is necessary as a whole for perceptual-
phenomenal consciousness. The concepts involved in specifying the basic package
have been further elucidated by examples. These have helped to illustrate how the
application of everyday psychological concepts depends to some extent on taking
account of interrelations among the internal processes of a system (Chapter 7). It
is important that having the basic package (being a 'decider') does not necessarily
involve having a language (Chapter 8).

The basic package, though necessary for perceptual-phenomenal consciousness, does not seem also to be sufficient, as consideration of the imaginary rabbitoid shows. So the second stage in dealing with the what-is-it problem has been
to explain what must be added to the basic package to guarantee that a decider is
perceptual-phenomenally conscious. The necessary additional feature is directly
active perceptual information, which has two aspects: instantaneity and priority.
To avoid a threatened dilemma, direct activity has to be conceived of holistically,
as a matter of integrated processes. However, the proposed account of perceptual
consciousness in terms of direct activity is not equivalent to one in terms of
'availability' or 'poisedness' (Chapter 9).

On the assumption that the basic package-plus satisfies the necessary functional conditions for perceptual-phenomenal consciousness, the sole-pictures
argument can be extended to rule out unconscious deciders-plus. I have argued
that the assumption is true: the basic package-plus does satisfy the necessary functional conditions for perceptual-phenomenal consciousness. So I conclude that

the basic package-plus is both necessary and sufficient for perceptual-phenomenal consciousness (Chapter 10).

However, the gulf between being the observer of a conscious subject and being that subject, and the associated gulf between viewpoint-neutral and viewpoint-relative concepts, are both wide. Even if I am right, those who have not gone step by step through the necessary philosophical reasoning will remain liable to seduction by the zombie idea. It will stay shimmering there, poised to dazzle and confuse.

Bibliography

Akins, Kathleen, 1996. 'Of Sensory Systems and the "Aboutness" of Mental States', *Journal of Philosophy*, 93: 337–72.

Anscombe, G. E. M., 1959. *Intention*, Oxford: Blackwell.

Armstrong, David M., 1968. *A Materialist Theory of the Mind*, London: Routledge & Kegan Paul.

Austin, C. R., and R. V. Short (eds.), 1972. *Embryonic and Fetal Development* (Book 2 of *Reproduction in Mammals*), Cambridge: Cambridge University Press.

Baars, Bernard J., 1997. *In the Theater of Consciousness: The Workspace of the Mind*, New York: Oxford University Press.

Baddeley, Alan, 1997. *Human Memory: Theory and Practice, rev. edn.* Hove, UK: Psychology Press (Taylor and Francis).

Baker, Lynne Rudder, 1985. 'A Farewell to Functionalism', *Philosophical Studies*, 48: 1–13.

Balog, Katalin, 1999. 'Conceivability, Possibility, and the Mind-Body Problem', *Philosophical Review*, 108: 497–528.

Bermúdez, José Luis, 1998. *The Paradox of Self-Consciousness*, Cambridge, Mass. and London: MIT Press.

Block, Ned, 1978. 'Troubles with Functionalism', in Wade Savage (ed.), *Perception and Cognition: Minnesota Studies in the Philosophy of Science*, 9/100: 261–325.

—— 1980. 'Are Absent Qualia Impossible?', *Philosophical Review*, 89: 257–74.

—— 1981. 'Psychologism and Behaviorism', *Philosophical Review*, 90: 5–43.

—— 1990. 'Can the Mind Change the World?', in George Boolos (ed.), *Meaning and Method: Essays in Honor of Hilary Putnam*, Cambridge: Cambridge University Press, 137–70.

—— 1995. 'On a Confusion about a Function of Consciousness', *Behavioral and Brain Sciences*, 18: 227–47.

—— 1997. 'Anti-Reductionism Slaps Back', in James E. Tomberlin (ed.), *Philosophical Perspectives 11: Mind, Causation, and World*, Boston, Mass. and Oxford: Blackwell, 107–132.

—— 2002. 'The Harder Problem of Consciousness', *Journal of Philosophy*, 99: 391–426.

—— and Robert Stalnaker, 1999. 'Conceptual Analysis, Dualism, and the Explanatory Gap', *Philosophical Review*, 108: 1–47.

—— Owen Flanagan, and Güven Guzeldere (eds.), 1997. *The Nature of Consciousness: Philosophical Debates*, Cambridge, Mass. and London: MIT Press.

Botterill, George, and Peter Carruthers, 1999. *The Philosophy of Psychology*, Cambridge: Cambridge University Press.

Braddon-Mitchell, David, 2003. 'Qualia and Analytical Conditionals', *Journal of Philosophy*, 100: 111–36.

Byrne, Alex, 1999. 'Cosmic Hermeneutics', in J. Tomberlin (ed.), *Philosophical Perspectives*, 13: 347–83

—— 2001. Review of Carruthers 2000, *Mind*, 110: 1057–62.

Campbell, John, 1994. *Past, Space and Self,* Cambridge, Mass. and London: MIT Press.

Campbell, Keith, 1970. *Body and Mind,* Garden City, NY: Doubleday.

Carruthers, Peter, 1996. *Language, Thought and Consciousness,* Cambridge: Cambridge University Press.

—— 2000. *Phenomenal Consciousness: A Naturalistic Theory,* Cambridge: Cambridge University Press.

Chalmers, David J., 1996. *The Conscious Mind: In Search of a Fundamental Theory,* New York and Oxford: Oxford University Press.

—— 1999. 'Materialism and the Metaphysics of Modality', *Philosophy and Phenomenological Research,* 59: 475–97.

—— 2002*a.* 'Does Conceivability Entail Possibility?', in T. S. Gendler and J. Hawthorne (eds.), *Conceivability and Possibility,* Oxford: Clarendon Press, 145–200.

—— 2002*b.* 'Consciousness and its Place in Nature', in Steven Stich and F. Warfield (eds.), *The Blackwell Guide to the Philosophy of Mind,* Oxford: Blackwell, 102–42.

—— 2003, 'The Content and Epistemology of Phenomenal Belief', in Q. Smith and A. Jokic (eds.), *Consciousness,* Oxford: Clarendon Press, 220–72.

—— and F. Jackson, 2001, 'Conceptual Analysis and Reductive Explanation', *Philosophical Review,* 110: 315–61.

Churchland, Paul, 1985. 'Reduction, Qualia, and the Direct Introspection of Brain States', *Journal of Philosophy,* 82: 8–28.

Clark, Andy, 2001. 'Visual Experience and Motor Action: Are the Bonds Too Tight?', *Philosophical Review,* 110: 495–519.

Conee, Earl, 1995. Review of Kirk 1994, *Mind,* 104: 645–50.

Crane, Tim, 2003. 'The Intentional Structure of Consciousness', in Q. Smith and A. Jokic (eds.), *Consciousness,* Oxford: Clarendon Press, 33–56.

d'Aguilar, J., J.-L. Dommanget, R. Préchac, 1986. *Field Guide to the Dragonflies of Britain, Europe and North Africa,* rev. and trans. by Stephen Brooks, Nicola Brooks, and T. S. Robinson, London: Collins.

Damasio, Antonio, 1999. *The Feeling of What Happens: Body, Emotion, and the Making of Consciousness,* London: Heinemann.

Davidson, Donald, 1982. 'Rational Animals', *Dialectica,* 36: 318–27; repr. in E. Lepore and B. McLaughlin (eds.), 1985. *Actions and Events: Perspectives on the Philosophy of Donald Davidson.* Oxford: Blackwell, 1985, 473–80 (to which page references refer).

—— 1984. *Inquiries into Truth and Interpretation,* Oxford: Clarendon Press.

—— 1987. 'Knowing One's Own Mind', *Proceedings and Addresses of the American Philosophical Association,* 60: 441–58.

Dennett, Daniel C., 1969. *Content and Consciousness,* London: Routledge & Kegan Paul.

—— 1987. *The Intentional Stance,* Cambridge, Mass.: MIT Press.

—— 1991. *Consciousness Explained,* Boston, Toronto, London: Little, Brown.

—— 1995. 'The Unimagined Preposterousness of Zombies', *Journal of Consciousness Studies,* 2: 322–6.

Dretske, F. 1993. 'Conscious Experience', *Mind,* 102: 263–83.

—— 1995. *Naturalizing the Mind,* Cambridge, Mass. and London: MIT Press.

Dummett, M. 1993. *The Seas of Language,* Oxford: Clarendon Press.

Dye, Frank F. 2000. *Human Life Before Birth,* Amsterdam: Harwood Academic Publishers.

Edelman, G. M., and G. Tononi, 2000. *Consciousness: How Matter Becomes Imagination*, London: Penguin Books (pub. in the USA as *A Universe of Consciousness*, New York: Basic Books).

Evans, G., 1982. *The Varieties of Reference* (ed. J. McDowell), New York and Oxford: Clarendon Press.

Fodor, J. A., 1987. *Psychosemantics: The Problem of Meaning in the Philosophy of Mind*, Cambridge, Mass. and London: MIT Press.

—— 1990. 'Making Mind Matter More', in his *A Theory of Content and Other Essays*, Cambridge, Mass. and London: MIT Press, 137–59.

—— and Zeno Pylyshyn, 1988, 'Connectionism and Cognitive Architecture: A Critical Analysis', *Cognition*, 28: 3–63.

Gallistel, Charles R., 1990. *The Organization of Learning*, Cambridge, Mass. and London: MIT Press.

Gazzaniga, Michael S., 1988. 'Brain Modularity: Towards a Philosophy of Conscious Experience', in A. J. Marcel and E. Bisiach (eds.), *Consciousness in Contemporary Science*, Oxford: Clarendon Press, 1988, 218–38.

Gendler, Tamar S., and John Hawthorne (eds.), 2002. *Conceivability and Possibility*, Oxford: Clarendon Press.

Giurfa, Martin, S. Zhang, A. Jenett, R. Menzel, and M. V. Srinivasan, 2001. 'The Concepts of "Sameness" and "Difference" in an Insect', *Nature*, 410/6831: 930–3.

Güzeldere, Güven, 1997. 'Is Consciousness the Perception of What Passses in One's Own Mind?', in N. Block *et al.* (eds.), *The Nature of Consciousness*, Cambridge, Mass. and London: MIT Press, 789–806.

Hacker, Peter M. S., 1990. *Wittgenstein: Meaning and Mind*, Oxford: Blackwell.

Hepper, P. G. 1997. 'Memory in Utero?', *Developmental Medicine and Child Neurology*, 39: 343–6.

Hill, Christopher S., 1997. 'Imaginabililty, Conceivability, Possibility, and the Mind-Body Problem', *Philosophical Studies*, 87: 61–86.

—— 1998. 'Chalmers on the Apriority of Modal Knowledge', *Analysis*, 58: 20–6.

—— and B. P. McLaughlin, 1999. 'There are Fewer Things in Reality Than Are Dreamt of in Chalmers's Philosophy', *Philosophy and Phenomenological Research*, 59: 446–54.

Hillyard, P. D. 1996. *Ticks of North-West Europe*, Shrewsbury: Field Studies Council for the Linnaean Society of London and the Estuarine and Coastal Sciences Association.

Horgan, Terence, and John Tienson, 1996. *Connectionism and the Philosophy of Psychology*, Cambridge, Mass. and London: MIT Press.

Humphrey, Nicholas, 1992. *A History of the Mind*, London: Chatto & Windus.

Hurley, Susan, 1997. 'Nonconceptual Self-Consciousness and Agency: Perspective and Access', *Communication and Cognition*, 30: 207–48.

Jackson, Frank, 1982. 'Epiphenomenal Qualia', *Philosophical Quarterly*, 32: 127–36.

—— 1994. 'Armchair Metaphysics', in John O'Leary Hawthorne and Michaelis Michael (eds.), 1998, *Philosophy in Mind*, Dordrecht: Kluwer, 23–42; repr. in his *Mind, Method and Conditionals*, London and New York: Routledge, 154–76.

—— 1998. *From Metaphysics to Ethics: A Defence of Conceptual Analysis*, Oxford: Clarendon Press.

—— and Philip Pettit, 1988. 'Functionalism and Broad Content', *Mind*, 97: 381–400.

Johnson-Laird, P. N., 1983. *Mental Models*, Cambridge: Cambridge University Press.

Kim, Jaegwon, 1993. *Supervenience and Mind*, Cambridge: Cambridge University Press.

—— 1998. *Mind in a Physical World*, Cambridge Mass. MIT Press.

Kirk, Robert, 1974*a*. 'Sentience and Behaviour', *Mind*, 83: 43–60.

—— 1974*b*. 'Zombies v. Materialists', *Aristotelian Society Proceedings, suppl. vol.* 48: 135–52.

—— 1979. 'From Physical Explicability to Full-Blooded Materialism', *Philosophical Quarterly*, 29: 229–37.

—— 1982. 'Physicalism, Identity and Strict Implication', *Ratio*, 24: 131–41.

—— 1986. 'Sentience, Causation, and Some Robots', *Australasian Journal of Philosophy*, 64: 306–19.

—— 1993. ' "The Best Set of Tools"? Dennett's Metaphors and the Mind-Body Problem', *Philosophical Quarterly*, 43: 335–43.

—— 1994. *Raw Feeling*, Oxford: Clarendon Press.

—— 1996*a*. 'Strict Implication, Supervenience, and Physicalism', *Australasian Journal of Philosophy*, 74: 244–56.

—— 1996*b*. 'How Physicalists Can Avoid Reductionism', *Synthese*, 108: 157–70.

—— 2001. 'Nonreductive Physicalism and Strict Implication', *Australasian Journal of Philosophy*, 79: 545–53.

Kripke, Saul, 1972. *Naming and Necessity*, Oxford: Blackwell.

LaBerge, David, 'Attention, Awareness, and the Triangular Circuit', 1997. *Consciousness and Cognition*, 6: 149–81.

Latham, Noa, 2000. 'Chalmers on the Addition of Consciousness to the Physical World', *Philosophical Studies*, 98: 71–97.

Levine, Joseph, 1983. 'Materialism and Qualia: The Explanatory Gap', *Pacific Philosophical Quarterly*, 64: 354–61.

—— 1993. 'On Leaving Out What It's Like', in M. Davies and G. Humphreys (eds.), *Consciousness: Psychological and Philosophical Essays,* Oxford: Blackwell, 121–36.

—— 2001. *Purple Haze: The Puzzle of Consciousness*, Oxford and New York: Oxford University Press.

Lewis, David K., 1966. 'An Argument for the Identity Theory', *Journal of Philosophy*, 63: 17–25.

—— 1994. 'Reduction of Mind', in S. Guttenplan (ed.), *A Companion to the Philosophy of Mind*, Oxford: Blackwell, 412–31.

Loar, Brian, 1997. 'Phenomenal States', in N. Block *et al.* (eds.), *The Nature of Consciousness*, Cambridge, Mass. and London: MIT Press, 597–616.

—— 1999. 'David Chalmers's *The Conscious Mind*', *Philosophy and Phenomenological Research*, 59: 465–72.

Locke, John, 1689/1975. *An Essay Concerning Human Understanding*, ed. P. H. Nidditch, Oxford: Clarendon Press.

Lockwood, Michael, 1998. 'Unsensed Phenomenal Qualities: A Defence', *Journal of Consciousness Studies*, 4: 415–18.

Lowe, E. J., 1996. *Subjects of Experience*, Cambridge: Cambridge University Press.

Lycan, William G., 1996. *Consciousness and Experience*, Cambridge, Mass. and London: MIT Press.

—— 1997. 'Consciousness as Internal Monitoring', in N. Block *et al.* (eds.), *The Nature of Consciousness*, Cambridge, Mass. and London: MIT Press, 755–71.

McCulloch, Gregory, 1994. *Using Sartre: An Analytical Introduction to Early Sartrean Themes*, London and New York: Routledge.

McDowell, John, 1994. *Mind and World*, Cambridge, Mass. and London: Harvard University Press.

McGinn, Colin, 1982. *The Character of Mind*, Oxford and New York: Oxford University Press.

—— 1991. *The Problem of Consciousness*, Oxford: Blackwell.

Marcel, A. J., and E. Bisiach (eds.), 1988. *Consciousness in Contemporary Science*, Oxford: Clarendon Press.

Milner, A. David, and Melvyn A. Goodale, 1995. *The Visual Brain in Action*, Oxford: Oxford University Press.

—— D. I. Perrett, R.S. Johnston, P.J. Benson, T. R. Jordan, D. W. Heeley, D. Bettucci, F. Mortara, R. Mutani, E. Terazzi, and D.L.W. Davidson, 1991. 'Perception and Action in Visual Form Agnosia', *Brain*, 114: 405–28.

Mulhauser, Gregory R., 1998. *Mind out of Matter: Topics in the Physical Foundations of Consciousness and Cognition*, Dordrecht: Kluwer.

Murdoch, Iris, 1970. *The Sovereignty of Good*, London: Routledge & Kegan Paul.

Nagel, Thomas, 1974. 'What is it Like to Be a Bat?', *Philosophical Review*, 83: 435–50; repr. in his 1979. *Mortal Questions*, Cambridge: Cambridge University Press.

—— 1994. 'Consciousness and Objective Reality', in R. Warner and T. Szubka (eds.), *The Mind-Body Problem*, Cambridge, Mass. and Oxford: Blackwell, 63–9.

—— 1998. 'Conceiving the Impossible and the Mind-Body Problem', *Philosophy*, 73: 337–52.

Papineau, David, 2002. *Thinking about Consciousness*, Oxford: Clarendon Press.

—— 2003. 'Theories of Consciousness', in Q. Smith and A. Jokic (eds.), *Consciousness*, Oxford: Clarendon Press, 353–83.

Peacocke, Christopher R., 2001. 'Does Perception Have a Nonconceptual Content?', *Journal of Philosophy*, 98: 239–64.

Pereboom, Derk, 2002. 'Robust Nonreductive Materialism', *Journal of Philosophy*, 99/10 499–531.

Perry, John, 2001. *Knowledge, Possibility, and Consciousness*, Cambridge, Mass. and London: MIT Press.

Putnam, Hilary, 1967. 'Psychological Predicates', in W. H. Capitan and D. D. Merrill (eds.), *Art, Mind, and Religion*, Pittsburgh: University Press; later retitled 'The Nature of Mental States'; repr. in his 1975*a*, 429–40.

—— 1975*a*. *Mind, Language and Reality: Philosophical Papers*, ii, Cambridge: Cambridge University Press.

—— 1975*b*. 'The Meaning of "Meaning"', in his 1975*a*, 215–71.

—— 1975*c*. 'Philosophy and Our Mental Life', in his 1975*a*, 291–303.

Robinson, Howard M., 1998. 'Materialism', in *Routledge Encyclopedia of Philosophy*, Edward Craig (general editor), London and New York: Routledge.

Rolls, Edmund T., 1999. *The Brain and Emotion*, Oxford: Oxford University Press.

Rose, Steven, 1976. *The Conscious Brain* (rev. edn), Harmondsworth: Penguin.

Rosenthal, David M., 1986. 'Two Concepts of Consciousness', *Philosophical Studies*, 49: 329–59.

—— 1997. 'A Theory of Consciousness', in N. Block *et al.* (eds.), *The Nature of Consciousness*, Cambridge, Mass. and London: MIT Press, 729–53.

Roth, Philip, 1976. *My Life as a Man*, London: Fontana (first pub. 1974).

Rufino, M., and D. A. Jones, 2001. 'Binary Individual Recognition in *Lysmata Debelius* . . . under Laboratory Conditions', *Journal of Crustacean Biology*, 21: 388–92.

Ryle, Gilbert, 1949. *The Concept of Mind*, London: Hutchinson.

Sartre, Jean-Paul, 1958. *Being and Nothingness: A Phenomenological Essay on Ontology*, tr. Hazel E. Barnes, London: Methuen; originally published in 1943 as *L'Être et le Néant*, Paris: Gallimard.

Searle, John R., 1980. 'Minds, Brains and Programs', *Behavioural and Brain Sciences*, 3: 417–57; repr. in D. R. Hofstadter and D. C. Dennett (eds.), 1981. *The Mind's Eye*, Brighton: Harvester, 353–72.

—— 1992. *The Rediscovery of the Mind*, Cambridge, Mass. and London: MIT Press.

Shallice, Tim, 1988. 'Modularity and Consciousness', in *From Neuropsychology to Mental Structure*, Cambridge: Cambridge University Press, 381–404; repr. in Block *et al.* (eds.), *The Nature of Consciousness*, Cambridge, Mass. and London: MIT Press.

Shoemaker, Sydney, 1975. 'Functionalism and Qualia', *Philosophical Studies*, 27: 291–315.

—— 1981. 'Absent Qualia are Impossible', *Philosophical Review*, 90: 581–99; repr. in his *Identity, Cause and Mind*, 327–57.

—— 1999. 'On David Chalmers's *The Conscious Mind*', *Philosophy and Phenomenological Research*, 59: 439–44.

Siewert, Charles P., 1998. *The Significance of Consciousness*. Princeton: Princeton University Press.

Skorupski, John, 1997. 'Meaning, Use, Verification', in B. Hale and C. Wright (eds.), *A Companion to the Philosophy of Language*, Oxford: Blackwell, 29–59.

Sleigh, M. A. 1973. *The Biology of Protozoa*, London: Edward Arnold.

Smith, Quentin, and Aleksandar Jokic (eds.), 2003. *Consciousness: New Philosophical Perspectives*, Oxford: Clarendon Press.

Stout, G. F., 1931. *Mind and Matter*, Cambridge: Cambridge University Press.

Strawson, Galen, 1994*a*. *Mental Reality*. Cambridge, Mass. and London: MIT Press.

—— 1994*b*. 'The Experiential and the Non-experiential', in R. Warner and T. Szubka (eds.), *The Mind-Body Problem*, Cambridge, Mass. and Oxford: Blackwell, 69–86.

Strawson, Peter F., 1966. *The Bounds of Sense*, London: Methuen.

Stroud, Barry, 2000. *The Quest for Reality: Subjectivism and the Metaphysics of Color*, New York and Oxford: Oxford University Press.

Tye, Michael, 1995. *Ten Problems of Consciousness: A Representational Theory of the Phenomenal Mind*, Cambridge, Mass. and London: MIT Press.

—— 2000. *Consciousness, Color, and Content*, Cambridge Mass. and London: MIT Press.

Unger, Peter, 1990. *Identity, Consciousness and Value*, New York and Oxford: Oxford University Press.

Van Gulick, Robert, 2003. 'Maps, Gaps, and Traps', in Q. Smith and A. Jokic (eds.), *Conosciousness*, Oxford: Clarendon Press, 323–52.

Warner, R., and T. Szubka (eds.), 1994. *The Mind-Body Problem: A Guide to the Current Debate*, Cambridge, Mass. and Oxford: Blackwell.

Webb, Barbara, 1996. 'A Cricket Robot', *Scientific American*, 275: 62–7.

Weir, A. A. S., J. Chappell, and A. Kacelnik, 2002. 'Shaping of Hooks in New Caledonian Crows', *Science*, 297: 981.

Weiskrantz, Lawrence, 1986. *Blindsight: A Case Study and Implications*, Oxford: Clarendon Press.

—— 1997. *Consciousness Lost and Found: A Neuropsychological Exploration*, Oxford: Oxford University Press.

Wittgenstein, Ludwig, 1953. *Philosophical Investigations*, tr. G. E. M. Anscombe, Oxford: Blackwell.

—— 1969. *On Certainty*, G. E. M. Anscombe and G. H. von Wright (eds.), Oxford: Blackwell.

Yablo, Stephen, 1999. 'Concepts and Consciousness', *Philosophy and Phenomenological Research*, 59/2: 455–63.

Index

a posteriori necessity 28–9
  and physicalism 14–17
a priori necessity 14–15
  as an epistemic notion 65
  need not coincide with c-necessity 65
  see also necessity etc.
aboutness, not a single relation 138–9
  see also basic package; de-sophisticating
    the framework; representation
absent-minded driver 59
  see also automatism
access consciousness 69, 193–5
  defined 70
  as distinct from phenomenal
    consciousness 70
  see also Block; phenomenal consciousness
acquaintance, *see* epistemic intimacy
d'Aguilar *et al.* 84
Akins, K. 92 n. 3
Anscombe, G. E. M. 95–6
Aristotle 92 n. 2, 196
armchair science 72–3
Armstrong, D. M. 59, 92 n. 2
  on introspection as inner sense 212
artificial giant 104–5
  its information and behaviour are not
    integrated 105
  is not a decider 104–5
assessment (of situation) 88–9, 90, 100–2
  see also basic package
attention 172
Austin, C. R. 102
automatism 178–9, 197
availability and poisedness 145, 190–1, 214
  contrasted with direct activity 157–8, 190,
    195
  see also direct activity

Baars, B. J. 199
Baddeley, A. 199
Baker, L. R. 205
Balog, K. 30, 46 n.
basic package 5, 88–96, 97–118
  capacities involved in 89–92; are not
    all-or-nothing 91; must be integrated 91
  descriptions to be taken in neutral or
    functional sense 89
  does not imply mindedness 118
  does not need language 119–20
  does not imply personhood 134–5

and goals 88
and how to tell whether a system
  has it 95–6
and the intentional stance 91–2
as necessary for phenomenal
  consciousness 93–4
and non-conceptual content 135–7
is not a natural kind 91
is not to be understood
  behaviouristically 91
and perception 92–4
and point of view 135
and rationality 134
and robots 115–17
seems insufficient for consciousness 141–3
as sufficient for perception in the
  full sense 94
unity of 89–92, 95
usefulness of the idea 96–6
see also bees; direct activity; reflex systems;
  simple organisms
basic package-plus 156
  and how to discover its presence 156
  is necessary and sufficient for perceptual
    consciousness 163, 164–98
  satisfies necessary functional conditions
    for consciousness 166–71
  see also direct activity
bees 98–101
  and abstract concepts 98–100
  need not be classified as deciders 99–100
behaviourism 24, 106, 203–4
  fails 204
beliefs 127, 130, 131
  and language 120, 122, 123, 132–4
  and possibility of being mistaken 132–3
Bermúdez, J. L. 103 n., 135 n.
  on concept-possession 122–3
  his 'priority principle' 122
  on the alleged structure of
    representations 128
blindsight 70, 141, 150, 175–8, 192, 193
  as evidence for indeterminacy of
    consciousness 160
  and information acquired 152
  not a counter-example to the basic
    package-plus account 175
  'superblindsight' 193–5
  'super-duper-blindsight' 194
  see also Block; direct activity